THE HIDDEN ABUSER

Learn to Recognize Subtle

Abusive Behavior

Dr. Audrey Snowden

The examples I have given from my own experience are true. Names of
individuals have been changed to protect their identities. This book is
intended to provide accurate information about abusive relationships. It is
not intended to replace professional advice such as counseling or legal
advice.

DEDICATION

To the survivors of domestic violence, may the strength of your experiences shed light on the darkness of this topic.

CONTENTS

ACKNOWLEDGMENTS

I'd like to acknowledge Michael Guinn whose unwavering support encouraged me to see the process through to the end. Mike has helped me with every part of this book at every step of the way. I'd also like to send a big thank you to Esmeralda Martin. She was a great contributor to the editing of this book and cover. Without her knowledgeable recommendations, this book would be much longer and much more repetitive.

CHAPTER 1
INTRODUCTION

"Every time we impose our will on another, it is an act of violence" – Gandhi

Some say if you want to cook a living frog, don't throw it into a pot of boiling water. The frog will jump out in an attempt to save itself. Instead, put the frog in a pot of room-temperature water, and very slowly, increase the heat. If increased slowly enough, the frog doesn't recognize that it is being cooked because it adjusts to the increasing temperature of the water.

Whatever folklore the frog story is, it describes a very important component to abusive relationships. In psychology, this component is called *grooming*, and in other fields it is known as *creeping normality*.

Grooming is the idea that subtle, inappropriate behaviors are introduced early in a relationship and are very slowly increased over the life of the relationship. These behaviors probably make you feel uncomfortable, but are not extreme, and so in most instances, they are overlooked as quirks, idiosyncrasies, or weird personality characteristics. These behaviors seem harmless at first. Over time, the unwanted behaviors become more intense, more unacceptable, and more alarming. By the time the more troubling behaviors show themselves, the victim is usually very deeply involved in the relationship and has a harder time leaving due to the enmeshment of their two lives together (i.e. shared bank accounts, shared transportation, shared residence, shared children, etc.). Grooming, in conjunction with the abuser's tactics, makes it very hard to recognize abuse for what it is when it does become alarming enough to question.

Personally, I have experienced grooming. I never recognized the abusive behaviors early on in the relationship: his constant nit-picking of me, his extreme need for control, the millions of arguments he would start over tiny benign things, the extreme highs and extreme lows of the relationship, his punishment of me when I didn't do something he wanted me to do. I never saw the warning signs: asking me to move in with him after 3 weeks of dating, asking me to marry him after 5 months of being together, asking me to add his name to my bank account and using my money to pay his bills. Instead, I believed that many of these things were signs of true love.

I made up excuses for his controlling behavior. I reasoned that all relationships take a lot of work and that I just needed to choose my battles more wisely. Although many of his behaviors were unacceptable, I didn't realize that they were abusive because they were seemingly so inconsequential. I didn't realize that all the little inappropriate behaviors were adding up to abuse, so that by the time he used recognizable abusive behaviors, I wasn't sure if what he was doing was abuse. This is grooming.

Over time he slowly increased his violent behavior. He started off with things like giving me the silent treatment. He progressed to things like social ostracism (leaving me out of family activities and making sure that he didn't invite me). He eventually began calling me names and telling me, "Shut the fuck up!" or "Get the fuck out of my house!" He increased the severity of his behavior to blocking my exits during scary arguments. He would charge at me during arguments, then stand over me, purposefully invading my personal space. He would yank items from my hands. This violent behavior further intensified to simple assault.

By the time he had become physically violent with me, I wasn't actually sure if it was abuse. He explained away all of his behavior. He persuaded me he wasn't abusive, and I wasn't sure, because like he said – he had never "beat" me.

Although seemingly benign, the subtle tactics, when taken together with controlling behavior add up to an abusive relationship. As the relationship continues, the subtle tactics will turn more threatening and violent. As many abuse counselors explain, the violence never becomes less severe, it always intensifies in severity. I hope that as you read this book, you will learn the subtle tactics that the abuser uses. These tactics are used to groom you, confuse you, convince you that you are not in an abusive relationship, and to keep you from leaving the abusive relationship. Lastly, by reading this book, my hope for you is that you will be able to recognize abusive relationships for what they are and avoid them in future situations.

Brief Explanation of Terminology

In this book, I use the terminology abuse, abusers, and survivor throughout. I define *abuse* as a pattern of behavior where the individual with more power consistently controls and forces another individual to do what he wants her to do by using the tactics outlined in this book. I use the term *abuser* to describe the person who is both controlling and who uses abusive tactics to get the other person to do what they want. The term *survivor* is used to describe the individual in the relationship who experiences the abuse.

I typically use several words interchangeably: domestic violence, abuse, and intimate partner violence. I use the words romantic partner, partner, intimate partner, and significant other, to describe one person in a romantic relationship between two people.

The majority of abusive relationships occur between a man and a woman, with the man being the abuser. One study found that 20% of women living with a male partner reported being victimized by the male partner, 11% of women living with a female partner reported being victimized by the female partner, 15% of men living with a male partner reported being victimized by the male partner, and 8% of men living with a female partner reported being victimized by the female partner (Tjaden & Thoennes, 2000). Because the majority of abusive relationships consist of heterosexual couples where the man is the abuser and the woman is the survivor, I use the pronouns "he" when discussing the abuser and "she" when discussing the survivor.

Abuse does occur in same sex relationships, and more rarely, in heterosexual relationships where the female is the abuser and the male is the survivor. However, the language of this book should not deter you from applying the information to the type of relationship you are or were in. Although I use "he" to describe the abuser, the principles, tactics, and abuser's way of thinking can be applied across all relationship types.

A Note on Power

Abusive relationships start with a power imbalance. One person has more power than the other. Having more power can mean being larger and more physically powerful than the other person, having more money and resources than the other person, and/or having a higher social status than the other person. The more powerful person then uses that power to gain and maintain control over the other person.

There are two types of power: *power to* and *power over* (Evans, 1996). *Power to* is a normal, healthy type of power to have. Power to is having control over yourself and creating good boundaries. It is acting in a way which is self-protective. It is declaring behavior that is not acceptable and creating boundaries to prevent harm to one's self. Power to does not decrease other's options, nor does it force others to change. When you have power to, you recognize that others may act how they want but that doesn't mean you have to put up with it. When you exhibit power to, you remove yourself from situations and people that are toxic or harmful to you. With power to, you utilize your options in order to do what is best for yourself.

Power over, on the other hand, is an abusive type of power. It is having power and control over others. When an individual uses power over, they are acting in a way that limits the other person's options in order to force that person to comply with their wishes. Power over is about getting what you want, when you want it, by any means necessary. It is about forcing others to change their behavior to suit you. Power over is controlling others and controlling others is abusive.

I think the serenity prayer explains power to versus power over in the most concise way: "Higher power, grant me the serenity to accept the things I cannot change, the courage to change the things I can, and the wisdom to know the difference." Power to is both changing ourselves and accepting the things we cannot change. We can change our reaction to the situation, what we do about it and how we feel about it. Changing these things is power to. However, we cannot control others. When we try to control others, we use power over. When we learn the difference between the two, we can more easily accept that we cannot change other people and instead focus on changing how we deal with the situation. In this one prayer, we begin to live healthy, set boundaries, become self-protective, and exert power to.

CHAPTER 2
BACKGROUND

What constitutes abuse?

There are three types of abuse: emotional, verbal, and physical. Most of us recognize physical assault (punching, kicking, choking, etc.) as abuse but rarely do we recognize constant lying, playing mind games, name calling, or put downs as abuse. Emotional and verbal abuse both consist of more subtle, hidden behaviors which are hard to recognize in relationships. Sometimes, emotional and verbal abuse are indistinguishable from one another. All three types of abuse consist of tactics, or behaviors which are purposefully used in order to get what the person using them wants.

It is important to recognize that the verbal and emotional tactics discussed in this book are abusive even without physical violence added into the equation. Being in a relationship with a person who uses verbal and emotionally abusive tactics is an abusive relationship. Controlling, verbally and emotionally abusive relationships are just as damaging as physically abusive relationships. Specifically, living with a partner who is controlling and who uses verbal and emotional abusive tactics can cause severe depression in the survivor (Anderson, 2008; Soenens, Vansteenkiste, Luyten, Duriez, & Goossens, 2005). Likewise, emotional and verbal abusive tactics are red flags for potential physical abuse. At the very least, learning to recognize the subtle tactics will allow you to avoid dysfunctional, tumultuous and

6

hurtful relationships in the future.

Typically, the tactics are used to gain control over the victim. All tactics are red flags for dysfunctional and damaging relationships. In this book, I will explain numerous tactics for each of the types of abuse and give examples which I personally experienced. This should help make the tactics more understandable and easily recognizable.

Why are some people abusive?

What many people fail to understand is *why* an individual is abusive. Abusers have an insatiable need for control over others. They believe that they know what is best for the survivor, more than the survivor knows what is best for herself. They feel entitled to have control over the survivor. They become abusive because they feel as though they are losing control over the survivor. They feel justified in their abuse of the survivor.

Abuse is centered around control. You may ask yourself, why is it important to know this? Knowing that control is the root of abuse is important for several reasons.

First, it allows you to recognize that the abuser wants his way and if he can't get his way, he will instigate a fight (either verbally, emotionally, or physically). You will learn quickly that the abuser will not take "NO" from you as an answer. This will result in the abuser using the tactics against you to force you to comply.

Second, as you probably have realized, gaining control of the survivor is at the center of the tactics. So, these subtle behaviors are controlling in nature. If you can recognize when others are trying to control you, you can set boundaries more quickly, or remove yourself from a potentially harmful relationship.

Third, controlling relationships lead to abusive relationships. The abuser may start off using the subtle verbal and emotional abusive tactics which are harder to recognize. However, as the relationship progresses, you may find yourself in a physically abusive relationship. This is because the abuser becomes more violent in his attempts to gain control over you, over time.

Who are abusers?

At this point, you may be asking: who are abusers, what are their goals, and why do they use tactics? These are all very great questions. Abusers can be anyone you are in *any* type of relationship with. They can be your boyfriend, girlfriend, lover, or spouse. Abusers can be your mom, dad, sister, brother, or other family member. They can be your neighbor, boss, or coworker. Abusers can even be your best friend. Not all abusers are the same. Some will never become physically violent, using only emotional and verbal abusive tactics to gain control. Others will use all three types of abusive tactics to get their way. Some may become violent quickly in the relationship while others may take months or years to become physically violent. The number of tactics used will differ depending on the abuser. Some may use only a few tactics, while others use the majority.

The nature of the relationship with the abuser may impact the type of tactics that are used as well. Physical abuse is more likely found in romantic and familial relationships than in workplace relationships. Similarly, work relationships are more likely to exhibit emotional and verbal abusive tactics. This is probably due to both societal expectations of the relationships and the ability to conceal the abuse. Although physical violence is illegal, it is easier to hide in romantic and familial relationships than in working relationships. Also, it is more likely that physical violence displayed in the workplace would be met with swift consequences like being fired and or jail time. Emotional and verbal tactics are very subtle and thus likely to not be recognized, even in work relationships. Therefore, the type and number of tactics used by abusers differs based on the relationship between you and the abuser.

What is the goal of the abuser?

The *goal* of the abuser on the other hand, is to use these subtle tactics to slowly train you to be submissive to them so that they can gain control and keep you under their control. Therefore, the function of the tactics is to keep you in a position where it is hard to escape and it is hard for you to recognize their actual intentions. The tactics are also designed to keep you continually working harder to please them. The tactics are so sneaky that without prior education on this subject it is very hard to recognize that you are *not in a normal relationship*. That is why it is so important to learn these tactics, because once you are in an abusive relationship, they are very difficult to recognize.

My goal is to teach you how to recognize controlling behavior and the subtle tactics that are used by abusive individuals. This knowledge will aid you in making better decisions about relationships, recognizing abusive relationships, and protecting yourself from them.

CHAPTER 3
EMOTIONALLY ABUSIVE TACTICS

There are two types of subtle abusive tactics: emotional and verbal. I will separate the tactics based on which type of abuse they fall under. However, it should be known that in many cases tactics can be both emotionally and verbally abusive. As you read through them it will become clear that the tactics are intertwined. Many times, more than one tactic is used in a specific situation.

To further your understanding of the ways an abuser might try to control you, I will give personal examples of how the tactics were used against me in my relationships. Most of the emotional and verbal abusive tactics by themselves seem innocuous (not dangerous). However, don't be fooled, taken together they paint a picture of tiny red flags for potential future physical abuse. In fact, experiencing emotional and verbal abuse from a partner is the greatest predictor of future physical violence (Tjaden & Thoennes, 2000).

The list of tactics below was created through extensive reading of the topic and my own personal experience living in abusive relationships.

Manipulation and Passive-Aggressiveness (Samsel, 2013)
First, it is important to understand that manipulation and passive-aggressiveness are tactics. Manipulation and passive-aggressiveness are ways to get you to do something without asking

and they are also ways that the abuser makes his feelings known without having to verbalize those feelings. Manipulation and passive-aggressiveness are very sneaky ways of controlling others. These tactics are used to control others without having to bark orders. They are both used to avoid directly asking for what one wants or needs and to avoid directly expressing what one feels.

Passive-aggressiveness is being used when a person makes you feel as though you have done something wrong but you aren't sure what. *Manipulation* is being used when someone wants you to do something but no one has asked you to do it. Many times, when a person is being passive-aggressive, they are also being manipulative and vice versa.

Typically, these two tactics induce guilt and guilt propels you into action. For example, a person being manipulative might yell, "Why am I the only one bringing all of the groceries in?" The person on the receiving end of this comment feels guilty that they aren't helping and they know that help is wanted, so they feel compelled to help. Another passive-aggressive manipulative example is, "God, I can't believe you wore that to the movies!" In this example, the abuser wants to control what the survivor wears by deterring them from wearing that outfit again (by making them feel guilty for wearing what they wore).

What passive-aggressiveness and manipulation looked like to me: *Abuser 3 was notorious for being passive-aggressive and manipulative. One night after sitting down and eating dinner as a family, I did not immediately hop up from the table to clean the dishes once I was finished eating. I continued to talk with the kids as they finished their dinner. Abuser 3 got up and started putting away the leftovers. He walked over to where I was sitting, grabbed the butter off the table, looked at me and said in a very sarcastic tone, "No, no, you just sit there, I got it." His comment made me feel guilty as though I was being lazy (passive-aggressiveness) and that I should be doing the dishes (manipulation). He was being controlling. He used this statement to get me to do what he wanted without having to ask me to do it.*

Abuser 3 would often precede his passive-aggressive manipulative comments with a loud, obnoxious sigh. For example, he would sigh loudly and then say, "Why am I the only one who takes out the trash!" This let me know that he was frustrated with me for not taking out the trash (passive-aggressiveness) and that I better take out the trash next time before he got to it (manipulation/control).

11

The purpose of passive-aggressive and manipulative behavior is to control the survivor without actually ordering or asking her to do it, and to express emotions without having to verbalize them. What is key in the passive-aggressive and/or manipulative behavior is that the abuser does not distinguish himself from you. He does not see you as a separate entity from him. You are an extension of the abuser. In the abuser's mind, he should not have to ask you to do anything, you should already know what he wants, needs, and feels. This goes hand in hand with the abuser's control over you. If you anticipate the abuser's needs and meet those needs without the abuser asking or manipulating you into doing it, the abuser feels he has absolute control over you.

Both manipulation and passive-aggressiveness can be found in the majority of the tactics list below. This means that the majority of the tactics you will read about will also be manipulative and or passive-aggressive.

Withholding (Evans, 1996)

Sharing information and feelings between two people is an integral part of a relationship. In romantic relationships, it is vital to share daily plans, future goals, in-the-moment feelings, and expectations. *Withholding* occurs when the abuser keeps vital information from you. By withholding important information, the abuser maintains his power over you, which puts you in a submissive position. How does this put you in a submissive position? First, you are unable to make good decisions because you do not have all of the important information. Second, it puts you in a position where you have to constantly ask the abuser about plans in order to stay informed. This not only creates a sense of insecurity in the survivor it also annoys the abuser and gives the abuser an excuse to start arguments with the survivor. Lastly, withholding can be used against the survivor in public to make her look uniformed and feel stupid.

What this looked like to me: *Abuser 3 would often withhold information from me and then surprise me with it. For example, he knew what day Meet the Teacher Night (a night where your kids get to meet their new teacher for the upcoming school year) was but did not tell me. When the day arrived, he stormed around the house yelling because I had not prepared for it by having the kids' clothes washed, having dinner cooked in time, or making the kids take baths before-hand. How was I supposed to know? He registered the kids for school and withheld that information from me.*

Abuser 3 also loved to surprise me with withheld information in front of people (friends/family) and then act astonished himself as though I should have known the information. For example, at the supermarket, we ran into the neighbors and Abuser 3 explained to them that we were going to have dinner at another friend's house in a few days. Because this was news to me, I was startled. Abuser 3 then turned to me with shock, "Don't tell me you forgot, I told you this last week!" This last example also falls under the Gas Lighting tactic.

Abuser 3 would typically withhold his daily plans from me but he would expect me to tell him all of my plans. Abuser 3 would decide to get a haircut after work (and not tell me) and this would make him late for dinner. When Abuser 3 did not show up for dinner at the regular time this put me in a terrible position. I would have to decide to either make the kids wait to eat dinner or eat without him. Either way Abuser 3 would use this as an opportunity to become enraged. Truthfully, it didn't matter which option I chose, Abuser 3 withholding the information was used to put me in a losing situation where he could start a needless argument.

Likewise, Abuser 3 would withhold financial information from me. He and I shared MY bank account. His money was located in another bank account that I did not have access to. He would often make purchases with my money and not tell me about it. This would create situations where my bank account would become negative because my bills were automatically withdrawn and there wouldn't be enough money in the account after his spending. When I would confront him about it, he would start an argument in which he blamed me for my inability to account for my finances appropriately. He would lie and say that we had discussed the purchase and that I had agreed to it. He would create these situations and then use the situations to make me feel as though I was incapable of taking care of my own finances.

Discounting (Evans, 1996)

When the abuser discounts you, he tells you that what you are thinking, feeling, or experiencing is incorrect. He attempts to invalidate your feelings. The most typical way the abuser discounts is by telling you that you are too sensitive or that you have no sense of humor. This tactic makes you believe that what you are feeling is wrong, that you are overreacting to something trivial, when the opposite is actually true.

You should be listening to what you are feeling because these feelings are alarm bells alerting you to the fact that something is wrong. In essence, when you believe the lies that you are overreacting or that you are too sensitive or that you have no sense of humor, you are turning off your natural warning system. You become desensitized to the abusive behaviors. This will then start to spill over into arguments. You may begin to "choose your battles more wisely" because you don't want to overreact to trivial matters. Slowly, you become (unconsciously) more submissive because you teach yourself that most things are trivial. Over time, you choose your battles so wisely that you don't realize you have given up control on almost everything.

What this looked like to me: *One argument I remember in the beginning of my relationship with Abuser 3 started with him yelling at me because I did not put noodles in boiling water. It was his turn to make dinner for the family. I was studying in the kitchen. He turned the stove's burner on high, put the pot of room temperature water on it and walked away. Ten minutes later he came back into the kitchen and was enraged when he saw me sitting at the table studying. He was pissed because I hadn't put the noodles in the water.*

First, he never asked me to put the noodles in the water. Second, it was his turn to make dinner. So, it made no sense to me why he was so pissed off. (He wanted control over me and he expected me to read his mind).

As we were yelling and arguing over who should have put the noodles in, I started to cry and hyperventilate, and he yelled at me, "Stop crying! Why do you always overreact to everything? How hard is it to put noodles in the fucking water!" In this situation, before he discounted me, I was feeling confused, frustrated, and angry. All of these feelings were trying to alert me to the fact that this was about control. He wanted control over me. He expected me to read his mind and put the noodles in the boiling water without actually having to ask me to do it. Abuser 3 created a situation that was set up specifically for an argument. Then he used the argument to discount my feelings.

This situation took me by surprise. I did not understand why he was so mad at me and this put me at a disadvantage in the argument. His anger, yelling, and arguing created a sense of fear and desperation in me. As soon as I began freaking out (which is what he wanted) Abuser 3 flipped the script, making it seem as though I was the one who started this madness over noodles. This is very subtle and very sneaky. By saying, "How hard is it to put the noodles in the fucking water!" Abuser 3 made me feel like I was making a mountain out of a mole hill, that I was stupid for not seeing the issue and fixing it before it became a problem and that it was such a trivial problem it could have been fixed without any of this unnecessary arguing. It also made me feel guilty as though I was being selfish for not putting the noodles in the water. In this argument Abuser 3 blamed me for his mistake which is another abusive tactic discussed later in the book.

Let me point out that this example is Grade A manipulation and control. It combined several tactics into one: discounting, ordering, guilt tripping, manipulation, blame, and crazy making. Sometimes discounting can be much simpler. For example, a friend may call you by a mean name (e.g. butter face, booty-do, thunder thighs, tool, choad, or douche, etc.) and when you confront them on it, they tell you it was a joke, or that you are being too serious.

In another example:

Abuser 3 discounted my feelings after I left him for becoming physically violent with me. He stated, "You don't need to be scared of me because I'm not violent when sober."

The truth of the matter is that I had every reason to be scared of him. When someone that you love is violent with you, there is a real reason to be scared. His statement not only disregarded and ignored my feelings on the issue, but he told me how I should be feeling. Furthermore, he trivialized and minimized his abuse.

Trivializing (Evans, 1996)

This tactic makes you feel like the things that are important to you are insignificant or lame. This is a sneaky way of putting someone down and making them feel worthless. The point of this tactic is twofold: first, it wears you down into thinking that your dreams, desires, goals and accomplishments are worthless; and second, you might attempt to work harder to gain the abuser's approval which is exactly what he wants.

What this looked like to me: *When I would go to Abuser 1 for emotional support, he would often mock me by saying, "Life sucks and then you die!" After studying extremely hard for a week straight, I aced my exam. When I excitedly told Abuser 3 that I made an A he said, "Come on, it wasn't that hard, you always make A's." This tactic makes your feelings or accomplishments seem trivial, as though you are over-reacting or that your accomplishments are not accomplishments at all but every day boring occurrences.*

This tactic can also be categorized under "discouragement."

After experiencing the trivialization of your accomplishments over and over, you may become so discouraged that you either stop talking about your accomplishments altogether or you might even stop working on the things that you loved. The latter is exactly what the abuser wants, especially if your goals are accomplished outside of the home, with other people, and without the abuser there. This allows the abuser more control over you as you become more isolated from others.

Undermining/Discouragement (Evans, 1996)
Similar to trivializing, this tactic makes you feel that your accomplishments are stupid, insignificant and worthless, and that you should quit trying. With undermining, instead of supporting you in your endeavors, the abuser discourages you from those endeavors. This tactic may be utilized by putting down anything you're interested in, claiming that the thing you want to do has already been done (so there's no point), putting your ability to do the thing down, or creating a reason why you shouldn't do it. For example, your significant other may discourage you from restoring old furniture by saying the furniture is so ugly, nothing will help it, or that you can buy new furniture for the same price so why bother, or that you don't know how to restore it and you will only mess it up.

What discouragement looked like to me: *As I was living with Abuser 3 I was also attending college. My major was originally math. However, I learned that it would take me four years to earn my math degree whereas it would only take me two years to earn my psychology degree. This was due to the university's scheduling of classes. I decided then to switch my major to psychology. My reasoning was that in the same amount of time (four years) I could have a Master's of Science in psychology. That night I told Abuser 3 about my changed major and my plans. I was expecting support, encouragement, and even excitement because I was excited about it. However, Abuser 3 was PISSED. He raged, "You can't earn shit with a psychology degree! How are you going to take care of the kids! How are you going to pay bills! How are you going to take care of this family! We had a deal!"*
After earning my Bachelors in Psychology, I decided that I really did want to go to graduate school. So, I applied. He tried to discourage me from applying as well. He said, "Don't you understand the chances of you getting in are slim to none?" (The graduate programs are super competitive but the point here is

that I wasn't being unrealistic, I knew my chances of getting in. He was using this to discourage me. He didn't want me to attend graduate school and he didn't want me to apply). He exclaimed, "How are you going to pay for it? How are you going to support this family!"

Although this made me feel bad this did not actually prevent me from applying or getting in (both of which I did). This tactic did however make me defend myself and promise many things in order to win the argument. So, I ended up promising that I would get a job and work while being in school full time. I also promised that if it was necessary I would take out student loans. Because I keep my word, these things made my life more of a living hell. This leads us to the "Double Standards" tactic. I was expected to go to school full time, take care of the kids and the housework, and work full time while Abuser 3 got to sit around. The amount of work expected of me was exponentially greater than the amount of work expected of him.

Sometimes, the abuser has (what seems like) very good reasons for not wanting you to do something. In the moment, these reasons seem very logical and this disguises the discouragement. In this case, it is extremely hard to recognize it for what it is during the situation.

For example, Abuser 3 limited what I wore by telling me that I needed to look more like a respectable parent, especially when dealing with the kids' school. He explained that I shouldn't wear band shirts or dye my hair unnatural colors because we wouldn't want to embarrass the kids and because those things were inappropriate. It seemed logical and I definitely didn't want to embarrass the kids.

Abuser 3 discouraged me in other ways. He would say, "I want to see you with normal hair." He would show me pictures of women's hair styles and say, "I think you would look really good with this haircut." When I would ask, "But what about my dreads?" knowing that I love them he would reply, "Aren't you tired of them? They don't look that good. They make you look like a ragbag."

The purpose of the discouragement tactic is to prevent you from doing something the abuser does not want you to do. It is about having control over you. It is also used to make you feel badly about your decisions, to make you feel insecure and incapable of making good decisions. I should mention that this tactic is really important in changing you. Through discouragement, you lose who you are and you change based on this constant verbal putdown of things that make you – you. You lose yourself and you become what the abuser makes you. This is one way the abuser gains total control over you without you realizing that it is happening.

Forgetting (Evans, 1996)

This tactic is exactly what it sounds like. The abuser pretends to forget a conversation, an argument, a date, or even a birthday. In a romantic relationship, the abuser may purposefully "forget" your birthday to make you feel unloved and worthless. The abuser may pretend an argument never happened to confuse you. Or the abuser may "forget" to pick up the kids from school to create a situation where he can blame you for not picking up the kids which makes you doubt your memory (and starts an argument).

What this looked like to me: *When I would confront Abuser 3 about an argument or something mean he had said, I can remember him yelling at me, "That never happened! You're high!" He also loved the phrase, "I never said that!" which relies on technicality to win the argument. As adults, we remember the gist of what other people say, our brains can't remember whole conversations verbatim (Brainerd & Reyna, 2009).*

The "forgetting" tactic has many purposes. First, it is used to cast doubt onto your ability to remember things correctly. The abuser is very convincing which makes the survivor question whether she is correct in what she remembered. This tactic is linked closely to Gas Lighting or Crazy Making. Second, this creates its own argument, deflecting whatever you were originally trying to bring up to the abuser (this is the Diverting tactic). For example, if you wanted the abuser to apologize for calling you a bitch, not only will you not get the apology, but now a new argument is on your hands (whether or not the abuser *actually* called you a bitch). Third, this argument is impossible to win, unless you have recorded all of your conversations. Lastly, this often leads to a childish argument where the survivor screams, "Yes you did!" and the abuser screams, "No I didn't!" There are three tactics used in this last point. The abuser is denying what he did, countering (disagreeing with you just to disagree), and stonewalling (shutting down communication and making it impossible for the argument to be productive).

Denial (Evans, 1996)

With the denial tactic, the abuser denies many things. This tactic is very similar to forgetting. The abuser may deny hurting the survivor (especially after being physically violent). The abuser might deny that a conversation took place, "I never said that!" Denial can also be used in conjunction with forgetting. For example, after "forgetting" a date with you, the abuser may say, "Jesus, I didn't know it was that big of a deal!"

What Denial looked like to me: *When I confronted Abuser 3 about his physical violence towards me he looked at me with all sincerity and said, "You know I would never hurt you!" During arguments, Abuser 3 would use denial by saying, "Are you calling me a liar?" Or, when I'd call Abuser 3 out on something he had said, he would reply, "You're putting words in my mouth, I never said that." After leaving Abuser 3 because of his violence, he told me, "I remember you saying on the phone that you needed to figure out why you wind up in abusive relationships, but baby our relationship wasn't abusive." In this statement, Abuser 3 flatly denies that he was abusive, and by doing so he also discounts my perspective, my feelings and my ability to think for myself or know my own mind.*

The purpose of denial is the same as the purpose of "forgetting." Denial works to make you question yourself, your perception and your sanity. Denial puts you in a position to lose the argument which forces you into submission. Also, by denying that the thing happened, the abuser does not have to take responsibility for his actions. Lastly, denial shuts down any productive communication.

Projecting (Freud, 1989)

Projecting occurs when the abuser accuses you of doing something that the abuser is actually doing. For example, if the abuser is cheating on you, he will accuse you of flirting with others, accuse you of cheating, or will call you a whore, or will want to go through your phone to see who you've been texting. The abuser who has a problem with outbursts of anger and violence may accuse you of having an attitude problem, always looking for a fight, or being out of control. Similarly, an abuser who is always hanging out with his friends may accuse you of never spending time with him.

What projecting looked like to me: *When I lived with Abuser 3, I would often bend over backwards to help him, even if it meant that I had to sacrifice greatly. When I refused to help him for one reason or another, he would then start an argument with me, "You are the most selfish person I have ever met! I can't believe you won't do X, after everything I have done for you! You're such a selfish bitch!!" Abuser 3 was projecting his selfishness onto me. He was the one who continued to take from me and not give back.*

The purpose of the projection tactic is to redirect your "vision" onto yourself. What I mean is, if your significant other is cheating on you, one great way of not getting caught is by accusing you of cheating. Now, you are so focused on proving that *you* are not cheating that you stop focusing on whether or not your partner is cheating. This is related to the "Diverting" tactic and is often used to thwart arguments. Projection can also keep you guessing. When projection happens, it seems like you are being accused of things that come out of nowhere. This is very unsettling and makes you feel on edge. You are never sure what you are going to be accused of, nor when you will be accused.

Projection, when used in conjunction with your insecurities, can make you reevaluate and second-guess yourself and can make you work harder at becoming a "better you."

For my case, I prided myself on being helpful. Therefore, I was insecure about others viewing me as "selfish." Abuser 3 picked up on this immediately and used it to his advantage to be able to shift the workload to his favor. Because I trusted Abuser 3 and his opinion of me, I often believed him when he called me selfish. This made me reevaluate who I was as a person. I believed that obviously I was not working hard enough and that I was not being considerate of others. This slowly shifted the workload as I tried harder to pick up the slack. This meant that I took on more work in an attempt to not be perceived as selfish while he did less. Lastly, projection works as a guilt trip. When my insecurities were touched on (being called selfish) I often felt guilty because I believed that I was being selfish. The guilt also encouraged me to work harder so I wouldn't feel guilty.

Black and White Thinking (Samsel, 2013)

Black and white thinking means that the abuser looks at the world through glasses which allow no middle ground. Things are either amazing or horrible, right or wrong, good or bad, sweet or sour, straight or curved. There are no in-betweens. There is no grey area.

This can be viewed as an absolute inability to bend the rules. It is also pinpointed when the abuser flips from acting like everything is fine in the relationship to screaming over something that seems miniscule.

Black and white thinkers often believe that their way is the correct way and any other ways are wrong. Black and white thinkers will not bend to or even listen to reason. Once a black and white thinker has made up his mind, there is no persuading him otherwise, even with conclusive evidence. Black and white thinkers refuse to bend from their "I am right and you are wrong" stance in an argument. However, black and white thinking goes beyond stubbornness. It is about being self-righteous. It is about them believing they are right so much so that they refuse to listen to others' point of view even when the other person is being calm and perfectly reasonable. The self-righteousness that the abuser feels is used as justification for the abusive behavior.

People who are non-abusers are able to take in information that disagrees with their perspective and understand it – even if they don't agree with it. Non-abusers respect that you have a different opinion, outlook, perspective, or way of doing things. They will attempt to compromise. They may agree to disagree. Abusers on the other hand, refuse to listen to your point of view and try to force you to acknowledge they are right by using other tactics like stonewalling, the silent treatment, etc. Abusers will also gloat when they feel there is enough evidence to prove to you that they are right.

What black and white thinking looked like to me: *When living with Abuser 1, I would often hear the phrase, "It's my way or the highway!" He always had to have things done his way, no matter if there were a million ways to do it. He also believed that his beliefs were morally superior to mine and he was very self-righteous. Because he often took a religious stance, he believed he was always right.*

Abuser 3 on the other hand would exhibit black and white thinking in arguments by screaming at me, "YOU ARE FLAT WRONG!" I remember this occurring in arguments where I knew I was right, and sometimes I could prove that I was right but I also knew that trying to prove that I was right would become an even greater fight. It would get me nowhere.

The purpose of black and white thinking is to prevent you from reasoning with the black and white thinker. They are completely stuck in their style of thinking, so nothing will persuade them otherwise. Reasoning with them is futile. Because of this, black and white thinking ends the conversation or argument. This tactic is also known as "Stonewalling." It prevents further discussion because black and white thinking shuts down communication. Lastly, because you cannot reason with a black and white thinker, and because communication has been shut down, your only option to ease the situation is to comply. This tactic forces you to do whatever it is the abuser wants you to do. Arguing with someone who says that you are wrong is pointless. It will end up pissing the abuser off more which may end in physical violence.

Stonewalling (Samsel, 2013)

The abuser stonewalls when he disregards the survivor's point of view. He completely cuts off communication. I like to think of stonewalling as talking to a brick wall. You can't get anywhere in the conversation with someone who is stonewalling you. Sometimes this can be a statement like, "This conversation is over" or "I am done with this conversation." Other times, stonewalling can be more forceful and aggressive.

What stonewalling looked like to me: *Stonewalling was almost always perpetrated during arguments. Some of Abuser 3's favorite stonewalling exclamations were:*

"YOU ARE WRONG!"

"SHUT THE FUCK UP!"

"GET THE FUCK OUT OF MY HOUSE!"

"GET THE FUCK OUT OF MY FACE!"

Many other times, Abuser 3 would give me the silent treatment. When he decided that he was done with the conversation he would completely ignore me, withhold all information from me, and purposefully exclude me so that I felt isolated and alone. He would do this by getting the kids into our room, have them take over the whole bed, turn on a kid's movie and let them eat whatever they wanted. He would not invite me and he would make sure that there was not enough room for me to invite myself. He would act overly loving towards the kids to gain their favor. He would not speak to me. He would give me looks of disgust when he walked by me.

The purpose of stonewalling is to shut down communication

which allows the abuser to gain power over the survivor. The survivor feels frustrated that she cannot express herself, that the abuser is not willing to listen to her, that the situation cannot be resolved, and the survivor often feels excluded and isolated. The silent treatment leaves the survivor in the dark, often wondering what she did to deserve this treatment. The only way to end the silent treatment is to grovel which puts the abuser in a position of power and the survivor in a position of submission. This is often achieved by the survivor apologizing for whatever she can think of, doing nice things for the abuser, and taking on more responsibility.

In my case, Abuser 3 would test me during his silent treatment of me. He would purposefully "forget" to take care of his responsibilities (taking out the trash, making coffee, or whatever chore he was supposed to do that day). He would expect me as part of my groveling to do them for him. If I did his chores, sometimes he would "reward" me by talking to me again. Or, if I did not do his chores, it would cause another argument where he would claim that it was my turn to do the chore.

Expecting Mind Reading (Samsel, 2013)

For this tactic, the abuser literally expects the other person to read his mind. In other words, the abuser will not ask for what he wants, the survivor has to figure it out. If the survivor does not figure it out and does not comply, the abuser will become angry. The abuser trains the survivor to anticipate his needs (read his mind) through passive-aggressive cues. When using passive-aggressive cues, the survivor figures out what is wanted through the abuser's sarcastic comments, inaction, and other tactics. For example, the abuser may say, "Just go! It's fine!" What this actually means is that the abuser wants the survivor to stay. In another example, if it's the typical time for dinner and it is the abuser's night to cook, the abuser will use inaction to passively-aggressively tell the survivor that she should cook instead. After being asked if it was his night to make dinner, the abuser might respond, "No. I thought it was your night." This tells the survivor that the abuser wants her to cook.

Other ways that the abuser can train the survivor to mind read is through expectations. Once a person has a routine, that routine is expected of them. For example, if the abuser gets the survivor to help him cook dinner several times in a row, it becomes an expectation that the survivor will always help the abuser cook dinner. If the survivor fails to help, this will lead to an argument or physical violence. In order to avoid future arguments and physical violence, the survivor feels she must anticipate the abuser's needs and meet those needs before he asks. This perpetuates the expecting mind reading tactic.

What this looked like to me: *I had arguments with both Abuser 1 and Abuser 3 about this. The arguments were almost exactly the same. The abusers said, "I should not have to ask you to do something, you should already know to do it without me asking!" Both abusers expected me to literally read their minds. They really believed that I should just "know" what they wanted and that they should really never have to ask.*

The purpose of this tactic is to gain total control over what the survivor does, without even having to ask or tell the survivor to do it. Furthermore, this tactic keeps the survivor guessing. When is the next fight going to be? What is it going to be about? In order to avoid fights, the survivor has to continuously anticipate the abuser's needs in order to satisfy them before being asked. This is an impossible feat which leads to more arguments and fights, which is exactly what the abuser wants. The survivor works overtime to try and guess what the abuser wants without much success. At the same time, as the survivor takes on more responsibility and works overtime to keep the abuser happy, the new responsibilities become routine and the abuser then begins to expect them from the survivor. Therefore, if the survivor does not live up to the new expectations, more arguments and fights will ensue.

Double Standards (Samsel, 2013)

Abusers do not abide by the same social norms and rules that survivors abide by. Double standards occur when rules placed onto the survivor do not apply to the abuser and when the abuser has higher expectations of the survivor than he does for himself. For example, the abuser may force the survivor to delete any male phone numbers out of her phone but the male abuser does not delete any female phone numbers from his phone. The abuser may expect the survivor to fill up the car's gas tank after every use but the abuser will bring the car back on empty. In an abusive relationship where double standards are at play, the survivor often has exponentially more work than the abuser. While the survivor is attempting to complete all of the household chores, the abuser may be watching TV.

What double standards looked like to me: *While I lived with Abuser 3 the workload was far from equal. I was required to take care of the house and the children while I worked and attended school full time. It didn't start out that way. The division of the chores in the beginning of the relationship was closer to equal with me having slightly more. Over time, Abuser 3 would complain about how much work he was doing and how little time he had, and how stressed out he was, and one by one, I took over his duties, thinking that I was being helpful. As I took them over, it became expected that I would continue to do them myself. Eventually, I was doing everything. The one chore I wouldn't do – mow the lawn – he paid a company to do. This left him with only school responsibilities, no household duties and no work responsibilities, while I had ALL of the household duties, plus outside work responsibilities, and school responsibilities.*

To further this double standard, it became expected of me that I would help Abuser 3 with any endeavor he got into so he wouldn't have to do it by himself. This meant helping him get the kids ready for school in the morning or helping him cook if he decided to do so, etc. So, I was completely overloaded, extremely stressed out and overwhelmed. When I thought I was going to lose it from the stress, I finally asked Abuser 3 for help. I begged him to take over some of the chores, even if only for a little while. This turned into a huge blowout fight. He screamed at me that I was the most selfish person he ever met. He belittled me for not being able to handle the work and stress. He told me I would have to quit school or work because I wasn't able to handle all of it.

Abuser 3, like ALL abusers, are completely unable to put themselves in your shoes, to empathize with you, or to understand where you are coming from. THEY are extremely selfish and create the double standard when they call you selfish. In this instance, it is also projecting.

Another example of double standards for me was that Abuser 3 would not allow me to wear shirts with band names or pictures of bands. His reasoning here was that band shirts were trashy and that I needed to look like a respectable parent. (Abusers can often make very reasonable sounding points which makes it harder to see that it is control. This is because they may not outright forbid you to wear certain things, they manipulate or reason you into it.) This was a double standard because Abuser 3 wore whatever he wanted and looked trashy as often as he wanted. The rules he made for me did not apply to him.

A last example of double standards that I experienced and you may have too, is that I was expected to maintain my composure during arguments. Abuser 3 pushed all of my buttons, but when I pushed Abuser 3's buttons he would flow over with rage, hatred, and violence. Abuser 3 would call me names, use low blows, and back up his points with long winded arguments, but I wasn't "allowed" to do the same thing. As soon as I defended myself using the same methods that he used on me, he would become physically violent.

The purpose of this tactic is to reinforce the power structure. The abuser has all of the control and power and can force or manipulate you into doing things, however, you do not have the power to influence the abuser on the same issue. This shows the survivor that the abuser has total control, whereas the survivor is in a subordinate position and has no say. The double standards tactic reinforces the idea that the person with the power can do whatever they want.

Toxic Delegation (Samsel, 2013)

With toxic delegation, the abuser asks the survivor to do something for him and then the abuser takes the opportunity to criticize the work, to say it's not good enough, or to make the survivor do it over. Here, the abuser may point to every flaw in the work and explain how to do it "correctly" while forcing the survivor to correct their "mistakes." This tactic can come from black and white thinking where the abuser has to have things done his way, otherwise it is not "correct." Similarly, this tactic can show up in the many rules the abuser has set up. For example, the abuser may have a set of rules for how the laundry must be done. If the survivor does not abide by the rules, then the abuser will punish the survivor. Punishment can be in the form of lecturing, forcing the survivor to redo the work, arguments, screaming, putting down the survivor, the silent treatment, intimidation, physical violence, or some combination of those. The antidote to this tactic is the saying "beggars can't be choosers." If someone really needs help, whatever help you provide them will be good enough.

What toxic delegation looked like to me: *Abuser 1 loved this tactic. He would start off by saying, "Audrey, I need your help." Then he would tell me that I needed to clean something, or help him do something. For example, after I cleaned the bathroom for Abuser 1, he would walk around the bathroom looking for flaws and pointing them out. He loved to say "You missed a spot!" This is an example of general nit-picking. Nothing was ever good enough for Abuser 1. After he walked through the bathroom pointing out my every mistake, he would then ask me if I listened to his instructions. He did this to make me feel incompetent, to imply that I was unable to even follow the simplest of directions. Abuser 1 would then demean me by re-explaining every step to cleaning a bathroom, using a deliberately slow verbal pace to emphasize that I was stupid and that I needed to be talked to as though I was stupid. He would then force me to reclean the bathroom. He would literally stand over me while I recleaned it, to force me to do it his way. That way, if I did something he disliked, he would be able to criticize me immediately and re-explain in slow motion AGAIN how to do it "correctly."*

This example actually includes a couple of tactics besides toxic delegation. Here Abuser 1 is using black and white thinking because he believes that the only "correct" way to clean a bathroom is his way. He is also using intimidation by physically standing over me. He also used criticism and constantly correcting as well.

Toxic delegation has several purposes. First, because you have already committed to the task at hand, you feel obligated to finish the task and to do a good job. This can create a feeling of stuckness because of the conflicting feelings (wanting to leave because of the poor treatment but also feeling obligated to finish the job). Second, completing the task allows the abuser to have total control over you. Third, by putting down your work, by criticizing you, and by talking to you as though you are stupid, the abuser undermines your self-esteem. Encountering many episodes like this where you have combined feelings of being stuck, having to obey, and being put down, can lead to a sense of total helplessness which leads to depression.

Raising the Bar (Samsel, 2013)

Raising the bar can be thought of in three different ways. The first is that the abuser gives you something easy to do and when you finish it, instead of praising you for your good work, he gives you something harder to do (raises the bar). The bar continues to be raised which prevents you from feeling successful.

The second way that raising the bar occurs is when the abuser asks you to do one thing for him and when you agree, he adds more things for you to do which you have not agreed to. For example, the abuser might ask you to pick up a few things from the grocery store and you agree. Then, as you are leaving for the store, he calls out to you, "Hey! While you're out, fill up the car with gas, take it to get the oil changed, and pick up my dry cleaning!"

Because you have already agreed to do the smaller task (picking up a few items from the grocery) you feel obligated to do the others. Also, because you are practically out the door, you feel rushed to make a decision and pressured to say yes. You also know that if you say no, it will cause a huge argument about why you won't do these other "small things." You know he will probably call you selfish, lazy, or a bitch, and you feel like it is just easier to say yes and avoid all of the hassle of saying no. In this respect, the abuser has used manipulation to get you to do what he wants. He has used your propensity to feel guilty and your good-hearted nature to help others – to manipulate you.

Third, raising the bar can be thought of as unrealistic standards and expecting perfection. No matter what or how much you do, to the abuser, you have never done enough and it's never good enough. The abuser will not acknowledge or praise you for any hard work you have done. The abuser may continue to compare you to others who either have done more than you or are better than you in some way. Like toxic delegation, after the work is done, the abuser may criticize the work instead of acknowledging it. The abuser may even compete with you. Instead of acknowledging the work you have done, the abuser might tell you how they could have done it faster or better.

What raising the bar looked like to me: *Abuser 1 typically raised the bar by comparing me to others who were better than me or by criticizing my work. For example, after asking me to do his laundry, he would tell me how I had folded it wrong and while showing me how to do it "correctly" he would say things like, "It doesn't take a rocket scientist to fold the laundry." Rarely was I told "good job." No matter how hard I worked or how hard I tried, it was never good enough for him. This left me feeling incompetent. Abuser 1 would also raise the bar by asking me to do small things which I would agree to and then he would immediately turn around and add more tasks onto my "to do list" without asking me first if I would be willing to do them.*

The purpose of raising the bar allows the abuser control over the survivor by continuously giving her more work. By never acknowledging the survivor's work, the survivor continues to try to work harder to please or gain the acceptance of the abuser. Raising the bar leaves the survivor feeling like she is not good enough.

Using the Children (Samsel, 2013)

When living with an abuser, the children can be used in several ways by the abuser to coerce the survivor into doing what the abuser wants. The purpose of this tactic is to gain control over the survivor through threats, wearing the survivor down, and other means. For example, the abuser may threaten the children to get you to do something:

> "If you don't shut the fuck up, I will kick you and the kids out on the street!"

> "If you leave, I will take the kids. You know the courts will side with me!"

> "If you leave me, I will kill myself and the kids."

> "Do you want me to hurt the kids? Because you know I will."

> "You're teaching the kids disrespect, arguing with me like that!"

> "Because you're such a bitch, the kids no longer get to…"

In other instances, the abuser may draw out court proceedings to wear the survivor down. The abuser may use visitation in order to control the survivor. This can be done by attempting to control everything about visitation. The abuser will determine what day, time, place, and setting he will pick up and visit the kids and when/where/how to bring them home. If the abuser has custody of the children he will have even more of an advantage which will allow him more control of the visitation (who will pick them up/drop them off, where, what times, what days, etc.).

What using the children looked like in my relationship: *The way Abuser 3 used the children was much more subtle and harder to detect. His tactics were: changing the rules, exclusion, and causing relationship breakdowns between me and the kids.*

Changing the rules occurred in a couple of ways. First, Abuser 3 had a different set of rules with the kids than the rules he allowed me to have with the kids. In other words, he would use me as the enforcer of the rules while he got to be the breaker of the rules. For example, he would become pissed off at me if I allowed the kids to have a big snack before dinner. But, when he gave them snacks, the rule didn't apply.

Second, Abuser 3 would tell me not to let the kids do something, and then when I would enforce the rule, he would immediately overrule me, telling the kids they could do it. For example, Abuser 3 would tell me not to let the kids have a soda with dinner. Then, at dinner, when I would tell the kids to pick something else to drink because they have had too much soda that week, Abuser 3 would then chime in, "You can have a soda tonight, but tomorrow you need to start drinking more water."

Another example of this is when the abuser discounts your enforcing of a longstanding rule, immediately after you enforce it. For example, the kids know they are not allowed to play Nerf guns in the house. When it would happen, I would tell the kids to take it outside. Abuser 3 would immediately discount my authority by saying, "Let them play it inside for once! Why are you always such a hard ass?!"

Using the kids by changing the rules has a couple of purposes. First, the survivor is forced to follow the rules that the abuser makes because of the arguments and fights it will cause if the rules are not followed. Second, changing the rules keeps the survivor guessing. You are never really sure when the rules are going to change so your best bet is to stick to the rules you know. Third, it makes the survivor look like an incompetent, powerless asshole. The kids are seeing you as incompetent because you don't seem to know what the rules are. The kids receive the clear message that the abuser is the one in charge and has the final say, thus, the survivor is not the one in control and does not have any power. Therefore, the kids learn not to listen to the survivor and the survivor's opinion doesn't count. They learn to listen to the abuser. Lastly, it makes the survivor look like an enforcer who is a stickler for the rules while the abuser looks like the fun one.

Abuser 3 would also use the children by excluding me from activities. When Abuser 3 and I would get into an argument he would punish me by gathering up the kids, being extremely loving and attentive to them while icing me out (ignoring me as though I did not exist). He would physically ice me out by inviting the kids to watch a movie in our room. They would take over the entire bed where there was physically no room for me. The room itself was small and was filled with dressers, a bookshelf, and a desk, so that physically, there was absolutely no way for me to join them. He would reward the children by letting them pick the movie they wanted to watch and allowing them to eat junk food while punishing me through exclusion. He would purposefully leave the door to the room open so I could hear them laughing and having a blast without me. When Abuser 3 was angry with me he would also use the kids by buying them things and bending the rules. This taught the kids that when I am punished, they are rewarded and that ostracizing me is fun and pleasurable.

Lastly, Abuser 3 would use the kids by causing fights between me and the children. One specific example I can recall occurred during one morning when the kids were getting ready for school. One kid asked to borrow my toothpaste. I said yes. My toothpaste was kept in the bathroom in a bottom drawer beneath the sink. Abuser 3 was a stickler about the drawers being shut all the way. He would throw tantrums when the drawers in the bathroom were left slightly open. After the kids were finished getting ready, I went back in the bathroom to brush my teeth. The drawer was left open with all of my things strewn about. Someone had taken all of my things and dumped them about in the drawer. I was angry. I approached the child and asked, "Why did you dump all of my stuff everywhere? That is so disrespectful!" The child immediately denied doing it, "I swear, I didn't dump your stuff out! I used your toothpaste and put it back, that was it!" I didn't believe the child. "Who else would have done that?" Then Abuser 3 walked up on our argument. "I dumped your stuff everywhere! The drawer was left open so I dumped it all out! Maybe next time the child will remember to close the drawers!"

This put me in a difficult situation. Who was going to fix the problem? The child didn't dump my stuff out, so who should reorganize it? However, Abuser 3 was definitely NOT going to clean it up. Abuser 3 was using this as a way to punish the child without having to actually do it himself. He expected me to make the child clean up the mess he made as punishment for leaving the drawer open. If I chose to clean it up myself instead of making the child do it, I would be punished and Abuser 3 would find another way to punish the child.

This type of situation puts the abuser in total control. This is because the abuser caused the chaos that erupted. Furthermore, the abuser caused distrust between me and the kids which eroded our relationship which then allowed the abuser to be in more control.

Gas Lighting/Mind Fucking/Crazy Making (Samsel, 2013)

Gas lighting is the same thing as "mind fucking" and "crazy making." With this tactic, the abuser does things and says things that make you feel, think, and believe that you are indeed crazy. With gas lighting, the abuser might move your things around and when you confront him, he acts like he doesn't know what you're talking about. For example, the abuser might put your keys under the couch and when you ask him how they got there, he acts like he doesn't know.

Circular arguments are what I like to refer to as a "mind fuck." This type of argument never gets resolved or goes anywhere, and often comes back to something that is construed as your fault. Typically, you can tell if you are in a circular argument if the conversation keeps going in different directions, you realize that the abuser is not listening to you, and the argument comes back to something you did that the abuser is pissed about (which can even be from years in the past!).

With mind fucking, the abuser uses all of the tactics in order to confuse you, to get you off topic, to gain control of the conversation, to avoid taking responsibility for his actions, and to make it so miserable for you that you want to avoid future arguments altogether. It seems as though the abuser uses all of the verbal abusive tactics in one argument, and this may be very close to the truth.

Crazy making, however, is more direct. The abuser will explicitly tell you that you are crazy and then give great examples to back up his assessment. Many times, gas lighting and crazy making are used in conjunction. First, the abuser will move your things, then when you accuse the abuser of doing such, he exclaims that you are crazy or that you are imagining things. Similarly, crazy making and mind fucking are used in conjunction. First, the abuser engages you in a circular argument. He wears you down and gets you really riled up. You may feel extremely pissed off. Then, when you explode, the abuser calls you crazy and lists all the things you have done where you have "acted crazy." This is also found under the "baiting" tactic.

What these tactics looked like to me: *Abuser 2 loved to mind fuck me. That was his M.O. Often the circular argument would start with me asking him to do something innocuous. "Hey Abuser 2, can you please clean up your milk glasses? They are starting to stink and grow trees." (Abuser 2 would leave dirty glasses and plates in our bedroom for months. They would smell horrible and grow mold.) Abuser 2, would become pissed that I asked him to do something and launch into a tirade. Sometimes it would start out by blaming me for doing something similar. "What the fuck? When was the last time you even did the dishes? You're such a bitch! You are always trying to start a fight!" In this tirade, Abuser 2 used accusing and blaming, criticizing, asking questions, name calling, and blocking and diverting in just five sentences. Often the circular arguments with Abuser 2 would go on for hours. Now, imagine what that could do to your self-esteem and your sense of sanity. It can make you feel crazy. I remember one argument that went on for so long that eventually I started trying to switch up my own tactics just to make it stop. Instead of trying to prove my point, I started to agree with everything he said. When that didn't work, I tried apologizing for everything just to get it to stop.*

Abuser 2 was also known for crazy making. He would mind fuck me until I was sobbing uncontrollably and unable to breathe at which time, he would tell me that I was "fucking crazy" and that I needed "some serious help." The point here is that Abuser 2 would make me feel crazy and then he would explicitly tell me that I was crazy. Over time, this made me believe that I was crazy.

Abuser 3 on the other hand, never really used the mind fuck method. He did gas light me though. One day, a huge box came in the mail. It was addressed to Abuser 3. He opened it and revealed that it was a very fancy remote-control car, one that was very expensive (hundreds of dollars) and could get up to 60 miles per hour. When he told me how expensive it was, I checked my bank account (the one with ALL of my money in it, NONE of his money, but he had access to) and found $400 missing. I was pissed. "You spent $400 of MY money on a toy car and NEVER asked me?!" Abuser 3 calmly replied, "We talked about this. I told you that I was going to buy a remote-control car and you agreed with me." We then went on to argue about whether or not we actually had that conversation. I can assure you, we NEVER had the conversation. However, we argued about it and Abuser 3 took the opportunity to make me feel crazy. After gas lighting me, he then went on to tell me that he was really concerned about me and that he believed I needed medical help because I couldn't remember important conversations. He really tried to convince me that something was seriously wrong with my memory.

Another time Abuser 3 gas lighted me was right after he brought home a puppy. The puppy woke me up at 3am with diarrhea. He had pooped in the closet. I took the puppy outside and then cleaned up the mess. This woke Abuser 3 up who bellowed, "WHAT ARE YOU DOING?!" I explained what happened and what I was doing. Abuser 3 went back to sleep. The very next day Abuser 3 found more poop in the kitchen. He began his diatribe, "Why is it that I am the only one cleaning up after this dog?!" I yelled back, "I don't know what you're talking about, I cleaned up diarrhea out of the closet at 3am!" He then gas-lighted me, "Bullshit! You have NEVER cleaned up any of this dog's shit!" I then tried to refresh his memory of him yelling at me asking me what I was doing in the closet at 3am. He then used the crazy making tactic on me, "Audrey, you're high. THAT NEVER HAPPENED!" I tried to defend myself, "What the fuck! ARE YOU SERIOUS?" He then countered with, "You're crazy! You have NEVER cleaned up this dog's shit!"

All 3 tactics work to confuse the survivor, make the survivor doubt her own perceptions, doubt reality, feel crazy, and prevent communication. All of this puts the survivor in a position to rely more on and trust solely the perspective of the abuser. The 3 tactics also allow the abuser to avoid responsibility for his actions. They wear down the survivor so much that the survivor regrets bringing up the issue. The tactics make it to where the survivor cannot win any argument and this discourages the survivor from future arguments with the abuser.

Intimidation

Abusers will often use intimidation to win arguments and to get their way. Intimidation lies on a spectrum from very subtle (i.e. body language) to very apparent (i.e. "acting crazy"). Intimidation may take the form of kicking holes in walls, punching holes in walls, throwing dishes, electronics, or other items, flipping tables, destroying the survivor's property, and verbal threats. Intimidation is also noticeable when the abuser stands over the survivor with crossed arms, physically blocks the exit when in an argument (cornering the survivor), and follows the survivor around continuing the argument even when the survivor tries to disengage and leave.

What intimidation looked like to me: Abuser 2 used more intimidation than any other person I have been in a relationship with. Abuser 2 punched walls, kicked walls and doors, and threw phones. When in an argument, I would try to disengage and put myself in another room to calm the situation down. Because Abuser 2 would follow me around to continue the argument, sometimes I would lock myself in a bedroom or in a bathroom. During these times, he would become so enraged that he would kick down doors, or break down the doors to continue his tirade. One time, after I locked myself in a room, I was so scared that he would hurt me if I didn't open the door, so I opened it. I was greeted with a bar stool thrown at me.

Abuser 2 would often force me into cars to finish the argument we started. Once I was in the car he would drive extremely fast and recklessly while also threatening that he would kill us both in a car wreck. Sometimes when Abuser

2 would begin to lose an argument, he would start to punch himself violently. This was to let me know that he really wanted to punch me but since he believed he wasn't an abuser, he wouldn't touch me. One very scary argument we had, Abuser 2 grabbed a gun that was kept in the house, pointed it at me, and then pointed it at himself and threatened to use it, "I'm so fucking sick of this! I will fucking kill you! I will kill myself, how about that? You would like that wouldn't you!" When I left Abuser 2 I knew he was thinking about how to get back at me. Because I was living with my parents, I believed that he was thinking of killing them. When I met with Abuser 2 for the last time to get the rest of my things, I begged him not to kill my parents. He told me that he had been thinking about it but that he had decided against it.

Abuser 2 also used more subtle forms of intimidation. When an argument was brewing but had not yet occurred, he would slam doors, throw his keys down on the counter, sigh loudly, and talk to me very matter-of-factly.

Abuser 3 (who was physically abusive) used very subtle intimidation tactics. He would often laugh at me during arguments. He would physically stand over me during arguments, crossing his arms and he would physically put himself in my space where he was touching me/towering over me. Imagine a petite woman sitting down with a guy standing so close to her that his big gut is touching her face. His crossed arms are almost resting on her head. This is what I mean by physically putting himself in my space. When we argued he would physically block my exit. Sometimes when we argued in the room, he would stand in front of the door so that I couldn't leave. His entire body blocked the opening. When I tried to leave, if I touched him, which was inevitable, this was viewed as an act of aggression which he could then use as an excuse to "defend himself." When I attempted to leave through the door, he would shove his shoulder and elbow into me like a linebacker. He would also force me to apologize, "EXCUSE YOU. Can't you see I'm standing here?!" If I wanted to leave without a fight or another argument I would have to ask politely, "Can you please move?" which gave Abuser 3 total control. He would often reply, "NO. You can sit down and shut the fuck up."

I recall one argument that was getting out of hand quickly. I disengaged and walked to the bedroom to watch TV and calm down. I wanted to give it some time before talking with Abuser 3 because the argument was going nowhere and Abuser 3 was getting really pissed. I shut the door behind me (I didn't lock it, I learned my lesson from Abuser 2) and I turned on the TV.

Abusers do not like it when you take control of the situation. It pisses them off. They are the ones who have to be in control. So, if you end the fight, they will follow you around and force you to argue until they are finished with you.

Abuser 3 then barged into the room, slamming the door open. He charged me (I was sitting on the bed) and yanked the TV remote out of my hand. He then turned off the TV. "You don't get to walk away in the middle of the argument!" He then threw the TV remote on the floor, crossed his arms, and stood in front of my exit with his legs apart.

I should mention here that controlling abusers often make you feel like a child living with a parent. The controlling partner does not let you have your own feelings, your own thoughts, or your own way of dealing with conflict. It is always "my way or the highway" with them. When you feel as though you are living with a parent instead of a partner, this is your body's way of telling you that the power dynamic is seriously off kilter. With a partner, all things should be equal. There should be equal power in the relationship. But when you live with a partner who tries to act like your parent, it reveals their controlling nature and your lower status (lack of power) in the relationship.

The purpose of intimidation is very simple; it is to gain control of the situation. It is to make the survivor do what the abuser wants. It is to force the survivor into a submissive position. Intimidation is used to gain power over the survivor.

Guilt Trips

Guilt trips are a manipulative and passive-aggressive way of getting a person to do what the abuser wants. The abuser says something which induces guilt in the survivor. This guilt makes the survivor feel that they need to take action in order to not feel guilty. Instead of talking about their feelings and asking for what they want or need, abusers will often use guilt trips to do both. Some examples are:

If you tell your mother you can't talk with her on the phone and she replies, "Fine, I really didn't want to talk with you anyway!"

Your partner really wants you to lose weight so he buys a gym membership for you.

"I have given everything to you, and this is how you repay me?"

"I have cleaned the entire house and you can't even take out the trash?"

"I have been nothing but nice to you and you have to start this shit?"

What guilt trips looked like to me: *Abuser 1 would say things like, "I've done everything for you! The least you could do is..." Abuser 3 however would use sarcasm to guilt trip me, "No, no, you just sit there, I got it." Abuser 3 would also guilt trip me then counter guilt trip me. For example, one time when I was sick I was lying in bed and said, "I feel so sick." Abuser 3 then said angrily, "Fine. I'll get you some soup." When I countered with, "I really was not trying to get you to get me soup. I really just wanted to express that I feel sick." He would counter guilt trip me with, "No, no. I will get you some soup (sarcastically). It's not like I was doing anything."*

The purpose of the guilt trip is to induce guilt so the person who feels guilty will jump into action. It is to gain control over the survivor by making them do something that the abuser wants them to do and to make the abuser look like the good guy, something he can use against the survivor in the future.

In the ways that I experienced it, guilt trips were used both as a way to control me and as a way to start conflict. Often, Abuser 3 would misinterpret things that I said as being a guilt trip (because he used guilt trips, he believed this was what everyone did to get others to do what they wanted - projection).

However, when I wanted or needed something, I would just ask for it. I didn't use guilt trips. Therefore, when Abuser 3 would interpret things I said as my trying to impose a guilt trip on him, it would frustrate me. I would try to explain that I was not trying to get him to do anything for me but he would interpret this as a further test. It would then turn into a guilt tripping contest to him. It would become an argument where I tried to explain that I did not actually want whatever it was that he was trying to give me and him arguing that he would give it to me. This gave him the upper hand because it allowed him to look like a good guy (doing something for someone) while also having something to be mad at me about (which he would use as an excuse to give me the silent treatment) and it gave him something to hold over my head in the future so he could get what he wanted again. "I went out of my way to get you soup when you were sick and you can't even take the kids to school today?"

Disengagement

With this tactic, the abuser will find ways to show you that he is not listening to you. This is a pure power struggle that can be found in many different types of interactions. Sometimes the tactic can be as subtle as someone picking up their phone whenever you talk. Other times the abuser does not respond to you during a conversation. The abuser may simply ignore you. It may be that the abuser turns on the TV while you are trying to have a conversation with him. The abuser may walk into another room while you are talking to him.

How I have experienced disengagement: *Abuser 3's favorite way to disengage was to pick up his phone whenever I would begin to talk to him. He would clearly ignore what I was saying. Every once in a while, he would look up from his phone and ask me to repeat myself. I would then repeat myself only for him to disengage and again ignore me by picking up his phone and reading it. In this case it was impossible for me to convey any important information to him. I constantly had to remind him of my plans because he would not listen to me.*

Just recently, I experienced this with a stranger. I went on a job interview. The interviewer started off by asking me a question. As soon as I started to answer it, he picked up his phone, began reading, scrolling, and texting. Then, he looked up from his phone and said, "Oh, I'm sorry, what did you say?" Again, as soon as I began talking, he began texting on his phone again. This happened every single time I tried to answer his questions.

This tactic lets the survivor know that they are unworthy of the abuser's attention. It also lets the survivor know that their thoughts and opinions don't matter. It is a pure power struggle. When the abuser disengages, it puts the survivor in a submissive position. This tactic can erode the survivor's self-esteem. This tactic also frustrates the survivor and blocks communication. When pointing out the issue of disengagement, the abuser can use the very subtle nature of this tactic to deny and discount the survivor's perception and feelings. "You are way too sensitive! Just because I was on my phone doesn't mean I didn't hear you!"

Pointing out the problem can also be used by the abuser to start a fight. Similarly, double standards are often at play. The abuser has most likely started a fight over the survivor's disengagement. However, the survivor is expected to just ignore the same behavior.

A note I would like to make about this tactic is that it is so subtle that you may recognize times when you have acted similarly. The question here is: are you disengaging? Are you listening and responding? If you are reading your phone while someone talks to you, you are not listening. Often when we are communicating with others we are multitasking. The difference between multitasking and disengagement is the engagement. If you walk away from your partner as he is talking but you state, "I'm listening" and you continue to respond to what he is saying, that is not disengagement. If you wait to turn on the TV until your partner has completed his thought and you have responded to what he has said, that is not disengagement. Disengagement is about making the other person feel they are not worthy of your time. Whatever you are doing is more important than listening to them. Disengagement shuts down communication.

As a side note, studies have shown that the human brain cannot effectively multitask. If attention is divided, all tasks suffer (Gladstones, Regan, & Lee, 1989). Even though you may not be intentionally disengaging, it's best, if possible, to give your full attention to one task at a time, particularly when dealing with people. When someone is speaking, show them the courtesy of listening. If you must, excuse yourself and let them know you *do* want to hear what they have to say, but you can't right now.

Competition

Living with an abuser is one big competition. Competition can be thought of as a struggle for power (McCarrick, Manderscheid, & Silbergeld, 1981). The abuser, in order to be in power and in control, believes that he needs to "win" at everything. When you, the one who is supposed to be submissive starts to "win" (whether it be achieving success, winning an argument, or being your own person, etc.), the abuser begins to feel powerless which fuels the competition.

So, what does competition look like in a relationship? Competition comes in many forms. Sometimes it can be one-upmanship. The abuser counters whatever you say with something better. In arguments, if you point out something the abuser did that was wrong, the abuser will one-up you by pointing out what you have done wrong. If you decide to run one mile, the abuser will exclaim that he is going to run two miles.

Competition also looks like the inability to celebrate the other's achievements. The abuser may sulk or make you feel like you are being braggadocious if you have achieved something great. The abuser may flaunt and brag when he has done something bigger or better than you. The abuser may rub it in when you have failed at something. Likewise, the abuser may discourage you from your goals and dreams in order to keep you from doing better than him, to keep you small and seemingly irrelevant.

What competition looked like to me: *When I would go to Abuser 1 for emotional support, for example, if I had had a bad day, he would one-up me by telling me how awful his day was. I was then expected to put my feelings and needs aside in order to comfort him.*

Abuser 3 was very competitive. If I expressed to Abuser 3 about how stressed I was by an upcoming exam, Abuser 3 would one-up me with how he had 2 exams and a paper that he was stressed about. If I stated that I was tired, Abuser 3 would start a rant about how he got up at 5am every day and never went to bed until it was late.

Notice that with one-upmanship, the abuser is also discounting and trivializing your experience.

With arguments, Abuser 2 would one-up me by increasing the ante. In other words, if I pointed out something that he did wrong he would then list all of the things he could remember that I had done wrong. During arguments, he would start to yell, then I would start to yell, then he would one-up me by throwing things.

As a side note, it is important to mention here that if you were raised in a house where your parents compared you to your better-performing siblings, and/or your parents constantly criticized you, then it is very possible that competition can be used against you to get you to take on more responsibilities. How does this work? If you were raised in a critical/competing environment you probably feel as though to be loved you have to work harder and perform better than others. You may also feel that in order to show someone that you love them, you do things for them. You may show them that you love them by helping them or by taking on more of their responsibilities which you see as making a noble sacrifice in order to gain their love. In a normal relationship, this is fine.

However, if you are in a relationship with an abuser, they will use this against you. They will pit you in competitions so that you will continue to show them that you love them by helping them more and more and by taking on more and more of their responsibilities. This in turn will fuel the competition, because as you take on more responsibilities and you achieve more and help more, this drives the abuser's insecurities and feelings of loss of control. You will never win this competition because you play by the rules, the unspoken rules of normal healthy behavior, and the abuser doesn't. The abuser's objective is to bog you down in so much work that you can't help but fail. But there may be many times you won't fail. You are strong and this makes the abuser feel like he is losing control over you.

Neglect

Living with a neglectful partner is quite simply living in a one-sided relationship. When the abuser neglects you, he will not help you when you ask for it and need it. The abuser does not support you in your decisions or what you do. You find yourself constantly fulfilling your partner's needs but your needs are left unfulfilled. The neglectful abuser may literally leave you stranded without money, a phone, or a way to get home. The neglectful abuser may abandon you in unknown areas and unsafe places. The neglectful abuser will not take care of you while you are sick and still expects you to fulfill your everyday duties. The neglectful abuser expects you to listen to all of his problems but does not have time for yours.

What neglect looked like to me: *When I lived with Abuser 2 I became very ill with food poisoning. I was having to run to the bathroom every 10 minutes. Because this continued for 12 hours, I became very dehydrated. As this was happening to me throughout the night, Abuser 2 never once got out of bed to help me or ask me if I was ok. In the morning, I woke him and told him that I needed to go to the hospital. Abuser 2 told me that I was being dramatic and that I was fine. I was enraged. I screamed, "Either you're going to take me to the hospital right now or I am calling an ambulance!" Although Abuser 2 agreed to drive me, he still believed that I was over exaggerating. He took me to the urgent care facility located within the hospital area. When the urgent care nurses saw me, they took my temperature and began to freak out, "You have to be admitted to the hospital right now! Your temperature is way too high!" In fact, it was so high, they refused to tell me what it was. By this point, I was so dehydrated I could not walk. I was extremely dizzy and could not stand. They placed me in a wheel chair and took me to the actual emergency room.*

As I was going through intake, Abuser 2 got up and left me. I have no idea where he went. What I do know is that he left me during a time when I was having to run to the bathroom every 10 minutes and I couldn't walk.

When I finally was admitted and given a room Abuser 2 reappeared again. I was so delirious at this point I could not remember my name or his name. He stayed for a few minutes and left again. Through the duration of the hospital stay I had no idea where he was. He left me, he never told my parents what was happening. He never took care of me. He left me alone in the hospital and I had no idea what was happening to me. When I was released, he took me back home. Never once did he ask how I was feeling or if he could help. He left me alone, in the room.

Abuser 3 also behaved similar to Abuser 2 when I was sick. Once, when I had gotten pneumonia, he refused to take me to urgent care. I was too sick to drive myself. I had to call my parents to pick me up to take me. Abuser 3 also expected me to continue fulfilling all of my "duties" while sick. It didn't matter if it was pneumonia, I better make dinner, fold everyone's laundry, clean the house, etc. Abuser 3 enjoyed punishing me when I was sick. If I was too sick to fulfill "my" responsibilities, Abuser 3 would ostracize me and give me the silent treatment.

Neglect is the lack of equal distribution (or the withholding) of resources by the powerful one. Resources consist of help, love, companionship, communication, and support among other things. The abuser refuses to help you when you need it, to support you when you need it, to communicate with you when it's needed, or to be an equal companion. Withholding the resources from you, makes the abuser feel more powerful.

When you are neglected, you feel as though you are in a one-sided relationship. You ARE in a one-sided relationship. You are doing all of the work and receiving nothing in return. Double standards are at play too because what is expected of you is not reciprocated from the abuser. In other words, you are expected to cater to the abuser when he is sick but the abuser does not cater to you when you are sick. To sum, neglect makes you feel as though you are alone in the world and that there is no point in asking for help because no one will help you when you need it.

Minimizing (Samsel, 2013)

This tactic is a mix of trivializing and discounting. The abuser convinces you that your perception is incorrect and insignificant. Most often, minimizing is used after physical violence. The abuser minimizes the abuse by claiming it isn't as bad as you believe it to be. The purpose of minimizing is to get the survivor to distrust her perception of the events and to minimize the abuse as well.

Minimizing works by desensitizing you to the violence. This is important to continue the cycle of violence. The survivor will be more likely to stay if she believes the abuse was not that bad or that it was a one-time thing. Minimizing is also used in conjunction with blaming. Typically, the abuser will tell the survivor that the abuse was not as bad as the survivor is making it out to be. Then the abuser will also tell the survivor that the abuse was her fault. If the abuser can make the survivor believe these things, the survivor will then perpetuate the cycle of violence by staying and trying even harder to be more "perfect" so she does not set the abuser off on another violent rampage.

What this looked like to me: *The first time I was physically assaulted by Abuser 3, we were arguing. I was attempting to leave the house because I could feel that the argument was turning violent, I knew that it was going nowhere and it was getting worse. The kids had hidden my car keys so that I couldn't leave. As I was searching for them, Abuser 3 screamed at me, "Get the fuck out of my house!" I put my hands in the air in the international symbol for giving up (both hands up, palms facing forwards, bent slightly back at the wrist and bent at the elbow), sort of the way someone would put their hands up if they were being arrested. At the same moment, I exclaimed, "I'm trying to leave but I can't find my keys!" Abuser 3 then rushed me. He charged forward forcefully shoving me. I nearly fell. He charged me again and shoved me backward. The third time he shoved me into the door. I scrambled to get the door open where I fled and he slammed it behind me. When we talked later about this incident I told him he was abusive. His expression was of utter shock and disgust. He exclaimed, "Are you serious? I barely touched you! I never BEAT you!" Abuser 3 then went on to explain to me, "When you threw your arms in the air, that was a sign of attack, and that is why I shoved you. I was defending myself!"*

In the first statement, "I barely touched you! I never BEAT you!" Abuser 3 minimizes the abuse. This tactic is used so that the abuser does not have to take responsibility for his actions. The next exclamation is blame. The abuser blames the survivor for the abuse. This puts the ball back into the survivor's court making her believe that if only she hadn't done X, or if she had worked harder, she would not have been physically abused. It makes the survivor believe that the violence was her fault and that she deserved it. This also excuses the physical violence.

No matter if the abuser grabbed your arm, shoved you, or

punched you, it is never your fault. The abuser is *always* in control of his actions. The abuser has purposefully used violence to control you. You do not make the abuser do anything. You do not control the abuser's actions nor are you responsible for the abuser's actions. Also, do not allow yourself to believe that the abuser "lost control." Many abusers will say this after being physically violent but it is absolutely not true. Physical violence is about control, needing absolute control over you.

Ingratiating Behavior (Samsel, 2013)

Ingratiating behavior is over-the-top niceness. Like the saying goes, "If it seems too good to be true, it probably is." When the abuser uses ingratiating behavior, he is being extremely nice in order to get something in return, perpetuate the "good guy persona," induce guilt, or confuse the survivor (especially after physical violence). This tactic is very subtle and hard to recognize.

When the abuser wants something, he may become overly nice, sweet, and charming to induce guilt and obligation in the survivor. Abusers know that giving gifts or compliments before asking for a favor will guilt the survivor into doing what they want. Thus, the survivor is more likely to give in to the abuser's demands.

Ingratiating behavior can be used by the abuser to confuse the survivor after physical violence. This is also known as the *Honeymoon Phase* in the Cycle of Violence. When the abuser switches from physically attacking to being sweet, loving, and charming, it can be very confusing for the survivor. The ingratiating behavior makes the survivor doubt her own experience of the violence and the severity of it. The overly loving behavior of the abuser reinforces his minimization of the abuse. The survivor starts to think things like: "He can't be all that bad, he can be so sweet and loving" and "The violence couldn't have been that severe, because he loves me, he would never really hurt me."

Furthermore, when the abuser uses ingratiating behavior in public but is violent behind closed doors, this emphasizes the extreme opposites of the Jekyll and Hyde personality of the abuser. Finally, this tactic consists of both manipulation tactics and guilt trips.

What ingratiating behavior looked like to me: *After being ridiculously callous to me, Abuser 1 would often buy me presents, take me*

44

shopping, or take me to lunch to offset the malicious behavior. This always confused me. I would feel extremely frustrated and angry with him for treating me horribly, for not listening to me, and for never apologizing for any wrongdoing, and then he would do something very nice for me like take me shopping. This made me feel obligated to let the issues go. It made me feel as though I owed him and that anything he did before was not allowed to be brought up any longer. Buying me presents and being overly nice to me gave him a free pass to treat me like shit. Often, I felt torn between the fact that Abuser 1 hated me and also loved me. When he would cater to me and shower me with gifts, I often forgot about the mean things he had previously done to me.

Abuser 3 also used ingratiating behavior. After Abuser 3 assaulted me, and realized I was leaving him, he would switch into an overly nice and apologetic demeanor in order to get me to stay. (The Honeymoon Phase in the Cycle of Violence is discussed in a later chapter). During these times Abuser 3 would say whatever he thought I wanted to hear in order to get me to come back. He would promise to quit drinking, he would promise to go to counseling, he swore that he would never hurt me again, that it was a one-time accident, and that he loved me more than life itself. He would then go out of his way to shower me with gifts, cards, flowers, and "love" notes.

At first this type of behavior really convinced me of what he was saying. It was used against me to make me believe that what he was saying was true and that we could work the relationship out and that I would be safe. In time, I realized it was B.S. because he continued to hurt me and he continued with this ingratiating behavior. It was a pattern for him and it is the typical pattern of every abuser.

What is the purpose of ingratiating behavior? This tactic is used to persuade the survivor that the abuse will not continue to happen and to confuse the survivor into staying in the relationship. The mix of violent behavior and ingratiating behavior adds to the extreme highs and extreme lows of the relationship. When it's good (during the Honeymoon Phase where the abuser uses ingratiating behavior) it feels like it is the best relationship you have ever had. The abuser can make you feel as though you have never been loved by anyone as much as the abuser loves you. However, when the violence happens, the relationship is at the lowest of lows and it feels as though the entire world is falling apart. Ingratiating behavior is one reason why the survivor might stay. It makes the survivor question whether the relationship is actually abusive and whether the abuse is really that bad. It also makes the survivor question their view of the abuser, "He can't be ALL bad, right?"

Self-Degradation (Buss, 1992)

This tactic is a form of manipulation and is a bit different because the abuser degrades himself in order to get the survivor to do something for him or to get out of his own responsibilities. Specifically, the abuser will degrade himself to make the survivor feel guilt, pity, or some other emotion which will prompt the survivor into action. For example, if it is the abuser's night to cook, he may say something like, "You know I'm terrible at cooking! I will just end up burning it anyway! Why don't you cook? We both know it will turn out much better!"

In this example, the abuser is putting himself down saying that he sucks at cooking to 1) make the survivor feel sorry for him, 2) get out of the responsibility of cooking, 3) make the survivor feel guilty that she is good at cooking and 4) get her to feel these emotions so strongly that she is motivated to cook.

What self-degradation looked like to me: *Abuser 3 used self-degradation a lot, especially when I asked for help and he didn't want to help me. One time, I really needed time to study for an upcoming exam so I asked Abuser 3 if he would take some of my responsibilities. I knew that he did not have any exams coming up so he should be able to help. To get out of helping me, he used self-degradation. He began to tell me how lucky I was that studying came so easily to me. He made me feel bad about getting good grades and making A's on my exams and classwork. He degraded himself to me saying that it was so hard for him. He had such a hard time remembering the things he read for class and that he couldn't remember the things he studied. He said he wasn't as smart as me. This made me feel guilty for being smart. Then he said he had to work twice as hard as I did to do as well. He could only take half the number of classes I could take because he had to work twice as hard to do well in those classes. I felt sorry for him and I actually believed him. Because I felt sorry for him and felt guilty for being smart, I lost the argument. I didn't get help with the things I had to do and nearly lost my sanity.*

Looking back at it now, I can see that what he was saying was total bullshit. He wasn't overwhelmed like I was. He had ample time to take naps and watch TV and do what he wanted to do, while I was working my ass off trying to stay afloat. He manipulated me and used my emotions, my good heartedness and vulnerability to get what he wanted – the ability to continue having less responsibility.

Let's be real. Abuser 3 believed that he was entitled to less responsibility.

He believed that those were my responsibilities in the first place and that he shouldn't have to do them. It was "women's work" and if I wanted to be able to go to school and chase my dreams then I better figure out how to do it while maintaining my household responsibilities.

Forced Teaming (de Becker, 1997; Samsel, 2013)

With this tactic, the abuser inflicts a sense of obligation in the survivor by telling the survivor that they have a common problem that needs to be fixed immediately. It is also implied that the best way to fix it is by both parties working together. This tactic is used by the abuser to short circuit the survivor's distrust of them. It is also used to get the survivor to come back to the abuser if she has left the relationship. If successful, forced teaming will allow the abuser to have control over the survivor once more.

It should be noted that even if there is a problem that the survivor and abuser have in common, it is not necessary to work on it immediately and it is unlikely that they both have to work on the problem together for it to be solved. Forced teaming is most clearly recognized by "we" statements.

What forced teaming looked like to me: *After Abuser 3 became violent with me, I left him. He wrote letters, emails, texts, cards, and he called me on the phone to try and convince me to come back to him using the forced teaming tactic. Here are some of the things he said using the forced teaming tactic:*

"Why throw it all away when we can fix it, and be back where we were just three days ago? WE CAN FIX THIS!"

"We have helped each other come back from very dark places. Why can't we try one more time. Please."

"We can't let this define the story of our relationship. We can beat this and be life-long lovers."

"Please don't let go of everything we have before we try everything we can to fix it."

"We have gotten through so much and improved each other and our relationship in so many ways together. I know we can come out of this

stronger than ever if we try. I promise!"

"We can fix the anger too and be even better."

I want to point out that in every one of these instances, Abuser 3 does not take responsibility for his violent actions. By him using the forced teaming tactic, he is essentially telling me that I too am at fault for his abuse of me, and that I also have responsibility in fixing it (blaming tactic).

Please know that if you are being abused by someone, their violent actions are their sole responsibility. You do not and cannot make someone become physically violent with you. They choose to use   violence.

CHAPTER 4
VERBALLY ABUSIVE TACTICS

Countering (Evans, 1996; Samsel, 2013)

This tactic can be thought of as never agreeing, someone who argues with you for the sake of arguing. Countering can be seen as arguing technicalities and constantly correcting. The abuser counters everything you say. It doesn't matter, even if you agree with him, he will find a way to disagree and argue with you. The abuser is so set on arguing for the sake of arguing that he will even disagree with things he originally said, just because you agreed with him.

It should be mentioned that countering is different than just disagreeing. In normal relationships having differing opinions is natural. You will not agree with everyone on everything. The difference here is that countering is a systematic and habitual way of disagreeing. Countering is repetitive. The abuser RARELY agrees with anything you say. He will act irrationally by disagreeing with his own opinions and statements in order to disagree with you. Some examples of countering are:

Survivor: "These shoes are too small, they pinch my feet."
Abuser: "No they don't, they're fine!"

Survivor: "It's cold in this house!"
Abuser: "No it's not, it's hot!"

Survivor: "Oh wow, it's set on 75, it must be hot!"
Abuser: "Are you kidding, 75 is cold!"

Survivor: "I feel so sad that Aunt Lydia died."
Abuser: "You're not sad. You were just laughing a second ago!"

Abuser: "It's not green, its teal."

What countering looked like to me: *When I lived with Abuser 3, countering often took the form of yes you did/no I did not type of arguments. There were many times I would say, "Could you please not talk to me like that?" and then he would counter with, "I never said that!" These types of arguments would quickly turn into "Yes you did!" and "No I did not!" arguments.*

Realize that countering is another form of discounting. While the abuser is arguing with you, they are pointedly denying your reality. They are attempting to make you believe that your truth is "wrong" while their truth is "right." This is also black and white thinking and is another form of stonewalling. When countering is used many times in one conversation this can even be a form of mind fucking, especially if the abuser disagrees with himself in order to counter you. Then you know the conversation is circular because the abuser's goal is to disagree with everything you say – not to actually have a rational conversation.

Other examples of countering that I experienced were, "I didn't call you a bitch, I said you were ACTING like one!" Other times when I would repeat back what Abuser 3 said to make sure I had understood it, he would say, "That's not what I said, quit putting words in my mouth!" Abuser 1's countering was very subtle. He would often correct me on my pronunciation of words and my use of grammar.

Abuser 2 often mixed countering with intimidation. One time, as we walked into the house, I smelled gas. We had a gas furnace, so immediately I knew we had a gas leak. Worried, I told Abuser 2. He countered me exclaiming, "I don't smell gas! There is no gas leak. Quit being so dramatic!" He then pulled his lighter from his pocket and began walking around the house lighting it to scare me and to prove to me there wasn't a gas leak. Thankfully, nothing blew up or caught fire. But, we did have a gas leak because a couple of days after that, he had to get treatment for gas poisoning.

Countering serves to gain control over you by wearing you down, frustrating you, blocking any real conversation, and confusing you. If the abuser is always right, the abuser has the power and control. Remember that the abuser believes that you are not a separate entity. You should not have thoughts and feelings outside of what the abuser tells you what to think and feel. Therefore, when you have your own thoughts, opinions, and feelings, the abuser becomes angry and feels a loss of control over you.

Baiting

Baiting occurs when the abuser says something nonchalant that is meant to hurt you deeply in order to elicit a reaction from you. Then, when you react, the abuser, in all their calm glory, calls you crazy, extremely emotional, and tells you to calm down. The comment used to bait you is typically regarding something that has happened to you that is very hurtful (i.e. death, divorce, adultery, bankruptcy) or something that you are insecure about (i.e. your weight, acne, scars, stretchmarks). Some examples are:

"Don't you think that is why your ex cheated on you?"

"Maybe if you lost some weight you would get more action in the bedroom."

"No wonder your kid doesn't speak to you!"

What baiting looked like to me: *Abuser 3 would say something very cutting like, "You are so emotional!" while doing things to purposefully push my buttons (like continuously interrupting me to counter my points) and when I started to yell because he kept interrupting me and because I was enraged, he would then ask me if I was on my period. He would say something like, "You know you always act like a bitch when you are about to start your period." Then he would act like I was crazy and tell me that I needed to get help. "You are such a piece of work, you know that? God, calm down! You are the most emotional person I have ever met! I seriously have never met anyone as emotional as you! You need to get help because you have some serious emotional issues!"*

After I left Abuser 3 he said things like, "What happened the other night was a serious misstep in what is normally a very calm relationship, even with your anger. I am not minimizing what happened at all."

First, Abuser 3 is trying to minimize the abuse and make it seem as though he is not abusive by saying that it was a one-time thing. In the same sentence, he then baits me by saying, "even with your anger." This is used to focus the attention away from his violence and redirect the attention to my supposed "anger." This statement is also used to blame me for his abuse. The next sentence really drives this home. Abuser 3 counters me by saying, "I am not minimizing." In fact, he is minimizing. He is trying to force me to believe that he is not minimizing, and in this way, the last statement is also stonewalling.

Abuser 3 refuses to recognize that I have a different perspective and is trying to force me to take on his perspective. He is essentially telling me that my perspective is incorrect and his is the correct perspective. This is both discounting and black and white thinking. In this example, his baiting tactic did not fully work. I never responded to any of his letters. However, when used in face to face conversation, you bet this tactic would have derailed any sort of productive conversation.

Baiting has several purposes. First, it makes the survivor look crazy while the abuser looks sane. If the abuser baits the survivor in front of other people, the abuser not only adds credit to his fake public "nice guy" persona, but the abuser also discredits the survivor by making her look irrational.

Second, the abuser is able to gain control over the survivor because he is able to get the survivor to react the way he wanted her to react. The abuser also feels good because he got the survivor to lose her shit in public.

Third, this tactic allows the abuser to play the victim. After baiting the survivor and then watching her flip out, the abuser can sit back, feign innocence, and then point out how crazy she is. This tactic also falls under crazy making. The whole method of baiting, feigning innocence, and then pointing out how "crazy" the survivor is can really make the survivor feel crazy and believe that she is crazy. What's worse is that when others see this happen, they fail to realize that the survivor has been baited, or they become so taken aback by the survivor's response that they only pay attention to that and they reprimand the survivor for her outburst.

Lastly, it allows the abuser to derail the conversation. It effectively changes the subject allowing the abuser to avoid taking responsibility for his actions.

"Jokes" (Evans, 1996)
With this tactic, the abuser uses "jokes" to hide putdowns.

These "jokes" are not funny. They are really hurtful things said and covered in laughter. When the survivor points out that it is not funny, or explains how the "joke" hurt her feelings, the abuser quickly discounts the survivor by saying things like:

"You are so sensitive!"

"You need to grow a sense of humor"

"Why do you always take things so seriously?"

"You need to learn how to take a joke!"

Some examples of abusive jokes are:

"Her head is stuck so far up her own ass, she can't even see the light of day!"

"She's not the sharpest tool in the shed, now is she?"

"I'm imagining what it would be like with your mouth sewn shut."

"You're not pretty enough to be this stupid."

What abusive jokes looked like to me: *When I would forget something, Abuser 1 would say, "You'd forget your head if it wasn't attached to your shoulders!" Once, while shopping at a store with Abuser 3, I had a polite conversation with the male clerk. As we were leaving the clerk said, "Hope you guys enjoy the rest of your day!" So, I replied, "Have a great day, yourself!" Immediately Abuser 3 snarls, "Why don't you just suck his dick while you are at it!?" This comment really embarrassed me. I was floored that he would say something like that. Also, Abuser 3's comment was used purposefully to discourage me from showing kindness especially to males and to discourage me from talking with males in general. Of course, when I brought up his disgusting statement when we were in the parking lot he claimed, "It was just a joke!"*

Once Abuser 3 said to me, "So many things that were supposed to be taken as "light hearted" have been taken the wrong way over the years."

These "jokes" are both passive-aggressive and manipulative.

They are used to belittle you, make you feel uncomfortable, and put you down. Sometimes the goal of the statement is to get you to do something (i.e. not talk to guys) while other times it is used to make you feel horrible. When these jokes are perpetrated around friends, often friends do not recognize the verbal abuse for what it is and they also join in laughing. They do not realize that the "joke" is at the expense of the survivor. Similarly, when the survivor calls out the abuser on his horrible "joke" and is discounted ("It was just a joke! Quit being so sensitive!"), this makes the survivor look overly emotional in the eyes of others. This further serves the abuser in that it makes him look like the sane one while the survivor looks crazy.

Sometimes, the abuser might jump out from behind a door or bang on a window from the outside of the house to scare the wits out of the survivor. Let me point out that this is really horrible. When a survivor experiences physical abuse, she often feels on edge, worried about when the next episode of violence will happen. This is another way to shove it in the survivor's face that the abuser has absolute control. The abuser can scare the wits out of the survivor whenever he wants and then minimize the severity of it by calling it a "joke," which makes this act especially horrid.

What this looked like to me: *Sometimes, when we weren't fighting, Abuser 2 would turn off the car's headlights while he drove on dark country roads late at night. He would laugh hysterically when I would begin to freak out about it. Other times when he drove at night, he would put on welding goggles to scare me. Welding goggles are especially dark so that the welder's eyes won't burn from the extremely bright light. When I expressed my fear and anger over the matter, Abuser 2 would scoff, "You really need to lighten up. I was just fucking with you. Nothing bad happened!" In this situation, Abuser 2 took away any control I had over the situation. Then, when I confronted him on it, he used trivializing, minimizing, and discounting to silence me.*

Blocking and Diverting (Evans, 1996)

Blocking and diverting are used during conversations and arguments to block and divert the conversation. Blocking is used the most in stonewalling whereas diverting is used the most in mind fucking. Both can occur in circular conversations.

To block someone during a conversation is to attempt to prevent the conversation from happening. To divert someone during a conversation is to attempt to change the subject which is also a way to avoid talking about something that a person does not want to talk about. Some examples of blocking are:

"End of discussion!"

"I've had enough of your crap!"

"That's a complete load of bull!"

"Just drop it!"

"This conversation is over!"

"Shut the fuck up!"

"Get the fuck out of my house!"

Some examples of diverting are:

"That's not what I said! Quit putting words in my mouth!"

"Me? What about the time when you…."

"I didn't call you a bitch, I said you were acting like a bitch!"

What blocking and diverting looked like to me: *All of the phrases above have been said to me or screamed at me. Abuser 1 typically said things like, "End of discussion!" or "That's a complete load of bull!" and "Just drop it!" Abuser 3 however, said things like, "Get the fuck out of my house!" or "Shut the fuck up!" and "I didn't call you a bitch, I said you were acting like a bitch!"*

The purpose of blocking and diverting is to gain complete control over the conversation. The abuser decides what can be discussed, when it can be discussed, where it can be discussed, and how it can be discussed. If the abuser does not like what you are talking about, he may choose to simply shut down communication. On the other hand, the abuser may decide to wear you down and frustrate you by diverting the conversation. The diverting tactic can also be crazy making because it often ends up in an endless argument that never gets resolved.

The survivor is a reasonable person and wants to make sense out of senseless conversations. Because she is reasonable and believes that others operate like her, she has a hard time seeing the circular conversations for what they are: diversion tactics aimed at avoiding talking about real issues.

Blocking and diverting tactics can also include many other tactics such as: denial, stonewalling, mind fucking, accusing and blaming, threatening, etc.

Accusing and Blaming (Evans, 1996)

With this tactic, the abuser accuses the survivor of doing something wrong and blames the survivor for the abuser's physical violence, anger, incompetency, etc. Several examples of accusing and blaming are:

"If you hadn't distracted me, I would have put the tire on right!" Here the abuser accuses the survivor of distracting and then blames the survivor for putting the tire on wrong.

"If you weren't such a bitch, we wouldn't be having this fight!" In this sentence, the abuser accuses the survivor of being a bitch and then blames her for the fight.

"If you had been watching the food, it wouldn't have burned!" The abuser accuses the survivor of not watching the food and then blames her for it burning.

"Maybe if you helped around the house more, I wouldn't be so stressed!" In this interaction, the abuser accuses the survivor of not helping around the house and blames the survivor for the abuser's stress.

What accusing and blaming looked like to me: *After both episodes of physical violence I experienced with Abuser 3, he accused me and blamed me for them. The first time was the incident where I threw my hands up in the air to show that I was giving up and that I was trying to leave. He then rushed me and shoved me several times. He claimed that had I not thrown my hands in the air, he would not have shoved me. He accused me of escalating the fight because I put my arms in the air and blamed me for his physical violence.*

The other time Abuser 3 physically assaulted me, we were arguing and again it escalated. Later, I tried to speak with him about the physical violence. I told him that what he did was domestic violence. He denied the abuse exclaiming, "I never beat you!" He also said, "You know what? You have a lot of responsibility in this too. If you hadn't pushed my buttons, then I never would have even done that! You're just as guilty for what happened as I am. YOU PROVOKED ME!" By explaining the reasons for his violence, Abuser 3 had also "justified" the abuse (Samsel, 2013).

After I left Abuser 3, he told me, "Our relationship is truly a constructive, happy relationship in spite of our anger problems." Here Abuser 3 does not take responsibility for the violence he enacted on me and he blames me for the abuse as well.

It is really important for me to mention here again that you are not responsible for THE ABUSER'S violent actions. When arguments occur, both parties say things that hurt and anger the other person. However, what you do with that anger is your responsibility. You decide whether to physically attack someone when you are angry or to walk away. Just like the abuser decides to physically attack or walk away. That is their choice.

The overall purpose of the accusing and blaming tactic is to divert the attention away from the abuser's actions and place the attention onto the survivor's actions. This is a way of controlling the conversation by redirection. At the same time, this is a way for the abuser to avoid taking responsibility for his own actions. This is part of blocking and diverting, denial, defining problems, stonewalling, and mind fucking tactics.

The purpose of accusing and blaming the survivor for the violence is to thwart their own responsibility for their violent behavior. Accusing and blaming the survivor for the violence allows the abuser to NOT have to take responsibility for his actions which allows the abuser to continue the abuse. Furthermore, by diverting the attention back to the survivor's behavior, the survivor now feels as though she has to explain or defend her behavior. This moves the conversation further away from the abuser's actions. Blaming the survivor for the physical abuse also makes the survivor believe that if she had only done X, the physical abuse would not have happened. This makes the survivor believe that the abuse is somehow in her control, which is the farthest from the truth.

I want to mention one other point here. The abuser never loses control of himself during a violent episode. Often, the abuser will tell the survivor some version of this: they saw red, they blacked out, they got so angry they lost control. However, this is absolutely false. During an argument, the abuser feels that they are losing control of YOU and in order to regain control over you, they become violent to force you into submission. This is especially true when you are "winning" the argument.

Defining Problems (Samsel, 2013)

I like to think of this tactic as reworking an argument so that what you did wrong is brought to the forefront of the conversation. This requires a certain amount of finesse. However, like accusing and blaming, abusers have a knack for turning something that they did wrong into something that you did wrong. This tactic can also be used first by the abuser to continually state all of the things you do wrong so that you are so focused on doing better that you never have a chance to bring up what bothers you about the abuser. Some examples of defining problems are:

When you tell the abuser he really hurt your feelings and instead of apologizing, he lists all of the times you have hurt his feelings over the past 5 years.

When you ask the abuser to stop calling you a bitch and he replies, "You're mad because I've called you a bitch?! What about the times when you called me a dick?!"

Your romantic partner is always pointing out the things you do wrong. But when you bring up the things he does that you don't like, he tells you that you're being insensitive and it's not the right time to talk about it. He also gives excuses as to why it's not the right time: someone died, he is stressed, he has something more important to do, etc. However, in reality, anytime you bring it up, it's never "the right time."

What defining problems looked like to me: *Abuser 1 and Abuser 3 both used constant criticism to keep me focused on fixing "my problems" and defending my behaviors. When I brought up things that Abuser 3 did, it was usually met with, "This isn't a good time to talk about this." Sometimes, when I really pressed the issue, Abuser 3 would shut down communication by using accusing, blaming, denying, stonewalling, diverting, and other tactics to avoid taking responsibility and avoid talking about the problem.*

Abuser 2, on the other hand, would barrage me with so many tactics that he would make communicating completely miserable. Abuser 2 would use mind fucking and circular conversations to wear me down and punish me for bringing up something that he didn't like. Usually, after the argument was finished I would feel completely worn out, exhausted, confused, and ultimately unsatisfied. Nothing would be resolved and the issue that I brought up was not addressed. Typically, by the end of the argument, I would have been given a long list of the horrible things I had done in the relationship, a list of things I needed to work on to be a better person, and a list of all the things that I had done wrong. I usually left these arguments in tears and hyperventilating.

This tactic keeps the survivor addressing and defending her own actions while never being allowed to discuss the abuser's actions. Like accusing, blaming, blocking and diverting, the survivor becomes preoccupied with listening to the long list of items that the survivor has done wrong while never getting the chance to bring up what the abuser has done wrong. This tactic is also part of the mind fucking and criticizing tactics.

Criticizing/Nit-Picking (Evans, 1996)

With this tactic, every little thing the survivor does is scrutinized and criticized. The survivor is left "choosing her battles wisely" because the survivor knows that any one of these criticisms can turn into an all-out war. It is with this tactic that the abuser finds fault in almost everything the survivor does. Some examples of criticizing and nit-picking are:

"Wow, you've worn a lot of makeup today!"

"You look really tired!"

"This roast would have been great, had you cooked it more."

"Your nails are too long."

"Why do you always wear jeans?"

"Why are you always frowning? You should smile more."

"You always have the TV too loud."

"Your handwriting looks so childish."

What criticism and nit-picking looked like to me: *Abuser 1 was the master of criticism. He had a million ridiculous rules that I could never remember, which required very particular ways of doing things. He was also a black and white thinker who operated under an "I am always right, you are always wrong" attitude. Putting this altogether, Abuser 1 was somewhere in between a Nazi and a tyrant. He would order me to do something like clean the bathroom, and then come back behind me and "check my work." He would use that as an opportunity to criticize and demean me.*

Abuser 1 often took the opportunity to criticize things about me to make me feel bad about myself. He often told me that my handwriting looked childish. He would say things like, "You would look so much prettier if you…." Sometimes he would give me a disgusting look and would say, "Are you really going to wear that?"

Abuser 3's nit-picking was different from Abuser 1's nit -picking. Abuser 3 made me believe that I was an extremely loud and obnoxious person by constantly criticizing me when I did things that made noise. He would often say things like, "You are so loud!" When I would accidently drop something like my phone or even a pen, he would say, "Why are you always so angry?" After I closed a door normally he'd exclaim, "Why are you always slamming doors?" He would even criticize me on things I could not control. I can never breathe out of one side of my nose. Sometimes it makes a whistling sound that I cannot get to stop even by blowing my nose or using nasal spray. When the very soft and hardly distinguishable nose whistling would happen, he would look at me with disgust and say, "Is that your nose?" With this constant criticism on my "loudness" I began to open and close doors so slowly that you couldn't hear them. I also tried really hard not to drop things.

Abuser 3 would criticize me in other ways too. When I would try to lay on him, with my head in the crook of his arm he would tell me to get up because my hair was too scratchy. This would make me feel unloved and I knew it was his way of trying to get me to change my hair. Sometimes I would dye my hair in the bathroom and Abuser 3 would exclaim, "Every time you dye your hair, you get the dye everywhere!" Which was a total lie. But, nevertheless, I started to dye my hair outside so I wouldn't have to hear the criticism anymore. Even then, he would complain about dye getting on the concrete or the grass, and so I'd end up standing on a tarp.

With criticism, the complaints are endless. They are all directed at getting you to do something differently or doing it their way. The constant nit-picking is really micro control, or tiny ways to control you. The abuser feels good when he can get you to do things his way. He feels in control. The constant nit-picking and belittling break the survivor down, causing lower self-esteem, a loss of sense of self, and even depression. When the survivor gives in, she often feels as though she is doing a great job of choosing her battles and keeping the peace. However, the survivor does not realize that during this time, she is losing herself. Everything that the survivor changes in order to keep the peace is another thing that she gives up control over and is another thing that the *abuser* gets control over. The survivor does not realize that this is part of the grooming process.

Threatening (Evans, 1996)

Threatening others is verbal intimidation. It involves statements which are intended to manipulate the survivor into doing what the abuser wants. Threats often consist of statements to reveal your secrets, to hurt or kill you, your kids, pets, or to destroy your things. The abuser may also threaten to commit suicide if you do not comply. Sometimes threats are vague. Some examples of threats are:

"Don't make me go there!"

"You do not want me to bring up…"

"You have three seconds to shut the fuck up!"

"If you don't come back, I will burn all of your things."

"If you don't shut up, I swear I will hurt the dog!"

"I will kill myself if you don't come back!"

How I've experienced threats: *Abuser 2 typically used forceful, scary, extreme statements to threaten me. He would force me into cars to continue arguments. While he drove erratically he would say things like, "I am going to kill both of us!" Other times he would say, "I swear to God I'm trying so hard not to kill you right now!"*

Abuser 3 used a variety of threatening statements in order to control me. One of his favorite threatening phrases was, "You're starting to piss me off!" He would usually say this in the beginning of an argument to "warn me" that the argument was escalating and that if I did not comply or stop arguing it would end badly for me. Another subtle threat was when he would try to force me to apologize to him. This was almost always after I had brought up something he had done that really upset me. He would then turn the argument back around to something I had done that pissed him off, that now I had to apologize for – OR ELSE. He would say things like, "All you have to do is say two little words!" This emphasized to me that I needed to say "I'm sorry" in order to make the fighting stop or to prevent the argument from becoming violent.

Other times Abuser 3 would use threats to get his way. For instance, after the first bout of physical violence, one of my conditions for coming back to him was that he would never drink again. Of course, that did not last long. Once Abuser 3 felt that I was committed to him, he cornered me and threatened to break up with me if I did not agree to his drinking.

Abuser 3 threatened me verbally before becoming violent. He would say things like, "You have three seconds to get the fuck out of my face!" When I told him calmly that I wasn't in his face he would scream, "IF YOU DON'T GET THE FUCK OUT OF MY FACE I WILL SHOVE MY ELBOW IN YOUR NOSE!"

When I left Abuser 3 after becoming violent with me the second time, he threatened, "If you don't come back, me and the kids will die." The threat was vague. I wasn't sure if he was trying to say that he would kill himself and the kids or if he and the kids couldn't live without me. Either way, it was a threat and an attempt to manipulate me into coming back to him.

The purpose of threatening someone is to scare them into submission. It is used to force someone into doing something she is reluctant or refuses to do. Threats are used to scare the survivor into silence, or into doing something for the abuser. Threats are used when the abuser feels he is losing control over the survivor and escalates the argument in order to regain control.

Name Calling (Evans, 1996)

Name calling is a tactic which belittles and puts down the survivor. The abuser uses name calling to make the survivor feel inferior. In turn, it also makes the abuser feel better about himself. Name calling can occur under the "jokes" tactic as well. This is true if the abuser calls you a name and then when you become upset, he says, "It was just a joke!" Some of the most common types of name calling occur in arguments: bitch, cunt, slut, whore, asshole, bastard, fat ass, dick, prick, hormonal, psycho, crazy, jerk, ragbag, cum dumpster.

What name calling looked like to me: *I experienced both common types of name calling and very subtle name calling. In arguments, I was often called a bitch, cunt, psycho, crazy, and ragbag. There was also very subtle name calling that happened. Abuser 1's nickname for me was "Butterball." This insinuated that I was fat, round, and greasy. Abuser 2's name of endearment for me was "Shithead." Most people call their loved ones' babe, baby, honey, sweetie, darling, bae, or love. He called me shithead. Abuser 3 never called me fat outright. However, Abuser 3 had a very sneaky way of calling me fat. He would point to women who were my size and shape and say that they were too fat for him, he would never date a girl that fat, and then he would tell me "we" needed to lose weight. When I put on my favorite shirt, Abuser 3 would say, "Don't wear that." When I asked why, he told me it made me look like I was pregnant.*

All types of name calling that I experienced made me feel horrible about myself. When the names were of "endearment" they also made me feel confused because I hated the nicknames but felt like I was supposed to like them. The subtle ways that Abuser 3 would call me fat without actually calling me fat got me to change my habits. I threw my favorite shirt away and I started a diet (and lost 25 lbs.). Some people might rejoice for losing 25 lbs but I was only 130 lbs to begin with, on a 5'3' frame. I looked emaciated. This just shows how much control he had over me. He knew what to say and how to say it to get me to do what he wanted.

So, what's the point of name calling? First, it puts the survivor in "their place," beneath the abuser. Second, it makes the abuser feel in control and better about themselves. Third, it makes the survivor feel horrible about themselves which is important to keep the survivor stuck in the abusive relationship. Name calling makes the survivor feel that they are not worthy of love and that no one else will love them as much as the abuser loves them. Finally, it can be used as a way to get the survivor to do what the abuser wants.

Ordering (Evans, 1996)

Ordering is flat out telling someone what to do. Ordering is about controlling you, getting you to do what the abuser wants, without having to ask you. Ordering shows ownership over you. In this aspect, the abuser does not see you as a separate entity but an extension of himself. Therefore, the abuser feels that he does not need to ask you. This tactic prepares and grooms you for *expecting mind reading*. Eventually, the abuser will no longer order you to do things but expect you to do them without having to tell you. Many ordering statements start with phrases like, "Get me..." or "Come get...." Or "I need you to..." or "Help me..."

Some examples are:

"Get me a beer."

"Get our friend a drink."

"Come clean up this mess."

"Come over here and sit down."

"I need you to shut your mouth and open your ears."

"Help me pick this up."

"Answer the door."

"Look at me when I'm talking to you."

"Tell them that story you told me."

"You're not leaving."

"You'll do as you're told."

What ordering looked like to me: *I've heard some version of all the above in the abusive relationships that I've lived in. Abuser 1 typically used the "Come do this" and "I need you to..." statements. Abuser 3 on the other hand would say things like, "Shut up!" "Get the fuck out!" "Calm down!" "Get the dog!" and "You're not leaving." Abuser 2 was different in that he would say things like, "Get me a drink, woman," "Make me a sandwich," or "Bring your ass over here."*

Ordering is used to make it known who is in charge. When the abuser orders you to do something, he is stating that you are the subservient one while the abuser is the one in power and control. You follow the rules; the abuser makes the rules. Ordering makes the survivor feel powerless and subjugated.

Constantly Interrupting

This tactic is very subtle. The abuser interrupts the survivor regularly, not only during arguments, but also in daily conversation. This can make conversing extremely frustrating for the survivor because the abuser is making it known that what the survivor talks about is not important and that whatever the abuser interrupts with is more important. Furthermore, the society we live in teaches us that when someone is talking we should listen which puts the survivor at a disadvantage. If she does not listen when the abuser interrupts, the survivor is interpreted as being rude. This tactic is a pure struggle for power. It creates a situation where the survivor is forced to stop talking and listen or otherwise face an argument or appear to be rude and aggressive. This tactic can be seen more easily during an argument when the abuser does not let the other person get a word in edgewise.

It should be noted that we all get excited from time to time and can't wait to share our information and so we interrupt others. This is different from constantly interrupting. To recognize this as a tactic, it is important to see it as a pattern of behavior. The abuser interrupts the survivor more often than not, the survivor waits patiently for her turn to speak, or the survivor just quits talking altogether. Furthermore, if the survivor brings up the issue, she is often met with crazy making, denial, trivializing, discounting, or projecting. The abuser may scoff and say, "God! I just wanted to show you a hotrod! Why are you acting so crazy?" Or the abuser might deny interrupting the survivor, "I never interrupted you. How can I interrupt you when you weren't talking?" The abuser may trivialize the situation, "I mean seriously, you were talking about dinner. It's not like you were saving the world." Or the abuser may discount the survivor's perspective, "It really wasn't a big deal. Why are you acting like such a bitch?!" Lastly, the abuser may use projecting, "You're pissed off at me for interrupting you ONE TIME?! You interrupt me ALL the time!"

What constantly interrupting looked like to me: *Abuser 3 was the worst at interrupting. Whenever we were in the car and I was talking he would interrupt me to point out random things: like a motorcycle, a hotrod, a turtle, a dog, a squirrel. The list of the random things he would interrupt with could go on forever. It frustrated me more than a lot of things. Sometimes I would say things like, "Are you done? Can I finish talking now?" Other times I would shut down midsentence and not say anything else. When I would explain how much it frustrated me that he continually interrupted me he used all of the tactics above to block and divert the conversation. Above all else, Abuser 3 LOVED to interrupt me during arguments. He knew it was a pet peeve; it frustrated me to no end. It was his way of taking control of the argument. He could force me to listen to him but he absolutely did not have to listen to me.*

The purpose of constantly interrupting is to gain dominance over the person being interrupted. It is a pure power struggle. It is used to put the survivor in a subjugated role. Constantly interrupting forces the survivor to listen to the abuser. It also silences the survivor.

Excessive Talking (Samsel, 2013)

Excessive talking goes hand in hand with constantly interrupting. A person who talks excessively commands the room and prevents others from getting a word in. When someone is talking, the norm is to stop and listen. If others do not stop and listen, they are perceived as rude. This is a very subtle control tactic. Typical tactics of excessive talkers are: taking over an entire conversation, speaking extremely quickly to not let others get a word in, speaking for a very long time so that others are forced to listen, and making the conversations about themselves.

What excessive talking looked like to me: Abuser 1 was an extremely excessive talker. At a table full of individuals, he would often take over the conversation, speaking extremely loudly and talking for long periods of time. He would also change the conversation for other people when he deemed it to be unpleasant. Abuser 1 would command your attention for long periods of time telling the same stories or re-explaining the same point for the tenth time in a row. He loved to talk about himself. He had a way to turn every conversation so that it was focused back on him.

The purpose of excessive talking is to draw attention to the abuser, who in his own mind is the only one worth listening to, control the conversation because he sees himself as the most knowledgeable, and to remain in control of others by forcing them to pay attention. This tactic is also a pure power struggle. When the abuser talks excessively, he feels very good about himself. At the same time, this tactic silences the survivor, frustrates the survivor, and controls the survivor's ability to get anything else done.

Asking Questions (Samsel, 2013)

This tactic can be thought of as giving someone the "third degree." As with constantly interrupting and excessive talking, this subtle control tactic commands attention and demands an answer. In society, we are trained that when someone asks a question, it is respectful to answer it. Not answering questions is perceived as rude and antagonizing. Furthermore, by continually asking questions, the abuser is able to control the conversation and the situation. This tactic is used by asking one question right after another, after another. Therefore, as soon as the person finishes answering one question, another is asked.

Other times the tactic is used by asking a question and then when the individual begins to answer it, they will be interrupted with another question. In this situation, a pure power struggle is happening. Sometimes the abuser asks questions that are inappropriate, or ones he already knows the answer to. Another way this tactic is used is by asking questions to make commands or to question the person's capability or competence. This is a tactic used often by police and military interrogators to throw a suspect off guard and prevent them from having time to formulate an answer or gather their thoughts. It's often accompanied by threatening or intimidating postures and tone of voice.

Questions used as commands:

"Where do you think you're going?"

"You actually think you are going out looking like that?"

Questioning capability or competence:

"Why are you doing it like that?"

"You've never heard of that?"

"Do you not know how to do it?"

"What are you saying?"

Other Questions:

"Where were you?"

"Who are you texting?"

"Who are you with?"

"Why didn't you pick up the phone when I called?"

"Where are you going?"

What asking questions looked like to me: *Abuser 1 would often ask me inappropriate questions. After handing my mail to me he would ask, "Why is X sending you letters?" Or after I opened a letter, he would ask, "What did it say?" When parking my car in the driveway he would suspiciously look in the windows and bombard me with questions like, "Have you gotten your car inspected?" "How many miles do you have on your car?" "When was the last time you got your tires rotated?" At first glance, these questions might sound like those of a person who cares about your welfare and that of your vehicle, but these questions are always asked in a tone of voice that implies incompetence on the part of the survivor and suspiciousness on part of the abuser. After answering a phone call or receiving a text both Abuser 1 and 3 would typically ask me, "Who was on the phone?" "What did they want?" "Who's texting you?"*

Abuser 3's favorite question, on the other hand, was, "WHAT ARE YOU DOING?" This was meant to make me feel like a kid caught with my hand in the cookie jar. When I would get up to go to the bathroom at night Abuser 3 would bark, "WHAT ARE YOU DOING?" When I put the dishes away: WHAT ARE YOU DOING? When I would go to the bedroom to watch a TV show that I wanted to watch: "WHAT ARE YOU DOING?" When I would stay up past 9pm studying: "WHAT ARE YOU DOING?" When I would accidentally drop something: "WHAT ARE YOU DOING?" This specific tactic was emphasized to make me feel like I was doing something that I wasn't supposed to be doing. Every innocuous detail of my life was suspect and open to scrutiny.

The purpose of this tactic in many respects is to take away your autonomy. By forcing you to answer nosy questions, all the information is given to the abuser. Information which is typically none of the abuser's business. By giving all of this information up, you no longer have any separateness from the abuser. You do not have your own mail, your own friends, your own conversations, or your own activities. Your right to privacy as an adult has been revoked by the abuser. This makes the abuser feel like he is in control of the survivor. All decisions must be okayed through the abuser. All actions must be explained to the abuser. All must be justified to the abuser. The abuser knows that information is power. That is why they often withhold information from the survivor while at the same time require the survivor to explain, justify and reveal all information to them (more double standards).

Many times, abusers will use the information that the survivor has provided – against the survivor. The abuser may start fights over phone calls, text messages, mail, or going out. The abuser might accuse the survivor of infidelity. Or the abuser may attempt to catch the survivor in a lie. This show of distrust in the survivor is used as leverage for more control. The abuser may demand the passwords to the survivor's phone, bank accounts and social media in order to fact check her. The abuser may decide to follow the survivor, put GPS on the survivor's phone or car or ask the kids where she went in an attempt to catch her in a lie. The abuser may even go as far as to call the survivor's friends, co-workers or family members to fact check the survivor.

The act of the survivor continuously giving up her privacy by answering questions and then being fact checked is used to groom the survivor into absolute disclosure to the abuser. This makes the survivor accustomed to habitually telling the truth and not leaving details out for fear of being accused of lying. In this respect, the survivor will find it very difficult to withhold information from the abuser, often offering up the information before the abuser even asks for it (also part of the expecting mind reading tactic).

Brain Washing

This tactic is best described by the idiom "beating a dead horse" or "hammering it home." The abuser verbally "beats" the idea into the survivor's head by repeating it over and over. Often, the abuser will act as though the survivor does not comprehend what the abuser is saying and will therefore continue to repeat themselves. Other ways this tactic is used is by repeating what has already been said very slowly to emphasize the survivor's incompetence. Or the abuser may bring up an argument that was resolved in the past to rehash it.

What brain washing looked like to me: *This tactic was Abuser 1's M. O. He would lecture me for hours while repeating the same things over and over. To make me feel stupid, he would repeat things very slowly. In arguments he would bring up things I had done in the past that had already been resolved to rehash them over and over. It was extremely difficult to communicate with Abuser 1. There was no resolution of conflict. I often felt exhausted, mentally beat down, incompetent, and incapable of completing even the simplest of tasks after his brain washing.*

The purpose of brain washing is to gain control of the conversation, to force the survivor to listen, and to wear down the survivor. This tactic is also used to block the survivor from resolving the conflict. The survivor has no control of the situation and even apologizing, complying, agreeing with, begging the abuser to stop, or screaming, "OKAY, I GOT IT" does not subdue the abuser. The abuser decides when enough is enough. It is used to force the survivor into believing that she is stupid, worthless, and beneath the abuser by repeating these ideas over and over. It also forces the survivor to believe that the abuser is "right" and the survivor is "wrong" through repetition.

CHAPTER 5
OTHER RED FLAGS OF
AN ABUSIVE RELATIONSHIP

Power plays

Power plays are a subtle, raw struggle for power. The abuser gains control over the survivor through various methods that are very difficult to recognize. Some examples of power plays are:

Taking your chair as soon as you get up.

Standing in your way so you have to go around them or so you have to say excuse me.

Talking loudly over you.

Interrupting you while you are speaking.

Ignoring you while you are speaking.

Changing the TV channel when you are clearly watching a show.

Ordering you to do something.

Taking the remote from your hand and turning off the TV.

Making you sleep on the couch when you are sick.

The purpose of the power play tactic is to push the survivor's boundaries and to gain control over the survivor in ways in which she might not recognize. This is part of the grooming process.

Male Privilege

Male privilege described in one word is patriarchy. Patriarchy can be thought of as a structural system in which men are given most or all of the power. Researchers explain that the hierarchical placement of men in structurally and socially higher status and more powerful positions creates the foundation for male violence against women. This violence extends past wife abuse to rape and other forms of male violence against women (Smith, 1990). Sonkin, Martin, and Walker (1985) sum this up very well:

"Wife beating has been translated into modern times as a custom, the unwritten terms of the marriage contract and the paternal hierarchical structure of the family. It is reinforced by religious doctrine, by family law, by non-enforcement of criminal law, by an economic system that keeps women dependent upon men, by service providers and therapists who reinforce sex-role stereotyping and maintain the status quo: the power of one sex (male) over the other sex (female)."

This structural hierarchy dates back to the beginning of time. Specifically, those who believe in the biblical account of the beginning of time, share the idea that women are supposed to serve their husbands. The idea discussed in the Bible is that women were created after men, of men, for men, and to serve men. Furthermore, Eve's punishment for the original sin was subjugation to Adam. Here many individuals who follow the Bible's teachings apply this to all male/female relationships, that men are supposed to rule over women. In less extreme terms it is often said that men are supposed to be "leaders of the household" and that wives should "obey their husbands."

In early American colonies, this was indoctrinated into laws. The 1769 Blackstone Commentaries stated, "By marriage, the husband and wife are one person in the law. The very being and legal existence of the woman is suspended during the marriage, or at least is incorporated into that of her husband under whose wing and protection she performs everything." This meant that women were property of their husbands and did not have any rights. Women were not allowed to own property, sign contracts, or appear in court. Any property held by a woman before marriage was given to her husband. Women were not allowed to conduct business dealings.

Throughout the 1800's states individually began to grant married women the right to own property, the right to have separate economy, and the right to control their own earnings separate from their husbands. It wasn't until 1972 that women were considered equal to men under the law. In the 1980's crimes against women were starting to be addressed and tackled. Specifically, in 1984 the Family Violence Prevention and Services Act was enacted in hopes of reducing violence against women by their male partners. Finally, in the beginning of the 21st century, a fight to stop crimes against women was really undertaken.

What this means is that domestic violence is a social problem based on the power difference men have continued to have over women in society. In fact, "…research shows that wife assault is more common in families where power is concentrated in the hands of the husband or male partner" (Tjadens & Thoennes, 2000). Even though the U.S. is founded upon the idea that "all men are created equal" and that women have been included in this idea for some time now, patriarchy can still be seen in its systems. Men hold the majority of powerful government and economically fruitful positions in the U.S. In 2017, men held 81% of the seats in the House of Representatives. Similarly, men make up 79% of Senators (Rutgers, 2017). To date, there still has not been a female president. Furthermore, only 26 of the top Fortune 500 companies are led by female CEOs (Deane, Morin, Parker, Horowitz, Wang, & Brown, 2015). Likewise, there are 14 self-made female billionaires as compared to 665 self-made male billionaires (Casserly, 2010).

According to Samsel (2013), "Male Privilege refers to the tendency of men to allow and expect women to take on an unequal division of labor, responsibility, and self-denial." This is often seen in relationships that keep traditional sex roles. Women are expected to be the sole care-takers of children in heterosexual relationships. Women are expected to maintain the household or take care of tasks "related to women:" cooking, cleaning, care giving, etc. Even when both the man and woman work outside the home, the woman is expected to come home after work, take care of the children, cook, and clean while these expectations do not hold for men. Women are also expected to please their husbands by having sex when the husband wants it. Many of these expectations are backed up by society's beliefs about women's responsibilities in the household. These are all double standards. The amount of work expected of women is far greater than what is expected of men. If you are wondering what male privilege looked like to me, see the "double standards" section.

The purpose of male privilege is to "keep women in their place." In previous history, laws were created for exactly that purpose: to allow men power and control over their wives. Although the laws have slowly changed over time, male privilege still exists. Because of its existence, it adds to abusers' beliefs that the survivor should be subjugated to them. Male privilege continues to excuse and perpetuate dominance over women. Thus, male privilege in the form of traditional sex roles can be viewed as a red flag for potential future abuse in relationships.

Past Violence

Past violence is a good indicator of future violence. It is especially a red flag in romantic relationships. If your partner tells stories of past violence, acts violent towards others around you, or has a history of past domestic violence, this is a huge red flag that your relationship will eventually also turn violent. Things that you want to watch out for are: stories from your partner or partner's friends of your partner becoming violent with others. This can include bar fights, road rage incidents, school fights, gang related fights, etc. You should be wary if you have witnessed your partner becoming violent with others. Witnessing road rage (pulling others off the road, displaying weapons to other drivers, running others off the road, etc.), witnessing bar fights, and seeing your partner start a fight to "defend your honor" are all red flags of future violence in your relationship.

The biggest red flag that you should be concerned about is past domestic violence. If your partner has told you stories of his past relationships where he has become physically violent with his partner for any reason (!) discontinue the relationship as quickly as possible. Furthermore, abusers are very good at giving reasons for their abuse. Do NOT believe them when they tell you that their ex was crazy/psycho/out of control and that is why they used violence on her. Know that if you stay with them long enough, not only will you experience their violence but they will tell those same stories about you too!

What this looked like to me: *I experienced all three, past-violence red flags with Abuser 3. In the beginning of our relationship he bragged about a fight so bad that he beat some people almost to death. He bragged about how he was trained to kill people.*

Likewise, throughout the relationship, I had seen Abuser 3 become violent with other people. During one incident, he was driving the car and I was in the passenger seat when he became enraged with another driver. He honked the horn and flipped them off. I am not even sure what they had done that pissed him off. He drove up next to their car, rolled down my window and started screaming profanities at the driver. He got the person to pull over at a gas station. Abuser 3 got out of the car, charged the driver, screamed, yelled, and threatened the driver. Abuser 3 pushed the driver who had gotten out of his car and attempted to initiate a fight. Thankfully, the other driver diffused the situation, refused to fight, and got back in his car and drove off.

I experienced most of these red flags with Abuser 2 as well. Abuser 2 had a reputation of being "wild" and "crazy." People told stories of him jumping off roofs, wrestling others and playing with pyrotechnics for fun. Although Abuser 2 never became physically violent with any of his previous partners (that I know of), there was one specific instance where I saw Abuser 2 become violent with another person. Unfortunately, the violent action was perpetrated in "my honor."

Abuser 2 and I were at a house party of a mutual friend. A previous boyfriend of mine had shown up. This guy had been spreading really horrible rumors about me to anyone who would listen. When the ex-boyfriend was alone in a room, Abuser 2 went in there, cornered him and attacked him. Abuser 2 jumped on top of my ex-boyfriend and they began to tussle. We all heard the commotion and ran to the room to see what was happening. When I got there, Abuser 2 was on top of my ex-boyfriend holding a knife to his stomach. Our mutual friends jumped in, grabbed Abuser 2, and flung him off of the ex. At the same time, other friends grabbed me and took me into another room. The ex left without a word. Even though I despised my ex, I was thankful that Abuser 2 did not stab or cut him. More so, I wish the fight had never occurred. Regardless, the red flags were there that these men would become abusive to me. But I did not understand that their past violent actions warned me of future violent actions that would turn in my direction.

Isolation

With this tactic, the abuser tries to isolate the victim from family and/or friends. This can be accomplished very subtly or very overtly. With subtle isolation, the abuser may be very persuasive as to why the survivor should no longer visit family and friends. The abuser may claim that the family member or friend is toxic or doesn't have the survivor's best interest in mind. To isolate the survivor, the abuser may start arguments with the survivor's family and friends in order to make it so uncomfortable for the survivor that she stops inviting them over. After arguing with the survivor's family and friends the abuser may claim that the survivor's family and friends are trying to tear their relationship apart, then request that the survivor no longer talks to them.

Another way that the abuser will subtly isolate the survivor is by finding things to dislike about the survivor's family and friends. The abuser may point out that the family member has differing beliefs on some issue and then make a manipulative statement like, "You don't want to hang around people like that, do you? It's probably best if you don't see them anymore." The abuser may come up with very logical reasons for moving the survivor to a state where she has no family or friends.

With overt isolation, the abuser may flat out tell the survivor that she can no longer see or talk with that family member or friend again. The abuser may block calls from friends and family of the survivor. The abuser might also take the survivor's cell phone and erase numbers and block calls from people he doesn't want the survivor to associate with. Another way that the abuser might overtly isolate the survivor is by declaring, "It's me or them!" In this way, the survivor is forced to choose between family/friends (or any outside influencer the abuser sees as a threat to his power) and the abuser. The abuser might take the survivor's phone away, have it turned off, or quit paying the bill so that way she has no way to contact anyone. The abuser may also refuse the survivor transportation. He might sell her car so she has no way of leaving him.

What isolation looked like to me: *Because I moved in with Abuser 3, he had final say over who could come over. He rarely allowed anyone to come* over. He did not want people to see how we lived. So, it was very rare that my parents came over. I never had any friends over. The whole time I lived with him I was never allowed to invite my sister over.

Abuser 3 was also very covert in his ways to isolate me. His typical pattern of isolation involved: agreeing to go to some family function, backing out at the last minute, and then making me choose between him and my family. When I chose my family, Abuser 3 would punish me with either the silent treatment, an argument, or some manipulative sarcastic remark about how nice it must be to have time to spend with family and friends. It was this pattern of behavior that encouraged me to avoid hanging out with them.

Another way that Abuser 3 would isolate me was by obsessively texting me when I went somewhere. If I went to get my hair done or to have lunch with friends I would receive tons of texts from him asking me: "Are you there yet? Who all is there? How much longer are you going to be? When are you getting home?" I felt that if I didn't respond to his barrage of questions as quickly as possible, he would assume I was lying to him or worse, that I was cheating on him. I often took pictures of what I was doing or where I was at and sent them to him to cover my bases.

There was never a time in our relationship that I was allowed to go somewhere without asking him first. I never could just go out to lunch with friends. I had to ask, and then prepare him. I had to continually remind him that the event was coming up and that it was important to me. I had to give him all of the details: where, what time, who was going, how long was I going to be gone, when was I getting home, how was I going to make up for the family chores that I was going to miss. I had to plan to cook dinner in advance or make the coffee before I left. If Abuser 3 was left to do any of the chores while I was gone, not only would I receive many more texts, but I would also return home to a passive-aggressive, angry, sullen, abuser. He would then punish me by giving me the silent treatment, being snarky to start a fight, or completely disregard his responsibilities so that I had to do them. In essence, Abuser 3 made it so miserable for me to spend any time with family or friends, or do anything that I wanted to do that I basically gave most of it up. Maybe once a year I went to get my hair done. I only saw my family on the holidays. I almost never spent time with any of my friends.

Lastly, Abuser 3 had tried to convince me to move to Colorado early in the relationship. I flat refused. There were no prospects in Colorado. He had no job waiting for him there, I had no job there. We would have uprooted ourselves on a whim with no plan, no money, and no way to succeed. It was a foolish idea. Later in the relationship, Abuser 3 tried to convince me to move to Saudi Arabia. He said that he would love to live there. Saudi has some of the most *oppressive rules for women. Again, I flat refused.*

The purpose of isolation is to remove the survivor's support system to make it harder for her to leave the abusive relationship. If the survivor has no one to escape to, no one to call to talk to about the abuse, then it is more likely that the survivor will feel as though there is no way to leave the relationship. Furthermore, as the support system of the survivor grows smaller, the more control the abuser gains over the survivor. The survivor now has to rely solely on the abuser for support. Moreover, because the survivor has no friends and family with which to discuss the relationship, the survivor loses out on having other perspectives which might disclose the relationship as abusive.

Dr. Jekyll Mr. Hyde Personality

Another red flag of an abusive relationship is the abuser's Dr. Jekyll Mr. Hyde personality. It is recognized by the survivor that the abuser has two distinctly different personalities. The abuser is quite charming, charismatic, outgoing, sweet, endearing, caring, has a great sense of humor, and is loved by everyone when he is in public. This is the abuser's public persona. On the other hand, the abuser is quite mean, caustic, unyielding, argumentative, stubborn, self-righteous, critical, and violent behind closed doors. This is the abuser's private persona.

The abuser's two distinct personalities serve several purposes. First, because people outside the home do not see the abusive behavior, when the survivor tells of the abuse, they have a hard time believing it. The survivor especially encounters this when disclosing the abuse to mutual friends. Often the friends are shocked and will say things such as, "Are you sure? He seems like such a nice guy! I've never seen him hurt anyone! I've never even seen him angry!" Second, because the survivor realizes that she will not be believed, it may discourage the survivor from disclosing the abuse. Third, when the abuser has a charming public persona and couples that with specific tactics that can make the survivor look emotionally unstable in public, this serves to discredit the survivor so that in the future, if she discloses abuse, it is less likely that she will be believed.

It should be mentioned that not all abusers fit this description. Some abusers are violent both inside and outside the home. Some will physically harm the survivor in public. However, this is less typical because it is easier for others to intervene and help when the abuse occurs outside the home. Likewise, when the abuse occurs in public, there are often witnesses which can make it easier for the abuser to be caught and punished by law enforcement.

What the Dr. Jekyll Mr. Hyde personality looked like to me: Abuser 3 was the epitome of Dr. Jekyll Mr. Hyde. He was very charming in public. Everyone loved him. He always knew what to say and exactly how to say it to make people feel at ease. Others were always drawn to him and his ability to lead others. Many admired him. He always seemed to have it together. Abuser 3 would constantly do things to enhance his public persona. He would stop and rescue turtles on the road. He donated money to charities (when it was asked for in public). He would help those who were sick or hurt. He would cry at movies, and he would express his feelings without any prompting. He was often outspoken for women's rights. He hugged other men. He always presented himself as kind and loving. All of this was great for hiding the controlling, abusive asshole that he really was.

Abuser 3 would call me names and discourage me from my dreams. He would shut down communication when it wasn't going his way. He would force me to apologize to him for slight grievances. Abuser 3 would corner me psychologically and physically. He often made my life miserable in order to force me to do what he wanted. Abuser 3 treated me as his personal maid. When things became really bad, Abuser 3 would become physically violent with me.

When I left him, and disclosed the abuse, most people couldn't believe that he was abusive. Most of our mutual friends continued to remain friends with him. He took no hit to his reputation. Abuser 3 was so good at separating his two personalities that many still believe that he never could have been abusive. Unfortunately, this unwillingness to believe the survivor adds to the minimization and trivialization of the abuse.

Love Bombing (Archer, 2017)

This tactic uses intense attention and affection to lure the survivor into believing the relationship is "true love," "love at first sight," or that you are "soul mates." The relationship begins in a swift whirlwind of romance. The survivor is bombarded with gifts, trips, love notes, flowers, and positive affirmation. The abuser will require all of your attention, talk with you for hours, declare that you are the perfect person for him, and he will say all the right things. The abuser will want to discuss at length with you about the future of your relationship. The abuser will ask you to move in with him within days or weeks of dating and ask you to marry him within a several months of dating.

This use of ingratiating behavior to capture you is the idealization phase. The abuser puts the survivor on a pedestal, believing and exclaiming that the survivor is the perfect partner for him. This is used as a reinforcement strategy. The ingratiating behavior rewards the survivor for behaving "correctly." However, the next phase, which is the devaluation phase, is used to punish the survivor for behaving in a way the abuser finds displeasing. The devaluation phase uses any and all of the verbally and emotionally abusive tactics to belittle, putdown, and discourage the survivor. This phase is also used to make the survivor feel worthless, to confuse the survivor, and to make the survivor feel as though she needs to work harder to regain the abuser's love. Typically, the devaluation stage occurs after the survivor does something that the abuser does not like. For example, the survivor may decide to go to lunch with her friends. Because the abuser feels like he is losing control over the survivor, the abuser will use emotionally and verbally abusive tactics in order to punish the survivor and to get the survivor to do what he wants in the future.

The love bombing tactic is used to gain further control over the survivor. It is also used to isolate the survivor from others. This tactic is comparable to the *cycle of violence*. The idealization phase of the love bombing tactic is very similar to the *honeymoon phase* in the cycle of violence. Likewise, the devaluation phase of the love bombing tactic is analogous to the *explosion phase* in the cycle of violence.

What love bombing looked like to me: *Abuser 3 definitely love bombed me. He showered me with gifts, love notes, and proclamations of his love for me very early in the relationship. Abuser 3 and I spent long hours on the phone discussing our relationship, how much we had in common, how much he loved me, and where our relationship was going. He often declared that there was no one else on earth quite like me. He told me how perfect I was and how I completed him. Abuser 3 told me that he loved me and believed we were "meant to be together" within one week of dating. He asked me to move in with him before we had dated for three weeks. By six months, Abuser 3 had asked me to marry him.*

Unbeknownst to me, getting me to move in with him and asking me to marry him so quickly are typical of abusers. The tactic is used to quickly gain control of you. Moving in with the abuser makes it easier for them to control you and it also allows them to devalue you much more often. Convincing you to move in with them allows them to keep an eye on you and to keep you under their thumb.

Getting you to marry them quickly is also a tactic of abusers. Once you are married to them, it is much harder to leave the relationship and the sense of commitment involved in marriage also makes it psychologically harder to leave the relationship when it turns violent.

The mix of love bombing and devaluation was very confusing and shocking to me. I often did not understand why I was being treated with such disrespect over such small matters. The devaluation really made me choose my battles more wisely because I did not realize the issue was about control. I did not understand that Abuser 3 was abusive and controlling. In order to stop him from devaluing me (or from using emotionally and verbally abusive tactics on me) I tried to avoid doing things which I was criticized for and I tried to do more of the things that he wanted me to do. Thus, I began to avoid friends and family and I began to not do things for myself (avoided self-care). I overworked myself taking on as much of his responsibilities that I could handle. In essence, I tried to become the most selfless being possible. But, as with all abusers, he was never satisfied.

Just because your partner sends you flowers and writes you love letters does not mean that he is love bombing you. So, how can you tell the difference? Love bombing is used to make you feel as though you are in love much faster than it would normally take a person to get to know someone and fall in love with them. It speeds up the relationship in order for the abuser to isolate you and gain more control over you. For example, the typical amount of time people take to say "I love you" is around six months. This also goes for moving in together and going on vacation together. The average amount of time that lapses before a couple gets engaged is roughly 2 years (Emery, 2016). One should be alarmed if these timelines are grossly shortened. It takes time to build trust and love.

In a relationship that involves love bombing, the abuser tries to short-circuit the survivor's alarm system by making them feel and believe that they love and trust the abuser before it's naturally possible to do so. Therefore, if the relationship is moving very fast, tell your partner that you would like to slow it down. In an abusive relationship, the abusive partner will use this either as a way to become even more forceful with ingratiating behavior (see stalking) in order to change your mind, or they will use this as an opportunity to devalue you. If you are in a non-abusive relationship, your partner will respect your wishes, may ask you how to take it more slowly and will follow your lead.

Mistreatment of Animals

Another red flag for abusive relationships is the mistreatment of animals by the abuser. Besides overt physical abuse of animals (punching, kicking, etc.), covert (subtle) mistreatment of animals is also a sign that you are involved with an abusive individual. Abusers may withhold food from animals to punish them. Abusers may force animals to eat spicy foods. Abusers may tease the animal with food that the animal can't have.

The same cycle of violence can be found with animals as with humans. In this case, sometimes the abusers are loving and kind to the animal, while other times the abuser is mean, harsh, controlling, and abusive to the animal. Abusers might also mistreat animals by shoving them, kneeing them, hitting them, kicking them, picking them up forcefully, shaking them, and throwing them. In the same way that these tactics are used against humans to gain control, they are also used against animals to gain control and compliance.

What mistreatment of animals looked like to me: *I experienced this once with Abuser 2. As we were lying on the bed, my cat jumped down from someplace high and landed on Abuser 2's chest. He immediately grabbed my cat with both hands and threw him across the room as hard as he could. My cat hit a row of cabinets and was dazed and confused. I was so shocked, angered, and saddened by his actions.*

Abuser 3 used grooming to normalize his mistreatment of animals. He started off by teasing the dogs relentlessly. He would tease them with steak and pork chops and other cuts of meat that he might or might not give them. He progressed to slathering whole jalapenos in meat juice and feeding them to the dog he despised. This would cause the dog to vomit, have diarrhea, and accidents in the house. He began punishing the dogs by slapping their behinds as one might a child. This slowly progressed to Abuser 3 using his foot to shove the dog across the floor. Other times he would knee the dog in the side when it was not doing what he wanted it to do.

He also enjoyed scaring the wits out of the dogs. While he was vacuuming, he would attach the suction part of the vacuum to the dog's butt or snout which would cause the dog to freak out. Towards the end of the relationship with him, Abuser 3 would kick the dog in the butt hard to get it to leave the kitchen. When the dog misbehaved, Abuser 3 would hit the dog in the snout as hard as he could with an open hand. Other times he would pick up the dog by the scruff of the neck and hit the dog across the face.

When I was in this relationship, I did not recognize that this was abuse. The abuse of the dogs happened so slowly and gradually during the six years that I didn't recognize it for what it was. Although I felt disgusted by the behavior, I did not understand that it was based on control and that it was violent. At the time, it seemed like it was along the same lines as spanking a child. Today I recognize that it is absolutely 100% animal abuse. Abuser 3 was using physical violence and fear to control the dogs, to force them to do what he wanted them to do.

Control

The abuser's goal is to gain absolute control over you. They want to be able to control your finances, your job, your dreams, what you do, where you go, who you see, what you wear, what you read, what you watch, what you eat, how you eat, and what you say. These are just a few of the things that the abuser tries to control.

Financial Control. One area that is important for the abuser to gain control is the survivor's finances. Having control over the survivor's money allows the abuser to limit the survivor's actions, forces the survivor to ask for money, which also gives the abuser the opportunity to ask what the money is for, and makes it much more difficult for the survivor to leave the abusive relationship. Limiting the money of the survivor also acts as a way to isolate the survivor. If the survivor does not have money the survivor is much less likely to do things independently of the abuser and is less likely to leave the abuser.

With financial control, the goal of the abuser is to gain access to the money while limiting the survivor's access to money. In some abusive relationships, the abuser may demand that the survivor give all of her money to the abuser. In other abusive relationships, the survivor may be manipulated into believing that the male is supposed to be in charge of the finances. Therefore, she may willingly give them up. In other cases, the abuser and survivor may share a bank account but the abuser uses all of the money before the survivor has a chance to do anything with it. In other instances, the abuser mooches off of the survivor, sucking the survivor dry of her earnings. In this aspect, the abuser does not contribute financially to any of the shared bills or expenses, leaving the survivor to provide for both parties.

In my relationship, Abuser 3 convinced me that we should share my bank account. What he meant by "share" was that I would add his name onto my bank account and that he would have access to my money. He explained that it would be easier to pay bills this way and that most couples share bank accounts. Because I believed that I was in a normal relationship, I was fooled by his reasons for wanting to put his name on my account.

Abuser 3 also had his own money. Although at first, he indicated that he would put his money in with mine, that never happened. He had a completely separate bank account which he never gave me access to. So, what started out as a show of love from me, turned into full control over me by him. He quickly signed up all of our bills to be auto-drafted from my account. We used my money first for everything. Once I ran out of money (which was very quickly), he still had his own stash of money separate from mine. This left me in a position in which I had to ask him for money for essentials.

He often spent my money on things that he wanted to buy for himself without consulting me first. This left me broke all the time. The only time I got to buy anything for myself was when he "graced" me with a shopping trip or I asked him for money. He loved that I had to ask him for money. This gave him all the power. Abuser 3 would sit there and ask me what it was for and why I didn't have the money to buy it myself. He would require me to give him all the details of where I was going and when. I would have to persuade him that I truly needed the item. Sometimes he would freak out on me about why there was no money in my account. He would treat me as though I didn't have any clue about how to manage money and that I shouldn't have let my bank account get so low. This infuriated me because he was the one responsible for making that happen, but to bring that up would be to start a war that I could not win.

Even before Abuser 3 physically assaulted me for the last time, I started to think about leaving him. I was searching the internet for cheap apartments. This left me in a very difficult position. I did not have the financial means to pick up my things and move into an apartment. I felt stuck. Because he continued to spend my money, I felt I had no way out.

During this time, I received a letter out of the blue from the comptroller of Texas. Abuser 3 tossed the letter at me, quizzically. He waited for me to open it. It was a check for $900 dollars. Somehow, some company had kept $900 of *my money when it was supposed to be given back. I was shocked with excitement. This was a God send! This was my way out! Abuser 3 noticed my excitement and asked, "What is it?" He walked over swiftly and snatched the letter out of my hand. He was thrilled. I could see him thinking about all the things he could buy with my $900. I immediately said, "I really need to fix my car. I think I'm just going to hold on to it until I am able to get some time to take my car in." In the back of my mind, I knew I was lying. I wanted to hold on to the money to be able to afford an apartment on my own so I could leave him. Of course, keeping my money to myself was not an option for Abuser 3. He did not want me to use my money. He wanted me to put the money in the bank so he could spend it. He then replied to me with, "You are the most selfish person I have ever met! You know we have to bills to pay! You have healthcare bills you need to take care of! The right thing to do is to put the money in the bank!" As I am sure you have realized, instead of dealing with Abuser 3's abusive tactics, I put the money in the account. All of the money was gone very quickly. I can't even tell you what Abuser 3 spent it on. I did not get to spend any of that $900.*

Job Control. One way that the abuser may try to control the survivor is through the survivor's job. Some abusers flat refuse to allow the survivor to work. This creates a dependency of the survivor on the abuser. In this case, the abuser is the one with money and therefore controls the finances (this is another form of financial control). The survivor has to ask and make a case for money from the abuser.

If the survivor is working at the time that the abuser and survivor begin to form a relationship, the abuser might order the survivor to quit working. Or, the abuser may persuade the survivor to quit her job by telling the survivor they should be home to take care of the children. Another way the abuser might manipulate the survivor out of a job is by showing up at her work and causing a scene in order to get the survivor fired.

What job control looked like to me: *When I lived with Abuser 2 we both worked for the same company. I was frustrated with things at work, and as any normal person would do, I vented these frustrations to Abuser 2. Instead of listening to me or helping me come up with solutions that I could implement to make my situation better, Abuser 2 went into the owner's office and quit for me. This means that he literally walked into the office and said something like, "Audrey quits. She no longer works for you."*

First, I was infuriated that he would make a decision like that for me. Second, I felt that I had no other choice but to accept Abuser 2's decision. It was a completely uncomfortable situation for me. I wanted to keep my job but I couldn't go against Abuser 2 and because he worked there, I couldn't pretend to quit and then go back. So, I lost my job because of him.

Abuser 3 was different. He never told me I couldn't work, he never quit a job for me, and he never tried to prevent me from working. He was much more manipulative and had a sneakier way of controlling me. It is important here to remind you that Abuser 3 already had access to my bank account. So, he wanted me to continue working so that he could continue paying his bills with my money and continue spending my money on the things that he wanted.

Abuser 3 tried to control my career prospects through discouragement and persuasion rather than other obvious methods. When I would discuss my career plans and future goals with Abuser 3, he would often try to discourage me from doing them. He would tell me that I couldn't make any money doing that. He would try to persuade me to go a different route by starting arguments with me and saying things like, "But how are YOU going to take care of this family!?" Having these arguments with Abuser 3 left me feeling completely unsupported and as though I wasn't allowed to make any decisions for myself. It frustrated me to have to constantly defend myself and my life's dreams to this person who constantly shot them down.

The goal of job control is ultimately financial control. If the abuser can get the survivor to stop working, the survivor is then solely dependent on the abuser for money. In this respect, the survivor has to ask or beg for money from the abuser. The survivor is often put in a position where she has to explain what the money is needed for and why she wants the money. This also creates a power differential. The one with the money has the power. The lack of money limits the survivor's options and makes it much harder for the survivor to leave the abuser.

Control of Daily Life. Abusers will attempt to control the survivor's daily life. Some abusers will control by ordering and demanding. This style is more overt because the abuser tells the survivor directly that she can't go out, see certain people, or wear certain clothes, etc. Others will control through nit-picking and criticism or simply not taking no for an answer. This style is more covert and manipulative because instead of demanding or ordering, the abuser may criticize her clothes in order to get her to change, or criticize her friends in order to get her to not hangout with them, or simply ignore her when she says no.

Others still will control via the mean-sweet cycle, rewarding you when they like what you do, and punishing you when they do not like what you do. This style is also covert and manipulative. Here, the abuser gets the survivor to stop seeing friends or stop wearing certain clothes by using abusive tactics to punish the survivor for doing so. The abuser may use the silent treatment to punish the survivor. The abuser may accuse and blame the survivor of infidelity to keep her away from friends or accuse the survivor of flirting because of a low-cut t-shirt.

What controlling daily life looked like to me: *Abuser 1 would control me in subtle ways. Sometimes, he would not accept my "no" as an answer. For example, Abuser 1 bought an all-natural remedy for depression with the intention that he wanted me to take it. He told me that it helps release Serotonin in the brain. I told him I wouldn't take it. He acted shocked and confused and asked me why I wouldn't take it. I explained to Abuser 1 that I wasn't depressed.*

This was all very absurd to me. Not only was I not depressed but I wasn't acting depressed and there was no reason for Abuser 1 to assume I was depressed. For whatever reason, Abuser 1 got it in his head that he believed I was depressed and that he knew what was best for me more than I knew what was best for myself.

Instead of taking my no as an answer and respecting it, he acted like he didn't hear it. Instead, he said, "But it helps the Serotonin in your brain." Then I explained again, "But I'm not depressed." Then Abuser 1 countered with, "What if I take it first?" Again, I said, "No. I won't take it." Abuser 1 replied, "Really, why?" I repeated myself for the third time, "Because, I am not depressed!" After this, he became frustrated with me because I wouldn't take it. He actually believed he was helping me!

Abuser 3 controlled many tiny aspects of my daily life that I did not even realize he was controlling until I left the relationship. This is because I often thought that I was choosing my battles wisely and avoiding small insignificant arguments. But, what was really happening was that he was controlling me and I was giving in to him in order to avoid abuse. Abuser 3 would typically use the nit-picking and criticizing tactics along with the punishment tactics in order to control me.

Abuser 3 controlled a lot of what I did. There were unspoken rules to follow at night: no flushing toilets, no turning on lights, no noise, no staying up past when Abuser 3 went to bed, and no snoring. Abuser 3 "groomed" these rules into me. He would often yell, "WHAT ARE YOU DOING?!" if I turned on a light, flushed the toilet, or made noise. This always made me jump and feel like a child, as though I wasn't allowed to be out of bed. I was so afraid of waking Abuser 3 that I learned to use the bathroom in complete darkness. Once, when I got sick, I was so scared that I was going to wake him up that I went into the backyard to throw up. Of course, I couldn't win here either. Abuser 3 was pissed that I made this decision and we had an argument about it. However, had I thrown up in the bathroom and woken Abuser 3 up, he would have been just as pissed. If I decided that I didn't want to go to bed at 8:30pm when Abuser 3 decided he wanted to go to bed, he would scream at me from across the house, "AUDREY IT'S TIME FOR BED, WHAT ARE YOU DOING?" He would claim that he wanted me by his side but the real issue was that I was making a decision on my own and this was never allowed.

The snoring problem was the worst. First of all, NO ONE can control snoring. It just happens. During the end of our relationship Abuser 3 was so controlling that he would wake me up in the middle of the night when he heard me snoring and force me to roll over onto my other side. If I rolled back over to face him, he would continue to wake me up and force me to roll over. It got so bad that I was spending 90% of the time sleeping on my right side. The whole right side of my body would become numb because I had to lay in the same position all night long. I would wake up with kinks in my neck because of it. Sometimes he would demand that I roll over and I would yell in defiance, "NO!" During these times, he would flop around on the bed to make it impossible for me to sleep. That whole time I believed that my snoring was obnoxiously loud. I also believed that I snored all the time. I learned later that I do snore, but only occasionally and very softly.

It seems as though the abuser has a million rules. This is the best way to describe what the abuser's control feels like. It feels as though you have to be perfect 100% of the time to not upset the abuser. This requires remembering all of their rules which is impossible to do because the rules keep changing.

Abuser 3 controlled me by creating a ton of bathroom rules. First, all showering items must be removed after the shower (except his of course). Second, any water on the floor must be wiped up. One morning, after I showered, I put my soaps in the cabinet and I wiped up the water off of the floor. I left and went into another room. Abuser 3 called me back into the bathroom, "AUDREY!" I went back into the bathroom to see what was wrong. I was sure that I had remembered to do everything. Abuser 3 pointed to the shower curtain which I had shoved to the side of the shower in order to get out. "Do you know how disgusting this is?!" I wasn't sure what he was talking about. I thought maybe because the shower curtain folds up on itself, it creates mold or something. I shrugged and looked at him puzzled. "You shoved the shower curtain right next to the toilet! Anytime anyone flushes the toilet, bacteria are going to collect on the shower curtain! When you get out of the shower, push the curtain to the other side." I looked at him like he was crazy, said, "OK" and walked away. There was one more rule that I had to remember.

Abuser 3 would criticize me to control me. I would yawn and he would say, "Jesus! You are the loudest person I know. Do you always yawn like that?!" Statements like these were meant to make me feel insecure about myself and they often worked. I worried that my yawn was obnoxious and that I was an extremely loud person. I often thought that I must really annoy others because of it. This sort of thinking would snowball until I changed my behavior. I started to yawn completely silently.

Abuser 3 would also use passive-aggressiveness and manipulation to control what I did. When I cooked, he would come into the kitchen where the mess was, sigh extremely loudly, and start to clean while acting extremely put out and annoyed. This created a lot of anxiety for me. This sort of behavior often started fights which were impossible to win and escalated rapidly. So, instead of waiting until after the cooking was done to clean up the mess, I cleaned while I cooked.

Abuser 3 also controlled where I went. First, this was done by limiting my money. Because I rarely had money, I rarely had the opportunity to go anywhere. Beyond this, Abuser 3 would become enraged if I did not answer his incoming calls and texts immediately after receiving them. "For safety" I was required to tell him where I was going, when I would be home, and who I would be with. I was required to text him when I got there and text him when I was leaving. (You know, in case I got kidnapped, raped, or murdered).

One day, Abuser 3 approached me. I was sitting at the table studying when he said, "I sent a link to your phone that I want you to accept and download." Not thinking, I said, "Ok. What is it for?" Abuser 3 replied, "It's a GPS tracker. It will allow me to track your phone in case of emergencies, like if you were kidnapped and the police couldn't find you." I was so shocked and scared because I realized how controlling this was. I responded, "Absolutely NOT! That is crazy! I already tell you everywhere I go, who I will be with, what time I will be back! I even text you when I get there and when I am leaving! No fucking way. I am not putting that on my phone!" Abuser 3 became pissed, "You got something to hide?! You cheating on me!? Only a person who was cheating on me would refuse to put this on her phone! I am trying to KEEP YOU SAFE!" I scoffed, "You're acting like a crazy controlling boyfriend right now! You can say whatever you want, but that THING is NOT

GOING ON MY PHONE!"

Abuser 3 continued to send me the link over and over in the weeks after that argument in hopes that I would forget and accidently click on it. I never clicked on it. I never put it on my phone. But, that doesn't mean that he didn't put it on my phone when I was in the shower or another room. That I will never know.

Abuser 3 also controlled what I wore. Besides no band t-shirts or unnatural hair colors, I also wasn't allowed to wear earbuds. I love to listen to music while cleaning but this was impossible in a house of 5. Listening to music would have required me to turn up the music louder than the multiple TVs and the vacuum. This would have annoyed the other individuals in the house. So, instead, I would listen to music via earbuds. One day, as I hummed to myself and cleaned, Abuser 3 was yelling across the house at me, "AUDREY!" Of course, I didn't hear him because of the headphones. This really pissed him off. How dare I ignore him when he called me! How dare I make him walk from one side of the house to the other to talk to me! He tapped me on the shoulder hard, "What THE FUCK! I've been calling you for the past ten minutes!" I took out my earbuds and shrugged my shoulders, "What do you need?" He snarled, "I NEED you to respond when I'm talking to you! What if there had been a fire?! No more earbuds in the house!"

He also controlled what I read. Abuser 3 would say things like, "It really bothers me that you are reading that. That book has to go." He would then yank the book out of my hands and throw it in the trash.

I was also told what I could and could not watch. Abuser 3 absolutely did not want the news on in "his house." He would become enraged when I watched the news and would force me to change it. He also really hated the TV shows that I enjoyed. So, the only times that I got to watch what I wanted was when I was at home by myself. At night, when we watched TV together, he chose the shows we watched, which were mostly things that I hated. Sometimes, when I had enough of watching that crap, I'd ask politely, "Can we PLEASE watch something else?" Often, his answer was "No."

Eating was the worst. Abuser 3 was so particular about what was eaten and how it was eaten. He started a campaign of "healthy eating" and forced me on it. Red meat was now on the "bad foods" list. Salt was on the "bad foods" list. He would watch me as I put salt on my food and then criticize me on it, "You put WAY too much salt on your food." Eventually, I cut out salt altogether so I didn't have to hear his nagging about it. He wanted all fat cut from meat. If some fat was left on the meat, it was expected that it would not be eaten. He emphasized that fat on meat was disgusting and he would dry heave whenever someone ate it.

Abuser 3 was the worst about chips. Seeing chips used to give me great anxiety. Normal people grab a chip, dip it in a dip, and then bite into it. Sometimes if the chip is small enough, people eat the whole thing in one bite. If the chip is too large, most people bite off the part that they can chew. When I ate chips the normal way, as people do, he would freak out, "You are the loudest person I know! I can hear your chip crunching all the way over here! If you can't fit the entire chip in your mouth, then you need to break it in half before you eat it!" So, I began breaking chips in half before eating them. He still criticized me, "Jesus! Is your mouth really closed? It sounds like you are chewing with your mouth open!" I eventually began to avoid chips altogether. His constant nit-picking of the way that I ate chips made me feel extremely self-conscious.

Sexual Control. Sexual control is hard to recognize. It is different than sexual abuse (sexual assault). Sexual abuse occurs when someone forces you to have sex or to engage in sexual acts against your will. They might hold you down, threaten you with a weapon, drug you, or manipulate the situation to where you feel you have no other option but to do what they want you to do.

Sexual control is slightly different. It is a little bit more subtle. As abusers love control, they also want to have control over the sexual part of the relationship. This means that they want to have sex when they want it, not necessarily when you want it. Thus, when you reject them, they will punish you. Punishment might include sexual affairs, rejection of you when you try to initiate sex, the silent treatment, name calling (whore, slut, frigid), accusations of cheating, destroying your property, "forgetting" plans, or any other mean thing that they can think of to seek revenge for your rejection of them. Abusers will also turn to pouting, guilt trips, and threatening sex with others to coerce you into having sex with them.

What sexual control looked like to me: *Abuser 3 was sexually controlling, but it was very subtle. I don't remember denying him very often, but the last time I denied him sex, he punished me by refusing my subsequent advances for the following 2 years. Yes, he refused to have sex with me for 2 years. Of course, he would make up excuses when I would come on to him: he didn't feel good, he was too worried about other things, he was too busy, etc. etc. But he let me know that he was not interested in having sex with me. He was still interested in sex. He left very visible clues that he was not too sick, too worried or too busy to pleasure himself. It was during this time that I started to wonder if he was having an affair. It is entirely possible, but if he was, I never found out.*

The purpose of punishment is to gain control over you sexually. You are taught with punishment that the abuser is the sole decider in when to have sex, how to have sex, and where to have sex. Your wants, desires, and feelings do not matter. If you refuse him, he will seek revenge and that revenge will teach you not to deny him what he wants. The abuser's revenge will make you feel insecure, unwanted, unattractive, and unlovable. When he finally does come back around to you, you end up feeling so grateful that you decide to give in to him in hopes that you won't have to face his punishments again (which you know will be worse the next time).

Accusations of Flirting/Cheating

Some abusers accuse their romantic partners of flirting or cheating because they view conversations with the opposite sex as a threat to their power. Even if there is no outside contact, the survivor's phone and computer are seen as potential avenues of contact. This serves to isolate the survivor to a greater extent. Survivors, in reaction to their partner's extreme jealousy, might quit talking to opposite sex friends (or same sex friends if in a same sex relationship) to avoid the accusations. Survivors may quit talking to retail or restaurant workers if the abuser is with them. The purpose of the accusations is to control the survivor's behavior. The survivor may learn that the only way to avoid embarrassing accusations and outbursts from the abuser is to keep her head down, avoid eye contact, and not speak to individuals that will enrage the abuser. To prove that she is not cheating and is trustworthy, the survivor may even hand over her phone to the abuser so that the abuser can check messages, emails, and social media accounts. This allows even further control over the survivor.

Sometimes however, the abuser accuses the survivor of cheating to hide the fact that the abuser is cheating. This is also known as projection. The purpose here is for the abuser to avoid being caught by keeping the survivor on the defensive about the abuser's accusations.

What cheating accusations looked like to me: *The only time I really experienced this was after talking with a sales person at a store that Abuser 3 and I were at. I exchanged pleasantries with the sales person and as we were walking away, Abuser 3 said, "Why don't you suck his dick while you are at it?" I felt extremely embarrassed that he would say something like that to me. It also made me question my behavior. Was I flirting? Did I say something that could be construed as inappropriate? Had I been too nice?*

I had a totally normal conversation with a retail clerk where politeness was exchanged. Abuser 3 took my politeness and exaggerated it into flirting. Because of what Abuser 3 said to me, I rarely spoke to retail clerks when we were out together. I often avoided eye contact with them. I would typically let Abuser 3 do most of the talking. Abuser 3 won in that regard. This made him look even more charming and outgoing while it continued to make me look more socially awkward.

Cheating

Repetitive cheating is emotional abuse. What makes cheating emotional abuse? I would argue that the same patterns of abusive behaviors are present during abusive cheating. The abuser denies cheating, lies about cheating, continues to cheat, blames the survivor for the cheating, minimizes the cheating, tells the survivor she is imagining things, refuses to talk about the cheating, does not take responsibility for the cheating, and may even use other abusive tactics in order to avoid having a real conversation about cheating (i.e. stonewalling, gas lighting, ingratiating behavior).

The survivor may feel as though the abuser is cheating or has proof that the abuser is cheating but the abuser flat denies it. The abuser may call the survivor "crazy" or cause such a huge argument about it that it makes the survivor question her instincts (crazy making). If the abuser is caught cheating with no way out, he might blame the survivor for it (i.e. "If you would have sex with me more than once a month, I wouldn't have to find it elsewhere!") or minimize the behavior (i.e. "I only kissed her! It wasn't cheating!"). The abuser may shut down conversation in order to avoid taking responsibility for his actions (i.e. "I never cheated on you! End of discussion!"). The abuser may even use physical violence against the survivor for catching him cheating!

In this manner, cheating is emotional abuse. The same abusive tactics used by the cheater are used by abusers.

On the other hand, if the cheater has not done so repeatedly, if he admits to cheating, takes full responsibility for his actions, is remorseful, does not blame the survivor, does not minimize the cheating, does not discount the survivor's perspective and feelings, does not attempt to shut down communication about the cheating, has not used cheating as revenge, and makes a wholehearted attempt to be faithful and remain committed to the survivor (if they decide to stay together), then I would argue that the cheating was a mistake and not abuse.

What cheating looked like to me: *I am not aware of any cheating in my past relationships with abusers. It is definitely possible that I was cheated on. Although I suspected it with Abuser 3, I never had any evidence that this was actually the case.*

Alcohol/Drug Use

Alcohol and drug use are related to domestic violence. Because the use of alcohol and drugs can cause people to become uninhibited, the propensity for extreme violence in alcoholics and drug users is there. In fact, women in relationships with abusers who use alcohol and drugs are at greater risk of being killed by their male intimate partners.

One study found that out of men who murdered their intimate partner, 80% were problem drinkers, who often binge drank, and drank right before killing their partner. In the same study, they found that those men who had murdered their intimate partner were significantly more likely to be drunk every day than abusers who did not murder their partner. Likewise, of the men who murdered their intimate partners, 67% of them used alcohol, drugs, or both during the murder (Sharps, Campbell, Campbell, Gary, & Webster, 2001). This does not mean that men who are sober will not be abusive. Sober abusive men can be just as brutal as inebriated abusive men. Do not let these statistics make you feel safe. If you are in an abusive relationship with a sober individual, know that you are in great danger. If your partner is physically abusive, the abuse itself is a huge risk factor for potential homicide.

What did alcohol and drug use look like to me? *When I began the relationship with Abuser 3, I was (and still am) completely sober. I wanted to be in a relationship with someone who also wanted to be sober. At the time that the relationship began, Abuser 3 was wearing an ankle monitor which assessed the amount of alcohol in his system. This should have been a warning sign to me – that Abuser 3 was an alcoholic, but he explained it away and I believed him.*

However, when we started dating, he professed his disdain for alcohol, how many problems he had because of it and how he never wanted to drink it again. I believed him. I realize now that he was saying what I wanted to hear in order to get me to be in a relationship with him. He knew that I was sober, that I intended to stay sober, and that I did not want to be around men who drank. Needless to say, as soon as the ankle monitor came off, he started drinking again.

Abuser 3 was always controlling; however, he was most violent after using alcohol and drugs. Just because he never physically assaulted me while he wasn't using, did not mean that his propensity for violence wasn't there. He definitely used physical intimidation tactics (blocking my exits, towering over me, invading my personal space, rushing me, etc.) when sober. These are, in their own way, a type of violence and indicate the possibility of him becoming physically assaultive even when sober.

Besides alcohol, Abuser 3 liked to use other drugs. During our relationship, he was hiding the fact that he was smoking K2. He started to behave oddly. He would come home and not want to come in immediately. He did not want to be greeted or talked to. He claimed that he needed his space. He would put down his things or change and then go outside. He would pretend to work on things in the garage or water the garden or work in the shed. He would smell weird when he came back in. He would act strangely. All of a sudden, he would be in a great mood and act very sweet. This would wear off hours later where he would become very mean. His feet began to smell very badly and he even began to throw up at random times.

In my heart and in my head, I knew that he was up to no good. I felt anxiety in the pit of my stomach. I knew that he was using something but I did not know what it was. I began to search for it. I looked in all the places an addict might hide their drugs. Finally, I found a pipe in the garage that he had made out of tools, and later I found a whole vase filled with empty K2 packages in the shed. I decided to confront him on it. He lied and denied that he was doing it. So then, I confronted him with the proof. I stomped into the garage, opened the drawer dramatically, pulled out the pipe and said, "Oh YEAH? You're not smoking K2? Then what's this?" I then stomped to the shed where I grabbed the empty packages and lighter. I confronted him again. With the evidence in front of him, he finally admitted it. He still would not stop smoking it and I couldn't force him to do it. He started to have health issues from it and that made him quit.

Later in the relationship, he started to take his mother's old anti-anxiety medication that she no longer used. He hid them from me in the top of the *closet, in a pair of shoes. I would often wake up to him getting pills out of their hiding place in the morning. The same pattern of behavior was there: he would become very sweet and loving when he was high and as soon as the drugs started to wear off, he would become increasingly mean, and agitated. Every tiny thing upset him. His anger was amplified. He was much more controlling and hid it much less. He would bark orders at me. He would start fights with me over any little thing he could find.*

He took the pills non-stop, all day long. He denied doing so. Anytime I tried to confront him on it or bring it up, he would become enraged and shut down all communication on the subject. I became extremely anxious during these times. When he left the house, I would sneak into the closet, and count the pills. I would steal 2 and throw them away. When he was taking a shower, I would steal a couple and throw them away. I knew that I couldn't throw them all away at once or it would cause a huge argument that could potentially end in violence. I counted the pills daily, subtracted the ones that I had thrown away and then subtracted the number of pills from the previous morning to figure out how many he was taking in a day. He typically took 6 or more. Meaning that he took one about every 2 hours. Finally, he ran out. This was no reprieve for me.

He then began to tell me all about his anxiety and how he needed to get a prescription for anxiety medication. He was trying to "warm me up to the idea" so that way I wouldn't fight him as much on it. He continued to wear me down on the subject until finally, he just went ahead and got them and my protest was not even heard. He was also drinking with them as well. It was during this part of the relationship, towards the end, that I started to really consider leaving him, but I had no money and nowhere to go.

I was constantly on edge, counting pills and counting beers in hopes of knowing when he was going to explode. He was ruthless during this time. He was so mean. He often kept me up late at night even when I begged and pleaded for him to let me sleep. If I mentioned that I had an exam the next day, he would make sure that I didn't get any sleep. If I did not stay up with him and do what he wanted to do, he would come into the room at 3am or 4am and turn on the TV to wake me up. If I wanted to be able to sleep, I would have to move to the couch. He loved it when I moved to the couch because it was a symbol that he had won. He had absolute power over me.

He made my life hell and the worst part was that I couldn't protest. If I fought back, pleaded or argued, he would turn it into world war three. I knew that the violence was coming but I just never knew when. So, I shut my mouth and took it in order to avoid the physical abuse. But the emotional and verbal abuse continued.

I want to mention here that using alcohol and drugs is emotionally abusive just like cheating. The same tactics are used here that are used with physical abuse and cheating: denying, lying, minimizing, blaming, shutting down communication, hiding alcohol and drug use, using other abusive tactics to avoid talking about it and avoiding taking responsibility for his actions.

CHAPTER 6
PHYSICAL ABUSE

According to Sonkin, Martin, and Walker (1985), "Physical violence is defined as the use of physical force to intimidate, control, or force another person to do something against their will" (pg. 37). Physical violence lies on a spectrum of severity. Society has a harder time recognizing and acknowledging less severe forms of violence, as physical violence. For example, pushing, shoving, grabbing and holding someone by the arm or face, physically moving someone, holding someone in place, grabbing and twisting someone's arm, tripping, hair pulling, pinching, holding someone down, sitting on someone, standing on someone, and slapping are forms of violence that are typically not taken as seriously as punching, kicking, burning, biting, choking, raping, and hurting someone with a weapon.

The reason why many of us don't recognize these "less severe" physical acts as violent is because we are desensitized to it. We learn norms by watching others, both in real life and also on TV. So, when we see physical abuse being portrayed in movies or on TV shows as severe physical violence, we believe that only severe physical violence is violence. Furthermore, as we see others engage in less severe forms of violence (whether on TV or in real life) and not suffer any consequences for their actions, we begin to believe that these forms of violence are not violent at all.

So, what does this mean for emotional and verbal abuse? If, as a society, we don't recognize pushing or shoving or slapping to be problematic, then we must view emotional and verbal abuse as even less problematic than shoving or slapping. We must view these types of abuse as *normal*. Therefore, if we see these as normal, then it is even harder to recognize it as abuse when it is happening in our own lives. "The more subtle forms of violence such as this are the most difficult to detect because most people do not associate that kind of behavior with violence" (Sonkin, Martin, & Walker, 1985; pg. 38).

What did physical abuse look like to me? *One night, while living with Abuser 3, I turned on the TV while we were both in bed. Abuser 3 immediately picked up his phone and started texting. It was clear he wasn't into the show. Halfway through it, something caught his attention. He looked up from his phone and asked, "What happened?" So, I rewound it, and explained it to him. He immediately picked up his phone and ignored me. He then put his phone down and asked me again, "O.K. What happened?" Again, I paused the show and tried to explain but he picked up his phone and ignored me again. Now I was really frustrated because of how disrespectful he was being. He then asked me a third time and in annoyance I said, "Oh my god." I then re-explained what happened for a third time. I could feel the tension in the air growing after that. I knew that by voicing my annoyance I was taking a huge risk. So, I tried to drop it. I let it go in hopes that it wouldn't start a fight. I dropped the tone in my voice and I set myself back to normal and played the show again.*

I got up out of bed and when I bent down to pet the dog, I saw Abuser 3 glaring at me. I could tell that Abuser 3 was pissed. He was beyond pissed, he was livid, and my letting it go wasn't going to work because he had heard the annoyance in my voice and now he wanted to confront me about it. He was in a mood to fight and so he tells me, "You know, I am getting really tired of the 'Oh my God' thing. You have been such a bitch today, all day, and I am sick of it."

I tried to deflect and rationalize at first and said, "Abuser 3, I haven't been a bitch all day. I had a reason to be annoyed with you a second ago. You were being rude when you weren't paying attention and then you kept interrupting the show to have me explain it to you, so I was annoyed. But it wasn't a big deal so I let it go."

As soon as Abuser 3 heard the word "rude" he knew he had ammunition to start a war. He really didn't even let me finish that whole sentence, I had to yell it over him because he cut me off to tell me, "You're such a FUCKING

BITCH! RUDE! I CAN'T FUCKING HEAR AND YOU KNOW THAT!"

Let me interject here that Abuser 3's hearing is totally 100% fine. This was a lie used to give him the moral upper ground in the argument, to justify his emotional and verbal abuse towards me.

I yelled back, "Yes, RUDE! You were sitting there on your FUCKING PHONE not paying attention to the show and then you kept making me rewind and explain it to you!!!" He countered with, "FUCK YOU AUDREY" and a nice shiny middle finger sat right in my face.

Here, I knew that it was going somewhere I didn't want it to go. It was already escalating to a point where I felt unsafe and I wanted to leave. Stonewalling me with a "Fuck you" did not leave much room for conversation. It essentially shut down conversation. But, because I did not understand that these tactics were abusive and that Abuser 3 was abusive, I still thought that I could reason with him.

I should point out here that abusive individuals cannot be reasoned with. Abusers are about control. They seek control over you and attempts to reason with them are futile. The only outcome the abuser is looking for is submission.

So, I tried to defuse the situation. In the calmest, most sincere voice I could muster. I said, "Abuser 3, I am trying to tell you that I didn't know that you couldn't hear, you were playing on your phone and weren't paying attention. That's why I got annoyed and it seriously wasn't even a big deal. I totally let it go."

There was no nullifying him. He was enraged. He would not listen to reason. He immediately told me, "FUCK YOU AUDREY" and kept going on about what a bitch I had been to him all day.

So, then I switched tactics. I told Abuser 3 still in the calmest voice I could, "Listen, you are seriously pushing my buttons. You keep telling me fuck you and you keep calling me names like bitch and that really makes me want to leave." Here, what I was really trying to express was that the situation was escalating rapidly, that Abuser 3 was absolutely not listening to me, and that I was scared and that is why I wanted to leave. So, Abuser 3 said authoritatively, "I DON'T CARE. LEAVE! AUDREY, GET THE FUCK OUT, I DON'T CARE."

After he said this I really should have left. That would have been the smartest play. However, he was trying to manipulate me into staying and it worked. To me, this was a test. He was testing me to see if I would leave. If I had left, he probably wouldn't have physically assaulted me but he would have punished me for leaving in other ways (using the children, silent treatment, etc.).

I continued to attempt to reason with him to alleviate the situation. "Abuser 3, you know it pushes my buttons when you say fuck you and call me names, I don't understand why you are doing this. We promised we wouldn't do these things anymore. Why can't you just let it go? It seriously wasn't a big deal." I think here he thought that he would get what he wanted: control and power. He thought he had me in a position he wanted, so he countered with, "You can make it stop with two little words. You were such a bitch all day. All you have to say is two words." In case you are wondering what those two words were, he was trying to force me to grovel for his forgiveness, on my knees begging him, by saying, "I'm sorry."

Needless to say, I got pissed. He was the one who started this whole issue by interrupting my show, making me pause it, and then making me explain it, all so he could ignore me and force me to do it again. He enjoyed having that power over me. Then, when I got annoyed with him, he had ammunition to start a fight with me. HE should have been apologizing to ME.

So, I told him that, via yelling: "REALLY? I WAS A BITCH ALL DAY? YOU WERE THE ONE BEING RUDE TO ME! SO, FUCK YOU ABUSER 3!" That is when Abuser 3 threatened me the first time. "You have three seconds to SHUT THE FUCK UP Audrey!" I was tired of him cornering me verbally, trying to gain control over me, and I was tired of feeling stuck, like I couldn't leave.

When I feel cornered, I start to fight back and I decided here that I was going to give it back to him verbally as good as he had been giving it to me. So, I started pushing his buttons. I got close to him and talked to him in a calm voice, "I'm not going to shut up. I am a grown ass woman who can talk whenever I want." He put three fingers in my face and said, "You have THREE SECONDS to get out of my face." I interrupted here with a calm voice, "Abuser 3, I'm not in your face." He got really angry and said, "You have THREE SECONDS to get out of my SPACE before I put my elbow in your face." So, I laid down on my side of the bed and got my phone and said, "Ok cunt. That's how you're acting right now Abuser 3, you're being a cunt." With venom he said, "You have three seconds to shut the fuck up, NOW YOUR PUSHING MY BUTTONS AND I'M GETTING PISSED."

What I think is interesting here, is that he was completely unwilling to listen to reason when I tried to ask him repeatedly to stop pushing my buttons. In fact, he laughed at me and continued to call me names and threaten me. But then, when I started to use the tactics on him that he was using on me, this is where the tables turned and Abuser 3 physically assaulted me. This is due to control. When I was verbally reasoning with Abuser 3, he still felt he had control over me. He believed that he could force me to apologize to him in order to quell the confrontation. However, when I began to defend myself by using those same tactics on him, he felt as though he was losing control over me and possibly even losing control over the situation. This loss of control is what prompted him to escalate the situation further by using physical violence in order to regain control over me.

"FUCK YOU ABUSER 3," is the last thing I said before he assaulted me. He jumped on top of me, with his knees on either side of my waist and he sat on my stomach with the full force of his 185 pounds. He grabbed both of my arms and squeezed them as tightly as he could while shoving them into my chest. He smiled a wicked smile, one that suggested that he was really pleased with the situation and with his actions and that he had total control over me now. I immediately started screaming, "GET THE FUCK OFF ME YOU FUCKING ASSHOLE!!" I squirmed and tried to break free but his grip was too strong and he knew it. AND HE LOVED IT. I looked into his eyes and I saw something I had never seen before. He was full of pure hate. He felt PLEASURE in the fact that he had me where I couldn't move, he felt PLEASURE now that he had control, and he felt PLEASURE because he was scaring me.

Next, as I was squirming to try to get free, he attempted to throw me off the bed. Two things happened here: one of his hands got right near my face and he lost his grip on my right arm. In one fluid motion, I bit his knuckle on his hand as hard as I could and I put my hand on the wall next to the bed to keep myself from falling off. He still had a hold of my left arm, but I was able to sit up super quick by putting my right arm under me. He let go of my other arm and I pushed him as hard as I could to get him off of me. But I was still no match to his 185 lbs. He was like a rock. He barely moved. He kind of chuckled and decided that he would lay back down as though nothing at all had just happened. He acted as if it was another day, as though he had been in bed watching TV all night.

I want to point out that Abuser 3 never "lost control." Abusers love to say they "blacked out" or "lost control" when they become violent, but that is 100% not true. They purposefully attack you and use physical violence to regain control over you. They feel as though they are losing control over you. This is known as escalation: using increasingly violent tactics in order to regain control.

Part of escalation is that the abuser becomes desensitized to using violence to gain control. As the survivor complies more and more often, giving the abuser more and more control over her, the abuser becomes accustomed to having that control. Therefore, the abuser needs even more control in order to feel as though he has control. So, when the abuser feels that he is losing control, he will use more violence in order to gain control. This is because less violent measures (emotional, verbal, and seemingly lesser violent actions) seem to no longer work. It's about *gaining* control, not just having it, and it's like a drug. The more control the abuser has, the more he wants and he has to use greater violence to get it. This is why the violence in abusive relationships becomes more violent, not less violent. This is very much a part of the Cycle of Violence.

CHAPTER 7
CYCLE OF VIOLENCE (WALKER, 1979)

Tension Building Phase

It is here that the abuser uses emotional, verbal, and "less" severe forms of violence to gain control over the survivor. The survivor does what she can to calm the abuser and to avoid escalation into physical violence. This phase consists of many minor altercations where tension begins to build. These altercations can include criticism, nit-picking, emotional and verbal abuse tactics, and arguments prompted by the abuser. The survivor may feel that she has to be "perfect" in order to avoid arguments. This feeling is captured by the saying, "I feel like I'm walking on eggshells." Furthermore, the survivor may feel as though she cannot do anything right. It is during this time that the survivor notices or feels that the abuser "is looking for a fight." The abuser becomes especially critical, nit-picky, and grumpy during this phase and utilizes the emotional and verbal abusive tactics. Because of this, the survivor will typically use coping skills in order to avoid the fight. Some examples of survivor's coping skills are:

Apologizing for any slight transgression

Apologizing even when it's the abuser's fault

Apologizing for things the survivor cannot control

Keeping the children quiet to not upset the abuser
Keeping the house spotless

Refusing to show any emotion (like anger, frustration or annoyance)

Staying out of the abuser's way

Catering to the abuser's every whim (becoming overly loving/nurturing)

Attempting to anticipate and meet the abuser's needs before being asked

Leaving the scene of an argument or altercation in order to deescalate the situation

Rehearsing what to say before saying it so as to cause the least Impact

Letting the issue go

Pretending not to be bothered by something that upset her (hiding true feelings)

Choosing her battles wisely (decides not to engage in confrontations)

What the tension building phase looked like to me: *I never realized how much I apologized for every little thing until I got out of the abusive relationship. I actually started to annoy myself with my constant apologies. However, when I was in the abusive relationship, apologizing was a way of avoiding a fight. I would apologize for dropping my phone, for shutting the refrigerator door too loudly, for accidently bumping the abuser, for putting the dishes away too loudly, for not taking out the trash before being yelled at, for not reading the abuser's mind, and for any other transgression that the abuser would point out.*

I would attempt to prevent fights by learning to anticipate the abuser's needs and meet those needs before being asked or told. This meant that I helped the

abuser do every little thing. I over-helped. I put in more effort at everything the abuser did so that it was apparent that I was helping. I catered to the abuser. I would take over the abuser's responsibilities and duties to give the abuser "time off." This meant that I overloaded my own schedule and stressed myself out with too many things to do while the abuser got to take naps and watch TV. I learned to not express, voice, talk about, or show my frustration and anger. I learned not to ask for what I wanted or needed because that too would start a fight. I gave into the abuser's demands and whims. I became a "yes man." I learned not to voice my own opinion. Instead, I figured out first what the abuser's opinion was and then expressed that.

The tension building phase was really hard for me to recognize while I was in abusive relationships. Even when I got out of the last abusive relationship, I had trouble really pinpointing it at first. I always felt this phase but never consciously recognized it for what it was.

It is a feeling of dread and impending doom. When the survivor feels as though the abuser is looking for a fight, or that the abuser wants to fight, the survivor is in the tension building phase. Recognizing that the abuser wants to fight and is purposefully finding things to fight about is the epitome of this phase. During this time, the abuser will not be happy or feel satisfied until he gets a fight (which is the Explosion Phase). The abuser might be edgy, anxious, grouchy, or have a bad attitude. It is during this time he becomes very critical and negative. As the tension grows, he may start to express his frustration and anger by sighing loudly, slamming things, or talking to you in a way that shows his disdain for you. It is during this phase that the abuser starts an argument with the survivor that escalates into violence.

The Explosion Phase

During this phase, the abuser erupts in violence, resulting in physical abuse enacted upon the survivor, a child or pet. Physical violence can also take the forms of: destruction of the survivor's property, verbal threats made against the survivor with or without weapons and/or even death of the survivor. The abuser also uses emotional and verbal abusive tactics in this phase. If the survivor attempts to flee the situation, some abusers may physically prevent the survivor from leaving. Other times the abuser psychologically traps the survivor. Out of all three phases, the Explosion Phase is the shortest. It is during this phase that the survivor may:

Attempt to reason with abuser

Attempt to subdue the abuser

Feel completely out of control

Defend herself by fighting back

Protect herself

Escape the situation by leaving

Call the police to stop the violence/protect herself

The explosion phase may look different depending on the relationship. In some relationships, the survivor may experience any one of the violent tactics listed under physical abuse. For others, the survivor may experience threats of violence, damage to property, or verbal/emotional abuse but not experience physical abuse. Regardless, it is important to note that the Cycle of Violence only becomes more frequent and more lethal over time (Sonkin, Martin, & Walker, 1985). This means that if you are experiencing emotional and verbal abuse but have not experienced physical abuse, eventually, the relationship is likely to turn physically abusive. Likewise, if you are experiencing physical abuse, it is very important to understand that the violence will only become more severe and more frequent over time. To be clear, the increase in severity of physical abuse means an increase in risk of death.

- Half of all female homicide victims are murdered by their male romantic partners.

- According to McFarlane et al., (1999), "Women are more likely to be killed by an intimate partner than by all other categories of known assailants combined."

- The murder of a woman by her partner is often preceded by physical abuse and the action of her leaving the relationship.

- Almost all of the women murdered by their intimate partners had experienced physical violence perpetrated by their partner in the past year.

- For 20% of women, the first physical violence experienced in the relationship ended in her death. This means that for every 5 women who were murdered, 1 never saw any signs of physical abuse until the assault which killed her.

- Half of women who had been murdered by their intimate partner had experienced violence by that partner in the past month.

- Forty percent of the women killed by their intimate partner experienced increasingly frequent violent episodes from their partner.

- Being choked by your intimate partner is a major risk factor for fatality. Twenty-five percent of women who were murdered by their partner were strangled to death.

- It is very important to understand that living in an abusive relationship can end in death (Arbuckle et al., 1996; Block, 2003; Browne & Williams, 1993; Campbell, 1992; Ellis & Dekeseredy, 1997; Kellerman & Mercy, 1992; McFarlane et al., 1999; Petrosky et al., 2017).

What the Explosion Phase looked like to me: *I experienced increasing severity within each of my relationships and also when getting into each new relationship. What I mean is that while in the relationship with Abuser 2, the violence became more severe over time as he progressed from punching walls to threatening to kill me. Abuser 3 progressed from yelling to using physical violence.*

When I would leave one relationship and get into a new one, the next abuser would be even worse than the first. Abuser 1's Explosive Phase typically consisted of verbal abuse. He would demean me, belittle me, and make me feel worthless. Abuser 2's Explosive Phase was worse than Abuser 1's. Abuser 2 would damage my property, threaten to kill me, threaten to kill me while displaying weapons, and generally act psychotic and scary. Abuser 3's Explosion Phase was worse than the previous two. He used physical violence during our relationship. For an in-depth look at his Explosion Phase, please see the Physical Abuse section. Because I did not realize that I was in abusive relationships, I did not learn the red flags which would have allowed me to avoid abusers. Unfortunately, I continued to seek out toxic and damaging relationships which were more and more severe.

The purpose of the Explosion Phase is to gain control over the survivor. The intent is to scare the survivor into compliance or submission. The abuser also uses physical violence to "punish" the survivor for perceived wrong-doing. The ultimate goal is to force the survivor into submission through fear thereby controlling her. The abuser's need for control is the motive for escalating an argument and using physical violence. In other words, need for control and the need to display that control drives the abuser to use violence to continue to gain compliance (Johnson, 1995). Although researchers admit, in some cases, no amount of compliance will satiate the need for control and thus, stop the violence (Smith, 1990). This is also why the violence increases over time in severity. As the abuser becomes accustomed to having more control over the survivor, the abuser is no longer satisfied with that amount of control. He always wants more control and the way he gains more control is by increasing his violence.

The Honeymoon Phase

During this phase, the abuser feels remorse, guilt, and acts very loving and kind to the survivor. The abuser may apologize to the survivor but there will be no real accountability. Any attempts to get the abuser to take responsibility for the physical violence or to admit the abuse is met with anger and frustration by the abuser. The abuser typically describes the abusive incident as "out of character" or a "one-time thing" or a "fluke" which is the opposite of the truth. The abuser offers an apology as a blanket statement in order to pardon, excuse, and avoid meaningful conversation about the behavior. Any real attempts to discuss the abuser's actions and force the abuser to take accountability for his actions are thwarted. This is often done through minimization of the abuse, (i.e. "I never beat you!") and blaming the victim for the abuse, (i.e. "If you had never…. I wouldn't have…" or "You made me do it!"). The abuser will never admit to being abusive (Samsel, 2013).

The abuser may also excuse the behavior by saying he got so angry that he "lost control." Do not believe this. The abuser does not lose control when he becomes violent with you. The abuser becomes physically violent in order to scare you and physically control you. This is because the abuser feels that he is losing control over you. Thus, when the abuser promises to "not lose control" again, this should not be taken lightly. The abuser's mentality feeds off of and revolves around controlling others.

It is during the Honeymoon phase that the abuser promises to never hurt the survivor again, to go to counseling, to attend Alcoholics Anonymous, to quit drinking, to quit using drugs, or to attend anger management in order to convince the survivor to forgive him, come back, or stay with him. The abuser will say anything he thinks the survivor wants to hear to preserve the relationship. If the abuser actually gets help, it is typically because the survivor has left him and has made it a condition on getting back together with the abuser. It should be known that in this situation, the abuser will attend classes until he feels that the survivor is back under his control and then the abuser will quit going.

During the Honeymoon phase the abuser showers the survivor with gifts, flowers, love notes, apology letters, and daily affirmations. The abuser may let you do things that he does not normally let you do. The abuser may take over some of the responsibilities or help you with things he wouldn't normally. Overall, the abuser is generally very nice to you (this is also known as ingratiating behavior). This contrast between the abuser being really mean and then being normal can make normal behavior seem extremely nice. When the abuser is very mean and then switches to being sweet, it can make the survivor feel as though everything is going to be better than ok. It is going to be amazing. Everything will work out. The contrast is what makes the highs seem really high in the relationship.

The purpose of the Honeymoon Phase is to regain control of the survivor, redirect focus away from the abuser's violence and onto the survivor's actions (to attach blame there), to avoid taking responsibility for the violent actions, and to sweet talk the survivor into forgetting/minimizing the violence. Often, the survivor withdraws emotionally, threatens to leave or leaves after the violent incident. When the abuser begins the Honeymoon phase, the survivor is sweet-talked, tempted into "remembering the good times," schmoozed into believing that the relationship is not an abusive one, that the abuse was a mistake, that all problems will be solved and that the violence will never happen again. The survivor is often tempted to go back to the abuser because of the manipulative and charming behavior. During this phase, the abuser is very good at minimizing the violence, making the survivor take half or all of the responsibility for the abuse and making the survivor believe that the relationship is wonderful and not abusive.

These tactics worked on me the first time and almost worked on me the second time that Abuser 3 became physically violent. Thankfully, I had a friend who took me to a women's shelter which offered free education on abusive relationships. I learned that indeed, I was in an abusive relationship. It was very hard for me to see at first that this was true. This was because I had never experienced the more extreme types of physical abuse: being punched or kicked, burned or choked. Because of this, I wasn't even sure that I was in an abusive relationship. Furthermore, because I did not know any of the subtle controlling tactics, Abuser 3 was able to use those tactics against me. He was able to convince me that the physical violence was my fault, and that the relationship was not abusive. However, after the second time Abuser 3 became violent, I began to learn more about abusive relationships which allowed me to determine that I was in one. Because of the knowledge and support I received from the shelter, I was able to leave the relationship for good. It allowed me to recognize Abuser 3 for what he was and I was able to recognize the "love" letters and gifts for what they were: The Honeymoon stage.

What the Honeymoon Phase looked like to me: *Immediately after I was able to get Abuser 3 off of me, I jumped out of bed, threw on my house shoes, grabbed my purse and left. I went to my parent's house in the dead of night. The next few days were filled with calls and emails from Abuser 3. In texts, letters, emails, and phone calls, he said to me things like:*

"This is completely different than the two times that I let alcohol make me lose my grip. I never beat you sweetheart, the two times that I lost my normally docile composure I quickly realized I was wrong, and quit. This is because at my core there is the gentle, loving man, who never wants to be associated with men who do this type of thing." —In this paragraph Abuser 3 minimizes the

abuse, denies that he is an abuser, blames alcohol for the abuse, and avoids taking responsibility for his actions.

"I told them that even though we both made mistakes, and got out of hand, ultimately you tried to get me to drop it, and that I should've never put my hands on you. I also told them that there are things that I need to do to repair it, with an end to my drinking being number one priority." —In this paragraph, Abuser 3 blames the abuse on me by saying 'we both made mistakes and got out of hand'. Abuser 3 then blames alcohol again for his abusive behavior.

"Our relationship was so full of happiness babe, I know you know this. We can be that happy again without real effort. As soon as I quit drinking when this happened the first time I became less able to be over stimulated and we virtually quit arguing except for quickly squashed episodes, and lately we had barely even done that. I came to the realization that I had taken Xanax the day before while at Scarborough faire, and there is always a tendency for me to have anxiety the day after, which was Monday, the day of the fight. I fully believe that along with alcohol, the constant stimulation we were both giving each other and both of our anxiety issues caused the whole problem honey. I have now quit drinking, and flushed the Xanax down the toilet."

—In this paragraph Abuser 3 tries to convince me that our relationship was amazing except for this one tiny problem which is black and white thinking and minimizing. Next, Abuser 3 blames the abuse on me, anxiety, and Xanax. Abuser 3 never takes responsibility for his actions. Abuser 3 also wants me to believe that because alcohol and Xanax caused the abuse, now that he has quit using them, there will be no more abuse.

Do not believe the abuser for a second. Once the abuser has you back under his control, he will immediately start drinking and taking Xanax again (or whatever it was that they promised not to do). Also, they are the ones responsible for their actions, not the alcohol or the Xanax. Because the abuser never takes responsibility, he will not change his controlling abusive behavior.

When Abuser 3 said 'We can be that happy again without real effort' understand that this is an excuse to not change his behavior and to avoid admitting that he was abusive. Abuser 3 actually, really believes this. He believes that he is not abusive. He believes that his behavior does not need to change because HE didn't do anything. Therefore, in his mind, things can be really happy again without any effort.

One last point here: when Abuser 3 said, 'Our relationship was so full of happiness babe, I know you know this, realize that he is telling me how I feel *and what to think. He doesn't even realize that I have a different point of view than him or that I have experienced things differently. This is because he does not see me as a separate entity. He views me as an extension of himself which is based on absolute control.*

"Please try to remember that the only time we ever had this issue, was when I had been drinking and even then, very rarely. Even though you believe this to be getting worse, it's not. I have gotten so much better over the years. I used to have serious anger issues but over the years I have calmed down. What happened the other night was a serious misstep in what is normally a very calm relationship, even with your anger. I am not minimizing what happened at all. I am telling you that I have known about this, but I thought I was over it. I knew as soon as I grabbed your arms that I had made a grave error. This is why I finally rolled over and said for you to leave. I was instantly embarrassed and telling you to leave was a defense mechanism. I do not like this person that comes out of me when I drink. Baby, I will never drink again! You mean way more to me than any other thing in this world and I will never ever take you for granted again. We have so much more positive than negative in our relationship, please remember the real level of our happiness. I know that you are scared, but there is no need to be as I am never violent when I am sober."

—Abuser 3 minimizes and blames alcohol again for the abuse. Abuser 3 then discounts my perspective (that the violence and abuse is getting worse) and he then counters me (tells me that it is not getting worse). Abuser 3 then goes on to minimize the abuse and blame me for it ("even with your anger"). That was really a nasty little dig. It was used to focus the attention on me, not his abusive behavior. It was also a baiting tactic. Abuser 3 then counters me again (I am not minimizing).

For Abuser 3 to tell me to leave directly after becoming physically violent with me is the epitome of controlling. In fact, Abuser 3 is so controlling that not only does he have to use violence to gain control but then he has to tell me to leave (while I'm in the process of leaving) to feel as though he forced me to leave, as though it was his idea.

When Abuser 3 promises to not drink again, it is an empty promise. Abuser 3 then uses ingratiating behavior to attempt to convince me to come back to him. The last sentence is really a doozy. Abuser 3 counters what I feel, tells me what to feel, discounts my perspective, and blames alcohol for the abuse (for the millionth time).

After reading these passages, you may notice a trend in the repetitive nature of what is being said over and over. This is the tactic brain washing being used at its finest. Abuser 3's points that he attempts to beat into my head through repetition are: alcohol caused the abuse, our relationship was perfect except for that one time…, I am at least partially if not fully responsible for Abuser 3's abuse.

Abuser 3 often used guilt trips to obligate me into coming back to him. The purpose here is to make me feel so guilty and feel so sorry for him that the only option is to come back to him. These statements were used in an attempt to manipulate me into coming back.

"My heart and soul has been ripped out and trampled on every second of every day since Monday. All I can think about is you and I am scared to death that I have lost you, my favorite person in the world."

"Also, I want you to know how much the dog misses you. He doesn't get up with me in the mornings, he stays asleep on the floor waits for you to get out of bed even though the door is open. I cried when I figured out why he did this. I cry a lot nowadays."

"This morning started out with the dog throwing up all over the kitchen. I'm a little worried about him as he doesn't seem like himself and didn't eat much. PetSmart and the grocery store were extremely tough because everyone knows you and I, and loves us. Everyone asked me where you were."

"It's not the fact that I am now tasked with all of the laundry, all of the cooking, all of the taxiing the kids around, all of the animal chores, or all of the housework that hurts me so badly. It is the fact that I am so alone."

"Well, at this point I have gotten used to having to run this house by myself. I have gotten used to having to tend to every single thing. The one thing I cannot get used to is the fact that YOU are not my best friend right now."

Abuser 3 is trying to make me feel responsible for his sadness and for all the work he now has to do because I am no longer there to do it for him but, HE caused this because of HIS violence. Abuser 3 is also passive-aggressive in several of the statements because he now has to carry the burden of all of the chores that I carried throughout the entire relationship. In being passive-aggressive Abuser 3 is trying to make me feel responsible for his problems.

Abuser 3 uses a lot of empty promises. At this point in the Honeymoon Phase, he is attempting to say whatever he thinks I want to hear in order to get me to come back to him. The problem with this tactic is that I have already heard all of these promises before. He has used these in the past in order to get me to come back, and after the first abusive incident, I did go back to him. He promised the same things.

If you are experiencing this, please know that this is a pattern of behavior that will continue. The abuser will become violent again. He will then make empty promises to get you to come back or reconcile. As soon as you come back or make up, the promises will be forgotten and the process will start all over again.

It is important that survivors recognize that these promises are shallow. They are intended to manipulate you into believing that things will get better, that the violence will not continue, and that the abuser will change. These are all lies.

What makes the promises empty is the fact that the one thing that actually needs to happen in order for the control and abuse to stop is that the abuser needs to take full responsibility for his violent actions and admit that he is abusive. The abuser is typically unwilling to do this. When the abuser is unwilling to own the violence and unwilling to admit abuse and control, no amount of counseling, AA, anger management, or whatever else promised will work. The relationship will still be based on the abuser's ability to have control over the survivor, which is the problem. Because of this, the abuser will not change and when the abuser feels that he is losing control over the survivor again, he will use violence in order to regain control.

One way for the survivor to know that the relationship will not get better and that the violence will continue is that the abuser blames the violence on other things: the survivor, alcohol, drugs, loss of control, etc. The abuser's sole purpose here is to get you back into their house so that they can have control over you again. Once they feel as though they have control over you, any of the promises that they had been keeping (sobriety, going to counseling, etc.) are discarded fairly quickly. Furthermore, if the survivor never intends to return to the abuser, as soon as the abuser realizes this, the promises are thrown out the window. This should make it clear to the survivor that the abuser is not trying to better himself but is doing what it will take for the time being to get the survivor back under his control. Here are some of the things Abuser 3 promised me:

"I will not let you down, I promise. I will quit the things that have caused this. I will never touch alcohol again, EVER. I will go to AA, couples

counseling (so we can learn not to antagonize each other), individual counseling, and anger management to learn to not put my hands on you again. I do not love to fight baby, I love my family and will do anything to have it whole again. I will do whatever it takes to win you back, and never make you feel the need to go again." —Notice in this paragraph Abuser 3 blames me for the abuse and believes that I need to go to counseling too.

"I have made an appointment for counseling, and will make us one when I go to this one, just in hopes that you will attend with me. I have quit alcohol." —Here he makes us a couples counseling appointment. This states that I too am responsible for his abuse. It also is a coercive way to get me to come back to him, and he does this without my consent. Abuser 3 never asks me if I would like to go to counseling or asks if I feel like I need counseling. This is typical of controlling abusers to do things without your perspective or your consent.

"I have an appointment this week with a counselor and am going to address my grief and anxiety problem. I would love it if you would come with me so that you could see the level of honesty and devotion with which I am trying to fix the only problem our happy relationship has had in the 6 years we have been together." —Again, Abuser 3 uses black and white thinking and minimizes the severity of the control and abuse.

"I will do anything, even give both my arms, my sight, my hearing or anything else that I have to give, to be back to the happy family that we were before Monday." —So, Abuser 3 is willing to amputate body parts to get me to come home to him but he is unwilling to admit that he is abusive and that he is solely responsible for his violence. Let that sink in.

"Never again will I put any mind-altering substances (either prescribed or store bought) in my body ever again, I promise you for ever and ever. I will not ever mention alcohol again, nor do I hold anything but loathing for it as it has brought me nothing but grief. I have already told everyone that I have had drinks with in the recent past about what happened, and that I will no longer be a drinker. They have been really supportive. I will drop them as friends if they are not, I promise Audrey." —I have heard this one before. The first time Abuser 3 assaulted me he told me he would never drink again. That did not last long. After I had made it known how committed to him I was, he started drinking again.

"I vow to never allow stupidity into our lives again." —It is hard to

recognize but even this statement is controlling. Abuser 3 here is making a decision for me without my consent or my input.

"I promise I will be the man that you want me to be." —He refers to the man he thinks I want him to be. *Never does Abuser 3 ask my input of what I think needs to change in order for this to occur. In fact, anytime I offered my opinion on this matter Abuser 3 has discounted my perspective, minimized, blamed, trivialized, denied, and stonewalled me.*

In most of his proclamations, Abuser 3 declares that he "will do whatever it takes" except, as it should be noted, take responsibility for his violence. That, he will not and does not do.

Abuser 3 also tried to charm me with ingratiating behavior to persuade me to come back. It should be known that this behavior is intended to make the survivor "remember the good times" and feel as though the abuser really loves her in order to trivialize and minimize the abuse to make it seem less severe.

The abuser can be really persuasive in this by mixing proclamations of love with abusive tactics such as blame. Furthermore, when the abuser claims that his behavior was a one-time thing, the statements of love are very hard to recognize as ingratiating, abusive, and controlling. Most individuals have a hard time distinguishing between sincere love and ingratiating behavior. However, "loving" statements are ingratiating behavior when there is a hidden agenda behind them. In the Honeymoon phase, the agenda is to prevent the survivor from leaving, to reconcile, or to get the survivor to come back to the abuser in order to gain control over her again.

Here are some of Abuser 3's charming statements intended to "win" me back. These ingratiating statements were mixed in with countless other abusive tactics.

"I think you are BEAUTIFUL and I would love to grow old with you. I love you to the core for being different, like me. I love you more than the sun, the moon, and all the stars in the sky."

"I love you so much Audrey. I think you are gorgeous and I think that we have a beautiful relationship that is so worth fixing."

"I miss my best friend, beautiful lover, helper, partner, confidante, and soul mate, oh so badly."

"I love you more than I have ever loved before."

"I love you so unconditionally and I think you are gorgeous, inside and out."

"I love you so deeply that I will do anything and I have never felt this way before."

Abuser 3 sent me an email containing a 44-item list of things he loves about me. Abuser 3 sent me an email with an article pasted in it which lists, "10 Things That You Learn When in a Good Relationship." Abuser 3 then compared our relationship with those listed items.

Abuser 3 also attempted to coerce me to come back to him. Coercion is attempting to force someone to do something by threatening them. Although Abuser 3 did not explicitly threaten me, the subtle threat of suicide is there. He was trying to make me feel as though whatever happened to him was my responsibility. He was trying to make me believe that his mental health was my responsibility and that I was the one causing his pain and sadness. Let us remember that his violence is what caused his pain and sadness. His threats are very vague, but nonetheless, the coercion is present.

"Without you here, the future is unsure."

"I am not doing OK Audrey. I am a total basket case and I can't keep it together. I feel so low; like I'm not good for people and that I ruined my entire life. I am scared for my future."

"This has been by far the worst week of my life. It has been a daily struggle to lift my head up off the pillow. I have never cried so much, or eaten so little. I truly feel like my soul is gone."

"Please don't let us die! Please!"

"Oh my god this is killing me! I am so not ok. I can't eat, I cry all the time, I can't sleep, all I can think about is you and I and the wonderful 6 year relationship that I am trying so hard to save."

"I don't think I can handle much more Audrey. It's been a really hard time since you left."

These coercive statements are also intended to be guilt trips. He wants me to *feel sorry for him. He is trying to make his feelings my responsibility, which they are not. In essence, he is blaming me for his sadness (because I left him) even though it was his actions (violence) that prompted me to leave. This is another tactic that abusers use to redirect your attention away from their violent actions and onto your own actions.*

During the Honeymoon Phase, Abuser 3 also sent flowers to my parent's house. He sent gifts to my parent's house. He showed up unannounced at my parent's house, at my work, and at my school. He mailed cards to me and emailed me letters. He sent tons of love letters. He had his family show up to my parent's house unannounced in hopes that he would be able to get them to convince me to come back. Abuser 3 went around to all the places he thought I might be in hopes of cornering me to "talk some sense" into me. I found this out through friends at those places. He called my cell phone and my parents' house phone repeatedly. He texted me obsessively. He left messages on my voice mail. He had his family call, text, email, and send me letters. He even had his family message me through Facebook. I received a multitude of unsolicited communications from Abuser 3 and his family every single day for two months straight after I left him.

To the average person who is not educated on abusive relationships, this looks like love. However, this is absolutely not love. Not only is this the epitome of the Honeymoon phase of the abuser trying to win back the survivor, but it is also stalking.

CHAPTER 8
STALKING

Although the legal definition of stalking differs by jurisdiction, stalking is defined by the National Violence Against Women (NVAW) survey (Tjaden & Thoennes, 1998) as, "repeated (e.g. two or more) occasions of visual or physical proximity, non-consensual communication, or verbal, written, or implied threats that would cause fear in a reasonable person" (McFarlane, et al., 1999). This fear can include fear of being harmed, fear of loved ones being harmed, and the fear of destruction of your property. Most often, victims are stalked by current or former romantic partners (Baum, et al., 2009; Breiding et al., 2014).

Stalking is more prevalent after the survivor has left the relationship as compared to those still in the relationship. However, that does not mean that stalking does not happen while the relationship is ongoing (Tjaden & Thoennes, 1998). The reason why stalking is more prevalent after the survivor leaves the relationship is because the abuser feels a loss of control over the survivor and therefore uses stalking as a means to regain power and control.

McFarlane and others (1999) explain that stalking is an extremely controlling and abusive behavior. Of women who reported being stalked, 81% reported being physically assaulted by the same partner who stalked them (Tjaden & Thoennes, 1998). Stalking can be deadly. Seventy-six percent of females who were murdered by their intimate partner had been stalked by that partner as well. Sixty-seven percent of the women who were murdered by their intimate partners had also experienced physical abuse by those same partners. Of the women who were physically abused and murdered, 89% of them had also been stalked (McFarlane, et al., 1999).

I highly recommend reading Spence-Diehl's book (1999), *Stalking: A handbook for victims*. Much of what I learned about stalking and how to protect myself when being stalked came from their handbook.

What are some behaviors that stalkers engage in?

- Stalkers will call, text, send emails, love letters, cards, and gifts wherever they believe you are staying.

- They will drive by your house, work, or other places you visit.

- Stalkers will show up at your house, work, and other places they believe that you will be.

- Stalkers will send friends or family members to the place you are staying, your school, or your work.

- Sometimes they will sit outside of your house, school, or work and wait for you.

- Stalkers will follow you.

- They will have their family and friends send unwanted and unsolicited text messages, emails, and letters to you.

- Stalkers will use the internet, private detectives, and public records to find you.

- Stalkers may coerce your friends and family into telling them where you are or giving them your phone number.

- Stalkers may use GPS and phone records to track you.

- If you still live with the stalker, they may use hidden cameras, voice recording, and telephone records, to keep track of you.

- They will also use your social networking sites to stalk you.
- Stalkers may damage your property like slashing your tires or throwing a brick through your window.

- Stalkers may break into your house and wait for you to come home.

- They might threaten to hurt you or your loved ones, including pets.

- Lastly, stalking, like abuse, becomes more serious over time.

What stalking looked like to me: *I immediately left Abuser 3 after he became physically violent with me the second time. I went to my parents' house. After about a week of talking with him on the phone to placate him while seeking information on abuse, I decided to go "no contact" with him because of the danger that was present for me. I explicitly told him on the phone that I no longer wanted to talk to him, I didn't want to receive phone calls, text messages, emails, letters, or presents from him any longer. I shut down all communication with him. I sent back my phone which he was paying for with a letter stating that I no longer wanted to receive any communications from him. This was both so that he couldn't call me or text me and also, he couldn't use the GPS on my phone to find me. I also explicitly stated that I did not want to see him or his family any longer. I did not want him or his family coming over to my parents' house, I did not want him or his family/friends showing up at my work or at places that I visit.*

Nevertheless, it continued. He flat ignored my requests and demands. Instead, he became desperate and angry bombarding me with everything that he could. He used multiple tactics daily to harass and stalk me. He called me multiple times a day. He texted me multiple times a day. He left multiple messages daily. He had his family call me and message me daily. He sent letters daily. He sent cards daily. He sent presents daily. He showed up at my parents' house unannounced. He had his family show up at my parents' house unannounced. He had his family send letters, cards, and gifts as well. He started to show up at my school and my work.

Abuser 3 hid his stalking under the pretext of "love." He never verbally threatened me. He used ingratiating behavior when he stalked me. Everyone around me believed that he was in love and heartbroken and that was why he was acting that way. To the untrained eye, he was showing me love. To those who are familiar with abusive relationships, he was in the Honeymoon phase and he was stalking and harassing me.

Do not let the abuser fool you into thinking this is about love. The abuser is doing this for control. It is to make you "remember the good times," make you feel as though you are wanted and loved and to make you believe that the abuser will never hurt you again.

Its purpose is to also scare you and keep you guessing. Is he going to be at my house when I get home? Is he going to follow me into the grocery store and make a scene? Is he going to break into my house at night while I'm sleeping and kill me? The abuser wants to overwhelm you so much that you feel the only way to make it stop is if you go back to him. This is about control. The abuser uses all the tactics in order to gain control over you again. The abuser becomes terrified when he can no longer control you. When Abuser 3 was stalking me he told me:

"I know that I am pushing you, and I am sorry. My quickness to rush to persuade you was because I feel like if you get away from me, you will forget how happy we truly are together without alcohol in our lives, and that you will be gone forever. This scares me to death."

What he is really scared of is losing his control over me. Again, do not be fooled, this is not love. One who loves you will give you space when you ask for it. One who loves you will trust that you know what is best for you. Someone who loves you respects your "no." One who loves you will back off when you tell them that they are scaring you. One who loves you will put themselves in your shoes and even if they can't understand your perspective, they will respect it.

While I was being stalked, I felt extreme fear. I feared for my life because I knew the violence Abuser 3 was capable of. I believed that it was entirely possible that he might kill me. I felt extremely jumpy, my heart stopping every time I heard a loud noise. I wasn't able to sleep. Fear short circuited my brain so that I couldn't plan to save my life if I wanted to. I was terrified to go to school or work because he might show up. I hid my car in the garage so that he would think that I wasn't home. I even left on multiple occasions to go to other places that he did not know about in order to feel safe. I eventually moved to a place that he was unaware of in order to feel safer. Even still, I worried that he would find me. I often worried that he would be waiting in the parking lot by my car after I got off work. I often worried that I would find my tires slashed or my car keyed. I often worried that he would plant some sort of improvised explosive device in my car because he knew how to make such things.

I learned that the majority of what I was feeling was a post-traumatic stress response (PTSR). This type of response is very normal after experiencing abuse in relationships and very normal when experiencing stalking. In fact, Baum and others (2009) indicate, "46% of stalking victims fear not knowing what will happen next." Similarly, 1 in 8 individuals who are stalked skip work due to the stalking and 1 in 7 individuals who are stalked move because of it (Baum, 2009).

What should you do if you are being stalked?

First, it is important for you to decide if you want to continue to have a relationship with this person, either now or in the future. If you are ready to end it and to move on, the best course of action is to go "no contact." This basically means that you will no longer have any contact with the abuser and that you expect the abuser to no longer have any contact with you. If there are biological children involved, this may not be as easily done. In this case I would recommend seeing a lawyer to understand your options to be able to protect yourself and your family from the abuser.

If you have decided that you are ready to end the relationship and move on, the most important thing to do is to make sure you tell the abuser clearly and seriously that you do not wish to pursue a relationship with him and that you no longer want any contact from him. The best way of doing this, in my opinion, is through email. This is because it is important to have proof of what day and time you told him for legal reasons. Having proof of going "no contact" will help you make a better case of stalking with the police if that is what you choose to do.

I DO NOT recommend telling the abuser in person that you no longer want to have a relationship with him. When the abuser realizes that he is losing control over you, there is a good chance that he will become violent. Therefore, if you tell him in person, you may be putting yourself in danger. I also do not recommend telling the abuser over the phone. He will try everything to dissuade you and abusers are very persuasive. He may threaten to kill himself, or destroy your property, or harm a shared pet in order to get you back.

Also, there will be no record that you went "no contact" with him. It will be your word against his. Texting him that you wish to end the relationship may work but you would need to take a picture of and print the texts. Or, you would need to call your service provider and have them send copies of the texts. Either way, it is more inconvenient than an email. Furthermore, it is easier to ignore incoming emails than incoming texts.

You need to understand that once you go no contact, the abuser will stalk you more intensely than ever. This is because the threat of losing control over you becomes very real to him. The most dangerous time in the relationship with the abuser is after you have left him and you have made it clear to him you are not coming back.

Next, it is important to start recording all of the abuser's stalking behaviors on an incident log. This will give you the evidence you need to make a case with the police that this person is stalking you. An example stalking incident log is provided in *Appendix A* and is called *Stalking Behaviors Record*. Record the number of times he calls, texts, and leaves voice messages. Save all voice messages and texts. Record in the incident log all the times he emails, sends letters, and sends cards. Save all the emails, letters, and cards as evidence. Record the times that he sends gifts. Record any times in which the abuser follows you. Record the times that he shows up at your work, at your home, at your school, and at other places you frequent. Also, document any property which has been vandalized or destroyed by the abuser. You can do this by taking photos and keeping them in a folder with the stalking incident log. Lastly, call the police for any crimes or suspicious behavior that the abuser engages in. For example, call the police if the abuser breaks into your home or is looking through your windows at night. Don't forget to record the incidents in the *Stalking Behaviors Record*.

Because stalking can turn deadly, it is very important for you to do things that enhance your safety and protect yourself. Your goal is to make it as hard as possible for the abuser to stalk you (meaning find you and communicate with you).

- Get a private mail box which is similar to a P.O. Box. Do not use a U.S. P.O. Box because the information is easily accessible on the internet. A private mail box can be rented at mom and pop mail stores like Going Postal or Pack N Mail. You can also find them at a UPS store or FedEx.

- If possible, move to a location that the abuser is unaware of. This means you should not live with friends or relatives that the abuser knows.

- Change your address on your driver's license. If you are able to put the P.O. Box as your driver's license address, do this. However, many states will not allow a P.O. Box address. In this case, ask a relative or a good friend if you can use their address as a permanent address. This should be an address that you are not actually living at.

- If you do use someone else's address, you need to make sure that they are aware of the dangers. The address will be able to be found publicly on the internet and the abuser may show up at that address looking for you. In this case, you should not give your new address to your friends or relatives. The abuser may try to coerce the information from them.

- After getting your driver's license updated with the new address, you may need to call your bank to update your billing address.

If you have a shared account with the abuser, remove your money and get a new bank account immediately.

- You will want to remove your name from the account

that is shared with the abuser. If you leave the account as is, the abuser has the opportunity to use the account in a way which can negatively affect your credit. I recommend talking to your bank at a time that the abuser will not know about.

- Tell your bank that you left the abusive relationship and that the abuser is now stalking you and you are trying to make a clean break from the abuser. The bank will often tell you what your options are and help you close the account.

- I recommend opening a new account in an entirely different bank. If this is not an option, open a new account with the same bank but make sure that your actual address is not used and make sure that they will ensure the privacy of your information.

- You will need to call all of the companies that you pay bills to and change your address with them as well.

The second most important issue to take care of is your cell phone. I would recommend getting rid of it completely. There are too many issues with a cell phone.

- If the abuser pays for the cell phone he can track your calls and text messages which will give him information about who you are talking to and what you are doing.

- If you had the cell phone while living with the abuser it is very possible that the abuser has downloaded an app or software to your phone which allows him to track you. Some spyware is designed such that the abuser downloads it to his computer, it sends him a code, and then the abuser types the code into your phone. Then the spyware is downloaded onto your phone. It can take less than 5 minutes. What the abuser has access to after that is astounding. The abuser has the ability to listen in to your phone calls, control your phone remotely, access your emails, access your call history, track you via GPS, and can set the phone to only accept calls from a list (Perry, 2012).

- If at all possible, get rid of the phone!

- You can take the battery out and run it over with your car.

- You can take it to the store where it was purchased, have them erase all of the data and give it to them.

- You can take the battery out of the phone and throw it away.

- If you are able to get rid of the phone, I strongly suggest copying all of your contacts, calendar, and other important information down first on a sheet of paper.

- Do not allow the cell phone company to electronically place all of your information from your old phone onto your new phone. It may transfer the spyware if there is any.

- Also, do NOT use the same provider as the abuser. It will be much easier for the abuser to walk into the cell phone store where personnel have seen both of you together and provide some sort of lie to them to get your new information. I would suggest getting a phone with a completely different company.

- One option is to go with a disposable prepaid phone. Prepaid phones can be found at Walmart, BestBuy, and other retailers. They are often a cheap alternative as well! Make sure that when you do get a new phone, you have a different number and keep it unlisted.

In order to keep your new address private, it is important to register to vote using either the P.O. Box address or your friends/family permanent address (where you do not live).

- At your new place, it is important to put the rental agreements in another person's name. This will make it harder for the abuser to find out where you live.

- Similarly, if at all possible, put the utilities in another person's name as well.

What should you do if the abuser confronts you at work?

If the abuser shows up at work or at other places you visit, remain calm and try to ignore him. If he confronts you remain calm and attempt to diffuse the situation. You know the abuser. You know what to say to keep him calm. If you must lie to him to keep him calm, lie.

- Inform your boss and coworkers that you are being stalked.

- Give them a picture of the abuser and a description.

- Tell them what kind of car he drives.

- Make sure the receptionist and security know.

- If at all possible, have security prevent the abuser from entering the building or remove the abuser from the building. If the abuser knows where your office is, ask your boss to arrange for you to move offices.

- Have the receptionist answer all of your calls in order to avoid contact with the abuser.

- If possible, work varying shifts to make it harder for the abuser to find and contact you.

- Try to avoid working alone.

- Furthermore, remove your name from any parking spots, business cards, or office doors to make it harder for the abuser to locate you or your vehicle.

- Make sure that all co-workers know they are not allowed to disclose personal information about you to anyone.

- Inform co-workers not to engage with the abuser in any way.

- Try to park in a well-lit and populated area. If at all possible, park in a secured parking lot.

- Always have someone walk with you to and from your car.

- Look for GPS tracking systems on your car. GPS tracking systems are small, black objects the size of a deck of cards which are easily placed onto the bottom of your car or in the wheel well or the bumper of your car via a magnet. Sometimes, the GPS device can be as small as a box of matches (Perry, 2012).

- As soon as you enter your car, lock the doors immediately.

- Take different routes to work and back home so that it is harder for the abuser to find you and track you.

- Pay attention to cars that may be following you wherever you go. If you are being followed, try to stay calm and drive normally. Drive directly to the nearest police station and honk the horn until someone comes out.

- If you park inside your garage at your house, remember to lock the car doors, shut the garage door, and lock the garage door.

- Make sure you look inside your car, under your car, and around your car before getting in. If the abuser is in the car, DO NOT get in. If you get into the car and the abuser is inside the car with you, attempt to throw your car keys as far as you can and run in the opposite direction of the keys. If you can throw the keys in bushes or tall grass, someplace that it is harder to find them, that is best. Call the police as soon as possible.

What should you do if the stalker shows up at your house?
If you come home to find that your front door is slightly ajar, your window is broken, or that your garage is open, do NOT enter the building.

- Immediately call the police or drive directly to the police station. Let them handle it.

- Similarly, if you come home at night and you feel that something is off (maybe your porch light is off or your back gate is open or drapes are closed when you've left them open), call the police or get a neighbor to go into your house with you.

- If you drive up to your house and find that the abuser is sitting on your front porch or waiting for you, do not stop. Drive directly to the police station.

- If you are home and the abuser comes over, do not answer the door. Do not acknowledge him. If he continues to bang on the door, or becomes violent, call the police immediately. Make sure you identify all persons before opening the door.

There are ways to enhance your house to protect you while you are both there and away.

- Install a wide-angle peep hole in all of the outside facing doors. This will allow you to see and identify exactly who is at the door.

- Have all repairmen and salesmen show identification before letting them inside your residence. Call the company to verify that they do in fact work for them.

- If you live in a house, make sure to lock the fuse box. This way, the abuser is not able to easily turn off your electricity. Do not rely on the key lock on the fuse box; it can be easily pried open.

- Keep battery powered lights/flashlights in each room.

- If the abuser has had previous access to the house, change all of the locks. He may have made spare keys. DO NOT keep spare keys in hiding places outside your apartment or home.

- Do not leave keys hanging on a hook near a door that has a side window. A stalker can easily break the window and reach in to get the keys.

- Get a safety deposit box and keep extra keys in there. Or you can give a spare key to a close family member or friend that you trust.

- Keep all doors and windows locked.

- Replace wooden doors with metal or steel doors. This will make it harder for the abuser to break into your home.

- Secure doors by adding deadbolt locks. Install deadbolts with screws that are two inches or longer.

- Do not rely on hotel style door locks. They are easily compromised.

- Get an alarm system for your house or apartment.

- Remove bushes from around the home to eliminate places that the abuser may hide. This will make it more difficult for them to surprise you. Trim any trees that may provide hiding places.

- Get motion sensor lights for outside your home. Have porch lights on the front and back porch. Try to find lights that are hard to remove.

- Place deadbolt locks on the bedroom doors inside your home.

- Install locks on the gates outside.

- Place blinds and curtains around all the windows to make it harder for the abuser to see inside.

- Install smoke detectors and carbon monoxide detectors inside your house or apartment.

- Keep fire extinguishers on each floor of your residence.

- Make sure that you keep your cell phone with you at all times. Abusers may cut the landlines and the electricity to your residence.

- If possible, get a dog. They are a great and inexpensive warning system. Some dogs can be great protectors as well.

- Tell neighbors or doorman (that you trust) that you are being stalked. Provide them with the abuser's information, picture, and cars he drives so that they can warn you when they see him or any suspicious activity.

- If you have children, make sure you walk them to and from the bus stops or school.

What should you do if you receive packages?

- Only open packages if you personally ordered the item.

- Do not accept or sign for any packages you are not expecting.

- If packages are sent to your home or work, DO NOT open them. Simply return the packages back to the sender. They are likely from the stalker.

- If the packages have no sender name or address and you are not expecting a package, call the police and report the suspicious package. Do NOT open or handle the package.

- Make sure to record that you received a package in the *Stalking Behaviors Record.*

What should you do to protect yourself online?

- Change all of your passwords to everything. It is very possible that the abuser has your passwords which will give him access to your banking, your emails, and your personal social accounts.

- If at all possible, get rid of all your social media accounts. I know that this is extremely difficult. So, if you do not want to do that, make sure that you block the abuser on all your social media.

Abusers use social media to find you!

- Review the privacy settings on all your social media accounts.

- Make sure that friends of friends cannot see what you post.

- Set your accounts to private.

- Stop posting pictures of where you are!

- Do NOT use the "check in" tool on Facebook.

- Absolutely DO NOT use the geotagging!

- Do not post about where you are going and where you have been.

- Do not post pictures which give information as to where you live, what you are driving, who you are seeing, etc.

- Do not post about new relationships as this can infuriate the abuser.

- Think very carefully before changing your status from married to single or from in a relationship to single or from single to in a new relationship. Any status change like this may trigger violence and rage in the abuser.

Many times, abusers will go to your friends and "friend" them in order to get your information. Once the abuser "friends" your friend, anything you post that your friend comments on, reposts, or is tagged in, the abuser will be able to see. This means that if you post a picture of you standing outside your new residence, the abuser now knows exactly what your place looks like! Likewise, if you post a picture of you in front of your car, the abuser now knows what car you drive.

Many cell phones now have automatic geotagging on them. This means that any photo that you take is tagged with the exact location that the photo was taken. Make sure that geotagging is not being used on your phone and that when friends and family take pictures with you, the location is not being geotagged.

To protect yourself from the abuser, make sure you block him, all his family, and his friends. If you do not block his family and friends, abusers will manipulate these people into going onto your social media sites and giving them your information. Sometimes they may even give the abuser access to their social media account so that the abuser can easily access your information. It is important to know that when you block someone on Facebook, they will not be informed that you have blocked them. With that being said, they will eventually find out (because they will no longer be able to access your information). To further protect yourself, do not accept friend requests from people you do not know. It is very possible that the abuser will create a fake account with an entirely different name and photo in order to get you to friend them.

Another way to protect yourself while online is to create your own "fake" account. In other words, create a social media account that uses an entirely different name, a random photo from the internet, a different birthday, and even use the opposite gender. Make sure that the fake account is believable. Use this fake account as your regular account. Inform and friend only trusted family and friends.

Lastly, if you have children that use the internet, make sure you educate them on how to stay safe online and keep up with their online activities (Perry, 2012).

Other ways to protect yourself from the abuser:

- Change your daily routine.

- Do not go to the same places you always go and do not go to those places at the same times.

- For banking, choose a branch location that is different from your usual location.

- If you tend to grocery shop on a Sunday in the morning, choose a different grocery store, shop on a Saturday in the evening.

- Find a new exercise center.

- Change the routes that you drive to and from work.

- Find a new church.

- If attending college or technical school, inform your school about the stalking and get educated on what your options are with them. Many schools offer assistance and protection to students from stalking, especially if the stalker also attends the same school.

- Try not to reveal too much about your upcoming plans, unless you really trust the person.

- Avoid going out alone at night.

- Avoid going into places where you are alone and could be cornered, like alleyways.

- If you have a restraining order, make sure to carry it with you at all times.

- Make sure that when you order items online, you do not put your name on the package. This will prevent the abuser from finding out where you live by checking the names of packages on the doorstep.

- Remember to shred any mail that you are discarding. Abusers are not above digging through your trash.

- Keep all your very important personal documentation (birth certificate, social security card, deeds to property or cars, etc.) in a safety deposit box at a bank.

- Keep one escape bag in the trunk of your car and one at a friend's house. An escape bag contains essential items for a one or two-night stay in an emergency. The typical escape bag may contain underwear, toothbrush, toothpaste, deodorant, socks, shoes, night clothes, day clothes, and money. This is important to have in place if the abuser becomes violent and you need to leave suddenly.

CHAPTER 9
HOW TO RECOGNIZE ABUSERS

When I left Abuser 3, I thought back on my other relationships to realize that they had also been abusive. I wondered: why do I keep choosing men like this? Part of the reason was that I felt like I couldn't recognize abuse for what it was. Even when Abuser 3 was shoving me into a door or holding me down, I wasn't completely sure it was abuse. (I have to add here that this is because abusers are very good at blaming you for their abuse and minimizing the abuse so that you doubt your own reality and your own intuition.) Like Abuser 3 always said, he never beat me. He never punched me or choked me or kicked me. Hell, he never even slapped me. So, I questioned whether being shoved or held down in bed was violent enough to count as abuse. I realized that I needed to get educated on what abuse is and what it is not. Since you are reading this book, you too wanted to become educated on the subject and I applaud you. Becoming knowledgeable is the first step to getting yourself out of this cycle.

In my quest to learn, I visited a women's domestic violence shelter and subsequently read many books on abuse. I learned that any form of physical touching that is unwanted is abuse. This can also be generalized to unwanted sexual touching. Therefore, shoving, and other seemingly "less violent" physical acts are in fact physical violence and abuse. I learned that intimidation is also physical violence. Some examples of intimidation include: towering over you, charging at you, raising a fist as though he is going to hit you, threatening to kill you, and standing in the doorway to block your exit. These intimidation tactics along with physical violence are used to scare you into submission.

After learning that what I had experienced was in fact domestic violence, I felt that something was wrong with me because I didn't recognize it as abuse beforehand. If I couldn't even see it when Abuser 3 was shoving me into a door, how could I see it before it happens next time? I felt as though I couldn't trust my own ability to identify future abusers. Furthermore, this wasn't the first time I had been in an abusive relationship. This was a pattern for me. It made me feel as though I was an easy target, as though abusers were able to identify me as an easy victim. I felt like I had a stamp on my forehead that read "VICTIM." This terrified me. Abusers could be all around me and somehow, I am sending them some kind of invisible signal that I would be a great victim for them to abuse. I believed that I would be victimized again by another abuser because I was unable to recognize abusers for what they were. To me they were wolves in sheep clothing and all I could see was sheep.

So how do we remove this "Victim" stamp? How do we recognize abusers so that we can avoid them and how do we stop broadcasting to abusers that we would make a great victim? First, I think that we need to learn the abuser's tactics and that these tactics are a pattern of behavior. Second, we need to learn the abuser's overall theme. All abusers have similarities to each other and these similarities will help you recognize an abuser much more quickly (hopefully before becoming too romantically involved with them). Third, it is also very important to learn why abusers are abusive so that way we can understand how they think and operate. Lastly, it is important that we take steps to remove the "Victim" stamp by making ourselves less attractive to abusers. To do this, we must learn to set boundaries. We have to find out who we are and what we want, and we have to undo the "training" that the abusers have instilled in us.

Tactics as a Pattern of Behavior

Before diving into this section and the sections to follow, I want to really encourage you to read Lundy Bancroft's book *Why Does He Do That?: Inside the Minds of Angry and Controlling Men*. He has brilliantly explained the abusers' overall theme, the abusers' way of thinking, and why abusers are abusive. I have gained a wealth of knowledge from reading it. Although I will briefly summarize some of his content with my own explanations, interpretations, and experiences, I still highly recommend reading his book. You will not be disappointed.

In order to recognize abusive men for what they are, it is imperative that you first learn the abuser's tactics (which you have already read in the beginning of this book). The abuser's tactics are the abuser's most visible attributes. Although the tactics range from very subtle to overt, most of them can be recognized once you have learned them. Unfortunately, once learned, you start to see the tactics used everywhere: by your friends, your family, your intimate partner, the shows and movies you watch, etc. This is similar to the new car effect. When you buy a car, you start to see your car everywhere, whereas before, you never really paid attention. Now that you have learned what to look for, you will start to notice when others use the tactics.

When this happened to me, I became very fearful. I felt like I didn't know who to trust because I didn't know who was abusive and who was not abusive. The best advice that was given to me was: in order to recognize and differentiate abusers from everyday folks, you want to look for a pattern of abusive behavior. Just because a person uses one of the subtle tactics once, does not make them abusive. (This does not apply to physical violence or intimidation. When these are used, even only once, it is absolutely abuse).

In fact, we are all guilty of criticizing someone or telling a bad joke or calling someone a name when we are angry. But the key difference is: abusers use tactics to gain control over you (to get you to do what they want), abusers use multiple tactics often (using the tactics is a pattern of behavior for them), abusers do not take responsibility for their actions (apologies are not counted as taking responsibility because abusers will often apologize and then continue the behavior), abusers will not make amends for their bad behaviors, abusers feel justified in their behaviors (they will make excuses for their behavior and often blame you or others for it), and abusers will not stop their behaviors when they are asked or told to stop.

The three phases of the cycle of violence are also a pattern of behavior found in most abusive men. The new relationship, like all new relationships, starts with feelings of closeness, love, lust, passion, feeling head-over-heals, "on top of the world," and like you are "walking on cloud nine." In a non-abusive relationship, these feelings develop more slowly over a period of time as the couple grows closer, learns more about each other, learns to trust one another, and becomes more vulnerable around the other. In an abusive relationship, these feelings typically occur very quickly due to "love bombing" or the Honeymoon phase.

Eventually, in an abusive relationship, the good feelings turn sour as the abuser uses verbally abusive tactics to degrade you and leave you walking on eggshells. During this phase (the tension building phase) the abuser makes it known that he is displeased with you. You feel as though you can do nothing right even though you are bending over backwards to please him. Then, the tension building phase gives way to the explosion phase. In an abusive relationship, this stage can be summarized as "he is looking for a fight." It doesn't matter to the abuser what you do, he will find something to become angry with you about and he will use that as justification to become threatening and or violent. After the violence, the abuser then goes back into the honeymoon phase, partly because he wants to keep you from leaving, partly because he wants to confuse you as to whether he really is mean and abusive, and partly to make you believe that he won't become abusive again (that it was a onetime fluke, an accident).

At a lower or less intense level, a similar pattern of behavior is played out by the abuser: intermittent normal, loving, or attentive behavior sprinkled with intermittent verbal or emotional abusive tactics.

First, it is the seemingly random pattern of behavior that keeps a survivor guessing what the problem actually is. The abuser switches from being loving and attentive to picking a fight over the smallest indiscretion. This keeps the survivor on her toes, trying to be perfect in order to avoid "causing" a fight.

Second, it is the intermittent intervals of normal behavior or attentive behavior that keep the survivor thinking that the relationship is normal. This normal or even loving behavior keeps the survivor in the relationship. She thinks, "See, he is not that bad. He does love me. I must be doing something wrong to piss him off so much."

Third, the contrast of the angry argumentative behavior with the normal behavior is exponential. In this type of relationship, the highs seem really high and the lows are really low. When the abuser is loving, the survivor feels on top of the world, as though no one has loved her this much in her entire life. But, when the abuser is being abusive, the survivor feels worse than she has ever felt in her entire life.

Furthermore, the contrast between the abusive behavior and

the normal behavior is so great, that normal behavior can be mistaken for loving behavior. The intermittent normal/attentive behavior and abusive behavior make for a roller coaster ride of a relationship. The abusive relationship is an extremely intense one where the survivor never knows when to expect normal, loving, or abusive behavior.

With non-abusive relationships there are no phases. There isn't much up and down. Sure, you will argue, the relationship will not always be sunshine and roses, but there are no extremes. A normal relationship feels eerily calm compared to the abusive relationship. There is no love bombing, tension building or explosions. There is no need for power or to be right. There is no need to shut you up. The non-abuser may not like what you say but can respect what you say. Arguments may end in an agreement to disagree or in a compromise. And most importantly, non-abusers can respect your decision to say no.

The Abusive Theme

Although abusers can differ from each other greatly in the tactics they use, what they control, whether they are physically violent or threatening, or how jealous they are, abusers also have many similarities. The similarities between them is what drives the abusive theme. All abusers need control over others, create many rules, exert punishment, are disrespectful, entitled, selfish, and vengeful, feel the need to compete with their partners, use manipulation, feel justified about their abuse, and exhibit charming behavior around outsiders.

Abusers feel entitled to have control over you. Control comes from a mix of selfishness and entitlement. The abuser is selfish because he believes that his wants and needs are more important than yours and that your wants and needs are of no concern to him. They are simply not his problem, they are *your* problem. The abuser believes that you are supposed to meet all of his needs but your needs are not his responsibility.

With regards to control, abusers create rules (either spoken or unspoken) that must be followed. The abuser believes that he is superior to you. He believes that his ideas, beliefs, and reasons are "right" or "correct" and that your ideas are "wrong" or "incorrect." He also believes that he should receive special benefits that you do not receive (i.e. making the decisions and not having much or any responsibility). In fact, he most likely believes that you owe him something. The abuser believes that he knows what is best for you and because of this, he is helping you by creating rules to follow. He also believes that you are so inept, that you need to defer to him for all things because in his mind, you will make poor decisions if he is not there to make those decisions for you. The abuser believes he deserves king status, which is the definition of entitlement. He should be able to make all of the rules, order others around and tell others how to do things but he should not have to actually do any of the labor himself.

With that being said, abusers do not always act like a king. There may be times when he will make dinner or split the chores with you. But he's not doing this out of love for you or a sense of sharing responsibility or a willingness to lessen your burden; he does it because it suits him at the moment. It's part of the 'benevolent dictator' mentality. The belief that he is entitled to king status is always there. He believes he knows best even if he listens to your opposing points of view. He has the last word. Whatever his decision is, you have to go with. He makes the rules. His needs come first.

The rules the abuser creates typically fall in the area of control that the abuser has over the survivor. If the rules are not followed, the abuser will punish the survivor. This is not dependent upon whether it is spoken. Even if you do not know that the rule exists, he expects you to read his mind and obey. He believes that it is your duty to obey the rules. He feels entitled to your subservience. If you do not follow his rules, the abuser will likely manipulate you to do what he wants or he will punish you for not doing what he wants. Sometimes abusers will come up with "creative" ways to punish you. Because abusers are entitled and selfish, they believe that they should get what they want when they want it and if you don't give it to them, this gives them permission to punish you by "teaching you a lesson."

Some abusers compete with their partners. The abuser's superiority is what truly drives their need for competition with you. It is all about winning with abusers. Winning arguments, winning power struggles, winning at parenting, winning at having the most friends, in general "winning at life." The abuser's stance is: "I am better than you and I know better than you."

Abusers believe they are right and you are wrong, that they

should win and you should lose, that they are smart and you are dumb, that they do much more work than you do, that they know what's best and you don't, and that whatever problems you've had, they've had it worse. Abusers believe this regardless of how untrue it is. When the abuser does get a glimpse that his beliefs are not true, that you are winning and that he is losing, that you are smarter or do something better, the abuser will punish, degrade, and sabotage you in order to "win" again.

When you compete with the abuser and "win" by being smarter, proving the abuser wrong, winning an argument, doing more work and showing the abuser that you handle it better, the abuser uses his trump card - abuse. If you look closely at your relationship, you might even find that the worse arguments and physical assaults have happened after you have succeeded at something, began to win an argument, proved the abuser wrong or refused to let the abuser tell you what to do. Abusers want to remain superior to you and anything that suggests that they are not superior is met with hostility, arguments, and physical violence.

Because of their entitlement and selfishness, abusers feel justified when they control, punish, and abuse you. Not only do abusers have justifications for controlling, punishing and abusing you, but these reasons are often used to persuade you that their actions are for your own benefit and the reasons sometimes seem fairly logical. For example, the abuser may want to control you by knowing where you are at all times. They may request or demand that you put a GPS tracking app on your phone. Their justifications, as they would explain to you, are that they want to protect you and keep you safe. Although wanting to protect you seems logical, tracking your every move is not, it's controlling.

Abusers also create justifications for abusing you. Because they are entitled and feel deserving of king treatment, if you do not give this to them, they feel justified in punishing and abusing you. Because they believe they are superior to you and know better than you, you should defer to them on all matters. If you do not follow their rules, advice, or decisions, they feel justified in punishing and abusing you by "teaching you a lesson."

Because abusers feel justified in their abusive actions, they will not take responsibility for the abuse. The justifications give them permission to blame you for the abuse. For example, an abuser may exclaim, "If you had shut your mouth, I wouldn't have had to slap you!" The abuser actually believes that he was justified in slapping his partner because she wouldn't shut up when he told her to shut up. Because of the entitlement and superiority, the abuser actually believes that the abuse is caused by his partner and not himself. He believes that if she wants him to change, she will need to change herself.

I want to point out here that this line of reasoning is preposterous. You do not cause abusive behavior. If this were true, then you would be responsible for all of his behavior. Did you cause him to go to the bathroom? Did you cause him to eat? The abuser is solely responsible for his actions just like you are solely responsible for yours. And as you *chose* your actions, *he too chose his.*

Another theme found with abusers is charm. Charming behavior is used by the abuser to present a "good guy" appearance to the outside world. This is especially important for two reasons. First, when the survivor begins to speak out about the abuse to family and friends, many will have a hard time believing her because, "he is so nice; he doesn't seem like someone who would be abusive." Second, this charming behavior makes the survivor feel crazy in a sense because she is the only one who endures the abusive behavior. This contrast is meant to make the survivor question her own perspective of the relationship: is he really abusive? Why does he only act that way towards me? Do I do something to cause him to act that way? All of these questions keep the survivor from seeing and acknowledging that she is living in an abusive relationship.

It is important to remember that abusers are all different. Some will be more charming than others. Some may have built up a "good guy" persona by volunteering at a homeless shelter, donating money to charities, starting a non-profit to fight for the rights of a marginalized group, rescuing animals, coaching little league, or mowing the elderly neighbor's lawn. Others might be the life of the party. Some may build a "good dad" persona instead of a "nice guy" persona. Others may exhibit all of these behaviors. And some abusers may not be charming in any of these ways but in their own way.

Although the "nice guy" persona is not wrapped up in entitlement or selfishness, is it wrapped up in manipulation. Its sole purpose is to set the groundwork to get away with their abusive behavior. It allows the abuser to convince others that he is such a nice guy that it is inconceivable that he would do anything abusive. Once outsiders start realizing that he is abusive, at that point, they believe that the survivor, herself, must have done something to cause the abuse. So, in essence, the "nice guy" front is a manipulation tactic employed to persuade outsiders and the survivor herself to believe that the abuser would never be abusive and that his abusive behavior had to be caused by something horrific the survivor did in which she *deserved* the abuse. In this way, the abuser has persuaded outsiders and even the survivor to believe the way he does – that he is justified in his abuse of the survivor.

Lastly, another theme that I experienced when living with abusers is the parent/child theme. Essentially, living with an abuser is like living with a parent-child. The abuser acts like both your parent and your child packaged in one person. The abuser acts like your parent in that he: orders you around, creates rules for you to follow, tries to control your movements and your friends, gives you a bedtime and a curfew, talks to you like a child, says he knows what's best for you, tells you what you can and can't wear, punishes you when you do something wrong, and just generally treats you like a child.

But the abuser also acts like a child in that he: is selfish, expects you to serve him, expects you to cater to his needs, requires you to give up your needs for his, can't handle criticism, throws tantrums when he does not get his way, and resorts to name calling and one-upmanship in arguments. Living with an abuser is like living with a 5-year-old that wants all of the freedom of being an adult and none of the responsibility.

To summarize, in order to start seeing abuse for what it is and abusers for what they are, you have to be able to recognize the abusers' theme, or what they do – their pattern. Seeing abuse for what it is comes from learning the tactics they use against you and from understanding how those tactics are grouped together to create an overall theme of: disrespect, needing control, creating rules, punishment, manipulation, competition, justifications, entitlement, selfishness, and charming behavior. If you look back at the tactics, you will find each one of the aspects of the abuser's theme.

Although understanding the abuser's theme is very important in the task of avoiding future abusive partners, half the battle is still understanding *why* he is abusive. In order to know this, we have to understand how he thinks. Knowing how abusers' think will allow us to not fall victim to their traps of blame, justifications, and excuses for their behavior.

The Abuser's Way of Thinking: Why He Doesn't Abuse

Before getting into why he *is* abusive, we need to understand why he *isn't* abusive. These are the myths that society has taught us. In truth, I myself have believed many of these myths. In this section, I have quickly summarized some of the most important falsehoods that I have fallen for. A larger list of myths described in much greater detail can be found in Lundy Bancroft's great book *Why Does He Do That?: Inside the Minds of Angry and Controlling Men*.

Falsehood 1: Alcohol makes him abusive. *This was the myth that I believed in the strongest. As a survivor, the worst times for me were always when Abuser 3 was drunk. This was when he was the most unpredictable, the angriest, the most demanding, and the most violent. During these times, everything else paled in comparison. So naturally, the more severe the abusive behavior became, the less I recognized subtle control and abusive behavior as abusive. In fact, I really could no longer see the control he had over me nor did I recognize that he was verbally and emotionally abusive to me on a daily basis. I felt and knew that he was a very critical person, that he was petty and nit-picky and spiteful but I didn't realize that this was part of the abuse. I thought his behavior was normal. Therefore, the only times I thought he might be abusive were the times he physically assaulted me and these occurred when he was drunk. I believed this so much so, that the first time he assaulted me, I demanded that he give up alcohol completely if he wanted me back in his life. I made him choose between the alcohol and me. And for the couple of years that he refrained from drinking, he did not physically assault me. He did however, continue to be abusive in the many other subtle ways that were discussed previously in this book (unfortunately, I did not understand at the time that this was still abuse).*

As Lundy explains, "Alcohol cannot create an abuser, and sobriety cannot cure one" (pg. 47).

As much as I believed that alcohol was the source of the problem, Abuser 3 used it as the excuse for his abuse. He initially blamed the alcohol for his behavior saying things like, "Baby, I would never hurt you! The alcohol caused me to lose control. I would never act like that sober! If I had never drank, this wouldn't have happened. If you just come back to me, I will never drink again, I swear!" But believe me when I tell you that this is a ruse. Eventually, the abuser will tell you that he is a grown man and "should be able to have a beer on the weekends." He will tell you that he feels controlled by you not allowing him to drink. He will even threaten to break up with you if you don't agree to his drinking – that is if he even agrees to stop drinking in the first place.

As he is sober, it may seem like he has become less abusive. However, do not be fooled, abuse and control are still at work. He may use more subtle tactics when sober, but he uses tactics nonetheless. Let's also not forget that abuse always gets worse and more intense – not better. So, even if he never drinks again, he will still progress from using subtler tactics to more scary and threatening tactics.

Therefore, I ask you, what tactics does he use on you when he doesn't drink? If he uses several of the tactics when he is sober, then it is time to realize that he is abusive all the time.

Falsehood 2: His parents were abusive towards him.
Another falsehood that I fell for was that being raised in an abusive home can cause a person to be abusive. Abuser 1, Abuser 2, and Abuser 3 all explained to me that they came from homes where their father was physically assaultive of their mother, of them, or both. These conversations seemed to imply: "I don't know how to communicate effectively because my family growing up used dysfunctional communication or violence to communicate," "I learned that violence was the way to solve problems," "I learned that the only way to get my needs met was through manipulation and intimidation," and "No one listened to me growing up so now I force others to listen to me."

Specifically, Abuser 1 told me many times (after being verbally and emotionally abusive to me), "I never learned to communicate as a child, so I just don't know how." Abuser 2 told me that he was beaten as a child and he watched his father beat his mother. When Abuser 2 would throw things, punch walls, kick down doors, kick holes in walls, punch himself, he would explain to me that he was preventing himself from hurting me by doing these things. Abuser 2 would say that when he got angry, he would "black out" and "see red." He said that by punching walls and kicking down doors, he was protecting me. He was avoiding becoming his father by taking out his anger on inanimate objects instead of punching me – which is what he really wanted to do.

Now, I encourage you to think about this more critically.

Because you are reading this book, it is probable that you have been the victim in an abusive relationship. Wouldn't you say that going through that experience makes you feel more in tune with others who have been victims of abuse? Wouldn't you agree that you understand how it feels to be abused and that you would never want that to happen to someone else? Wouldn't you also agree that you would want to make sure that you never treated another person the way that you were treated because it was so awful? In that aspect, you have become more sensitive to what could be abusive behavior. Like me, you probably worry more about being equitable to others, treating them with fairness and splitting everything 50/50. You probably have become more egalitarian, believing others should have rights equal to yours. In essence, you treat others like you want to be treated.

Abusers on the other hand, do not identify with this. Instead of being careful to not treat others how they were treated, they use the childhood abuse as an *excuse* to not change their abusive behavior. When you point out their abusive behaviors and ask for real change, they say things like, "I never learned how to communicate as a child," "I never learned how to use words, only fists," or even, "I am not abusive, I never (did what my parent did)."

Falsehood 3: He doesn't know how to control his anger. After abusers become physically assaultive, you may hear them say something like, "I don't know what happened, I just totally lost control" or "I became so enraged I just blacked out" or "One minute we were arguing, the next minute I saw red." As Lundy points out in his book, abusers never lose control of themselves or their actions. In fact, it is quite the opposite. Often, when they are being abusive they are constantly thinking about whether their actions will get them into trouble, whether their actions will become known to the neighbors or others, and whether their actions are crossing some "abusive threshold" in their minds. Abusers are aware of their surroundings and the possible consequences of their actions at the time. They allow themselves to use those behaviors because they do not believe them to be abusive.

Importantly, abusers have a "threshold" of abusiveness in their minds. They have an idea of what constitutes abusive behavior and which behaviors make someone an abuser. It is those actions that they deem morally wrong and abusive, and it is those actions that they will not engage in (until they decide to, at which point, they increase their threshold). For example, Abuser 3 believed that a "real abuser" was a man who punched, kicked, choked (or worse) his girlfriend/wife. He considered this to be beating her. And, because he had never done those things to me, he did not believe himself to be abusive. His threshold was punching. Anything worse than punching, he considered to be abuse. Anything less severe than punching, he considered to be normal, non-abusive behavior.

All abusers have their own threshold. Some may punch their girlfriends or wives but "would never choke her." Others would choke their girlfriends or wives but "would never kick her." And so on and so forth. What should be known here is that as the intensity of their abuse grows, the threshold becomes higher and higher. The abuser has to readjust his idea of what constitutes abuse so that he can continue to deem himself "non-abusive" even though he is abusive.

An interesting point that Lundy makes about this is that, "An abuser almost never does anything that he himself considers morally unacceptable" (pg.34). Let that sink in for a moment. Not only does the abuser believe that he is not abusive, but he also believes that he is morally right in his horrible treatment of you. He believes he is justified in abusing you. He has come up with reasons why he needs to use abusive behavior on you and he feels self-righteous in doing so. The self-righteousness and justification continue to protect the abuser's fantasy that he is not an abuser because it allows him to believe that he *had* to use those behaviors because of something *you* did. In essence, he continues to abuse you because of his beliefs that you cause the abuse, you are responsible for it, and you therefore deserve it.

To reiterate, abusers do not lose control of themselves. They choose to be abusive. They allow themselves to use abuse to get what they want. At some point in the argument they decide they have had enough and they pull out their "trump card" (abuse). During the abuse, they keep in mind their idea of what an abuser is, their "threshold" and they try not to cross it. They are also aware of their surroundings. They consider the consequences and try to protect themselves from being found out or caught. If the police show up, they stop their abusive behavior and turn on the charm. When they think a child might walk in the room, they stop being abusive and act as though nothing is going on. Don't get me wrong, there are plenty of abusers who will abuse their wives or girlfriends in public or in front of children. The point is that the abuser knows what is going on around him. He does not lose control. He considers the consequences not only legally, but morally (his version) and avoids behaviors that he thinks will make him look bad or cause himself harm.

Falsehood 4: He bottles his emotions up until he explodes.
I also fell for this one too, wholeheartedly. With Abuser 2, a disagreement would turn into an argument which would progress into him basically exploding. He would clench his teeth, his face would turn extremely red, and he would shake with anger. This would turn into him lashing out by destroying things or by punching himself in the face and head. Abuser 3 on the other hand, would become very quiet for long periods of time. He would show me that he was angry with me by being passive-aggressive and by punishing me but he would not tell me what was wrong or why he was angry (tension building phase). This would then progress into an argument. He would either find something else that I did wrong to start the argument or I would point out that he had been treating me poorly which would start the argument. The argument would progress into him needing to be right and me needing to be wrong, where he would try to verbally force me to apologize and be subservient to him. This would then lead to physical assault when I did not cow down.

Experiencing these situations, it did intuitively feel like they withheld their emotions until it was bothering them so much that they exploded. And I even tried to remedy this in my relationship with Abuser 3. I believed that if he would just tell me the things that bothered him when they were small things, they wouldn't turn into big things.

If you are thinking about doing this, DO NOT DO THIS.

It opened me up to so much more control and abuse. This was his golden ticket to nit-picking and criticizing me to death in order to "confess" all the "small things" that I did that bothered him. He now had free reign to control me and I had to change these things or they would become "big problems." He loved this so much that he would often criticize things that I had no control over and things that made up the essence of who I am. He criticized my breathing. He expected me to change the way I yawned and how I sneezed because they bothered him. In doing this, I essentially gave him permission to control everything about me in order to avoid being physically assaulted.

Let's examine more closely the falsehood that abusers withhold their emotions until they explode. Abusers are very selfish and entitled. They know very well what they are feeling and they believe that you should too. They believe that their feelings, wants, and desires are more important than yours and that you should put your needs on the backburner in order to tend to their feelings. Anytime the abuser feels negative emotions, he expects your world to stop in order to fix his frustration, anger, disappointment, discomfort, or sadness.

In reality, the abuser expects you to cater to him and his feelings but he does not give you the same respect. Think about it, when does he put his needs on hold to help you deal with your needs? If you were both sick at the same time, who would be expected to run the house and take care of the others? If you are upset with him, do you have to consider everything that is happening in order to plan a "good time" to bring it up? Does he do the same for you? Does he expect you to change all the things that you do that make him upset? Does he change the things that he does that make you upset? How many times does he tell you that he is upset with you for some minor thing you did – either verbally, passive aggressively, or by punishing you? How often do you get to air your grievances with him?

The answers to these questions should lead you to the realization that he is not in touch with your feelings, perspective, needs and desires but, he *is* in touch with *his* feelings, perspective, needs and desires. Moreover, he believes that his feelings, needs and desires are more important than anyone else's. He also believes that you should be the one to fix his problems. And he believes that if you are the cause of the problem, then you should change. In essence, the abuser over-expresses his emotions verbally and by using tactics. He doesn't bottle up his emotions and then explode, he continues to express his emotions and his wants because he believes them to be more important than your emotions and wants.

Falsehood 5: The Post-Traumatic Stress causes him to be abusive. Although those who suffer from PTS often have symptoms of irritability, PTS along with other mental illnesses do not cause men to be abusive. The individual's belief system causes him to become abusive. Mental illness, including PTS, can influence the severity of their actions. In Lundy's book, he explains that abusers who use the most severe physical violence often have higher rates of mental illness. This may be because the symptoms of mental illness cause the abusers not to care as much about the consequences of their actions. What should be noted here is that mental illness is a separate issue from abuse although they can interact. There are many men who are *not* mentally ill who *are* abusive and there are many men who *are* mentally ill who are *not* abusive. The two can be mutually exclusive.

I encountered this falsehood with Abuser 3. He self-disclosed to me that he used to have PTS before we met (and seemingly, he did not experience the symptoms anymore). I had empathy for him and wanted to make sure that he felt safe and secure with me. Unfortunately, he used PTS as an excuse to control me in our relationship. Loud noises bothered him, so I had to learn to open doors where they could not be heard. I had to learn to close doors in such a manner that they could not be heard. I had to learn to put the clean dishes away "softly." I was not allowed to read certain books because of his PTS. He also used PTS as an excuse when he became physically violent with me. The first time he assaulted me, he told me that because he had PTS, when I threw my arms in the air in the symbol of giving up, he said that he interpreted that as a threat, which is why he attacked me. Lastly, even the police were on this bandwagon. When reporting his assault of me, the detective asked if he had PTS as though that alone excused his behavior.

And here's the kicker, abusers do use mental illness, including PTS, as an *excuse* for their behavior. They reinforce this myth that mental illness causes a person to be abusive in order to be able to *not* change their behavior. They use the cover of mental illness to avoid taking responsibility for their actions.

As Lundy explains, if mental illness really did cause abuse, then the medications available to treat mental illness would cure abuse, but they don't. Even when it seems as though the abuse becomes less severe with certain medications, the overall control, subtle abusive behaviors, abusive theme, and the thinking that cause abuse are all still there. Thus, even if the abuser stayed on the medication, over time, the abuse would become worse.

In this section I have summarized what I think are the most prominent myths about abuse that are still believed today. These are only 5 of the 17 myths that Lundy explains in his book. In some cases, I combined a few of the myths into one where it made sense. However, I really want to motivate you to read his book. It was life changing for me and I believe it can be for you as well.

The Abuser's Way of Thinking: Why He Abuses

So, if it isn't his alcohol use, being abused as a child, or mental illness, why does he abuse?

The simple answer is that he is abusive because he chooses to be abusive. The abusive behavior gets him what he wants, when he wants it, and he allows himself to use it for that purpose. The abuser is selfish, controlling, entitled, feels justified, vengeful, punishing, manipulative and charming. He feels entitled to what he wants when he wants it and if he doesn't get it, he feels entitled to use abusive behavior to get it. The abuser feels *justified* in using abuse to get what he wants. Because of his black and white thinking, his belief that he is right and you are wrong, his belief that he knows what is best for you, he believes he is right in punishing you when you don't do what he wants, and he believes he is correct in using violence to get you to do what he wants. Many times, the abuser believes that he is helping you (because he believes you are not as competent as he is, nor as self-sufficient) when he is abusive towards you. In essence, the abuser's entitlement, selfishness, and justifications are his ways of thinking and believing that drive his abusive behavior.

Still, I wondered, is it his personality? A person's beliefs, thoughts, feelings and behavior make up who they are as a person, so I wondered, could it be an abusive personality? I think the answer is yes. He could be narcissistic, Machiavellian, psychopathic, and or sadistic which are all personality types that have been shown to be related to abusive behaviors. These four dark personalities make up what is called "The Dark Tetrad" (Buckels, Jones, Paulhus, 2013). I believe abusers exhibit these dark personalities which also explains their abusive behavior.

The dark personalities are related to each other through their common core of darkness: being callous and unemotional, meaning that they are cold hearted or heartless towards others (Paulhus, 2014). People who are narcissistic, Machiavellian, psychopathic, or sadistic share many similarities with abusers. In fact, I believe that if we were to assess how narcissistic, psychopathic, sadistic, and Machiavellian abusers are, they would exhibit high rates of these personality traits. I think it is likely that abusers' personalities are made up partly by one or more of these dark personalities.

The most important understanding to come out of this line of work, is that the dark personalities occur on a continuum. This means that we can assess each person's level of narcissism, Machiavellianism, psychopathy, and sadism, and each one can range from: non-existent to extreme (Paulhus, 2014). At the extreme end of the spectrum are where Narcissistic personality disorder and Antisocial (psychopathic) personality disorder lie. These are clinical diagnoses. However, just because a person falls in this extreme range – with diagnosable levels of the dark personalities – does not mean that they have been clinically diagnosed. Some individuals who have clinical levels of these personality disorders remain undiagnosed and untreated, and therefore, still fall into the "normal" or "subclinical" groups. Therefore, do not be fooled by the term "normal," it does not mean less severe (Furnham, Richards, & Paulhus, 2013).

In fact, many everyday people who have "normal" ranges of the dark personalities often exhibit socially aversive behaviors that are controlling and abusive. I think once you understand the characteristics of each of the dark personalities, you will see how they are associated with or similar to both the abuser's way of thinking and the tactics that the abuser uses.

Narcissists are extremely selfish individuals who are completely self-absorbed. They constantly talk about themselves, brag about their exploits, make themselves the center of attention, and act and feel superior to those around them. Narcissists feel very entitled. Because they believe they are superior to others, they also believe that others should submit to their demands. They are very controlling of others. They are so self-righteous and arrogant they are unwilling to understand another person's differing opinion or view point. Narcissists tend to do what they want when they want regardless of how it makes others feel or if it infringes on another person's wishes. The narcissistic individual will disparage others in order to feel superior to them. Narcissists are very intolerant of criticism, often responding to ego threats with hostility by belittling, insulting, and blaming others (American Psychological Association, 2013).

Machiavellians can be thought of as master manipulators (Paulhus, 2014) who will strategically plan (Jones & Figueredo, 2012) your takedown if it benefits them. Machiavellians get what they want by any means necessary. They will lie to you, they will cheat you, they will charm you, coerce you, or threaten you into giving them what they want. No tactic is out of bounds for the

Machiavellian. At the same time, they are very cynical (Furnham, Richards, & Paulhus, 2013), believing that others are just like them: cheating, stealing, and manipulating to get what they want.

Psychopaths have been thought of as the most malevolent of the dark personalities (Furnham, Richards, & Paulhus, 2013). However, now that everyday sadism has been added to the dark personalities (Paulhus, 2014) this may change.

Psychopaths are charming, impulsive thrill seekers focused towards immediate gratification (Jones & Figueredo, 2013; Paulhus, 2014; Semenyna & Honey, 2015). They are known to remain calm, cool, and collected in times of stress or anxiety (Paulhus & Williams, 2002). Psychopaths are known for their instrumental aggression, hurting others for the sole purpose of coercing others into doing what they want. Psychopaths feel a lack of remorse after hurting others. Probably because of this, they are much more likely to have "run-ins with the law" than Machiavellians or narcissists (Furnham, Richards, & Paulhus, 2013).

Everyday sadists enjoy hurting others both verbally and physically (Paulhus, 2014). They find cruelty towards others exciting and pleasurable and will go out of their way to find instances in which they can exercise their ruthlessness (Buckels, Jones, & Paulhus, 2013). Specifically, everyday sadists hurt others to gain control over them, to exact punishment, to get revenge, and to degrade them (Mededovic & Petrovic, 2015).

Importantly, researchers have found a direct relationship between the dark personalities and psychological (verbal and emotional) abuse. Those who scored highly on Machiavellianism and psychopathy reported perpetrating more verbal and emotional abuse; and psychopathy alone also predicted physical and sexual abuse (Carton & Egan, 2017). Other researchers find that narcissism and psychopathy are associated with domestic violence (Ryan, Weikel, & Sprechini, 2008; Swogger, Walsh, & Kosson, 2007). Similarly, Kiire (2017) found that psychopathy was strongly positively correlated with physical abuse, intimidation, control, verbal abuse, sexual abuse, financial control, and stalking. Narcissism was associated with verbal abuse, sexual abuse, and financial control. Machiavellianism, on the other hand, was only correlated with sexual abuse.

Lastly, the dark personalities have been found to be related to stalking. All four predicted cyberstalking, or the tendency to stalk someone through the use of electronics such as: concealed video and audio recording devices, GPS tracking, spyware, and fake profiles on social media (Smoker & March, 2017). Comparably, psychopathy is linked to typical stalking. "People with psychopathic traits tended to show escalation in frequency, severity and/or diversity of their stalking, they were noticeably unrepentant regarding their actions, and they selected victims with financial or employment problems – factors often associated with the severity of future stalking" (Storey, Hart, Meloy, & Reavis, 2009, pg. 244). The authors of this scientific paper also indicate that psychopaths may stalk to gain dominance and control over the victim especially when the stalker believes that the victim has wronged him and for the sheer pleasure of scaring/hurting another person.

CHAPTER 10
IMMEDIATE EFFECTS OF ABUSE

Before and during the violence, the sympathetic nervous system activates the fight or flight response. This results in a bodily response which prepares you to fight or run. However, although the survivor may fight back or attempt to flee, there are many times when the survivor endures the violence and protects herself as best as possible. In this case, the most obvious immediate effects of violence can be bruising, bleeding, broken bones, loss of consciousness, redness, swelling, physical pain, and sometimes even death. However, less obvious are the immediate psychological effects of violence. The survivor may feel extreme fear and stress, powerlessness, a sense of loss of control, and feeling cornered or an inability to escape. When the violence ends, the survivor may feel an extreme sense of relief.

Coping Through Leaving
In order to deal with the immediate effects of the violence, the survivor may attempt to cope in different ways. Leaving the situation is one way that survivors may cope with impending physical violence or violence that just occurred. Leaving is prompted by fear. It is a means to immediately remove one's self from harm's way. Leaving is a positive coping mechanism which may help to deescalate the situation. Even if the survivor only leaves long enough for the abuser to calm down, this coping

strategy may be helpful in preventing violence.

However, some abusers may become enraged by the survivor leaving because it is interpreted as the survivor gaining control over the situation and the abuser losing control over the survivor. This may be detrimental for the survivor who may experience even more severe violence as she attempts to leave or once she returns. Therefore, it is the survivor who should base her decision for leaving or staying on her intuition of how the abuser will respond. In other words, if you believe that leaving an argument before it becomes violent will result in more severe violence, then it is probably better to deescalate the situation in another way. On the other hand, if leaving the situation before the argument becomes violent has worked in the past to prevent violence, then this approach is helpful. Leaving the relationship for good is the most helpful tool to prevent future violence, however, it is also the deadliest time for the survivor. Therefore, leaving for good should be well planned and well thought out before enacting. Planning to leave for good is discussed in the next chapter.

Coping Through Psychological Control

Another coping mechanism is psychological control which is "…the belief that one can determine one's own behavior, influence one's environment, and bring about desired outcomes" (Taylor, 2009). This is the idea that if one can control what is causing the abuse, then one can stop, prevent, or make the abuse less extreme.

First, it should be pointed out that you are not responsible or in control of another's actions. You cannot control the physical violence, no matter what you do. Only the abuser can control his actions and decide to not be physically violent. Therefore, no amount of cleaning, agreeing, apologizing, begging, perfection, or keeping the kids quiet will prevent the abuse.

However, even though this is true, many survivors still engage in behaviors which attempt to prevent or subdue the violence. I myself, did this. In attempting this, many survivors become extremely conscientious, hypervigilant, anxious, and worried about perfection in order to avoid abuse. In this respect, the survivor's belief that she has some control over the abuse may reduce the stress involved with abuse and it may also keep the survivor in the harmful relationship. Interestingly, believing one can control the abuse through actions may actually prevent the survivor from developing depression and this is protective.

Some survivors may try to give control to the abuser before he tries to take it. This may mean that the survivor tells the abuser where she went, what happened, who she saw, what she did, and who she talked to before the abuser asks her for this information. The survivor might voluntarily hand over her phone to the abuser to prove that she has nothing to hide. The survivor might start to explain any phone conversation immediately after having it before the abuser can ask, "Who was that?" and "What'd they want?" In some ways, this may make the survivor feel more in control because she is *deciding* to give up control on her own terms. These actions, in the short term, may quench the abuser's thirst for control. However, the abuser's thirst for control is insatiable and eventually, what the survivor gives up is never enough.

Coping Through Depression

When living in an abusive relationship, the survivor deals with an extreme sense of loss of control. While some survivors may cope by controlling what they can, others may use coping methods which may feel helpful in the immediate situation but are harmful long term. Some of these coping mechanisms are: bouts of uncontrollable crying, learned helplessness and depression, self-harm, eating disorders, and alcohol and drug use.

Coping with loss of control, one may experience uncontrollable bouts of crying. Although crying can be helpful to work through pain, anger, and sadness, it can also trigger panic attacks especially if the crying comes from feeling overwhelmed, feeling a lack of control, feeling sorry for oneself, and an inability to calm oneself. Uncontrollable crying can also indicate depression.

Depression is the feeling of overwhelming sadness, emptiness, numbness, and a feeling of absolute lack of control over the situation. It is as if nothing you do matters, there is nothing that can change the situation you are in, you feel completely stuck and helpless (this is called learned helplessness). When the individual feels as though nothing that they do will help or change the situation, they give up and they stop trying to change it. In this sense, a survivor may cope with the abuse by giving up and succumbing to it. The survivor may experience depression in regards to this learned helplessness. As they begin to feel stuck and that nothing works, they may become overwhelmed with a sense of sadness, grief, loss of oneself, and loss of control.

Although long term depression is not helpful (because the survivor quits trying to leave or protect herself and gives up control) it may serve to protect the survivor psychologically during the emotional, verbal, and physical abuse. This is because depression is centered around self-deprecating thoughts. Essentially, the severely depressed survivor becomes her own worst enemy. She takes on the role of the abuser, thinking horrible thoughts about herself. As she is even more critical and belittling of herself than the abuser, this relieves the hurtfulness of the abuser's verbal tirade. In essence, no one can hurt the depressed survivor more than she can hurt herself. The belittling inner dialogue of the survivor protects her from the harmfulness of the hateful words spoken by the abuser. This allows her to cope with the abuse by becoming numb to it. Nothing can hurt her because she has said much worse to herself.

Unfortunately, depression and learned helplessness prevent the will to escape the abuse. Therefore, it may be even harder for a survivor who feels depressed to leave her oppressor. This creates a circular environment which feeds off of itself. Abuse may cause depression and depression may prevent someone from leaving abuse. To get out of depression, the two most helpful cognitive behavioral tools are:

1) Recognize what you do have control over and begin to exercise control over it

2) Replace the harmful inner dialogue with a supportive, praising, realistic inner dialogue

For example, with control, the survivor needs to begin to recognize that although she may not have control over the abuser's behavior, she does have control over how she reacts to it, what she does about it, and what she thinks about it. She can control whether she shuts down, screams, cries, or leaves. She can control whether she will continue to live with the abuser, call the police, go to a friend's place, fight back, get counseling, go to a shelter, or go to a neighbor's residence. She also has control over what she thinks about it: whether she believes he is responsible for his own behavior, whether she believes she causes it, or whether she deserves it or not. She can decide and control her own beliefs. She can choose to believe that she does not deserve the abuse and that she cannot control the abuser's behavior.

Similarly, she can change her hurtful thoughts into positive ones. Instead of saying things to herself such as: "You're stupid," "You deserve what's coming," "You're a worthless piece of shit," "You can't do anything right," "You would be better off dead," she can change them into: "You made a mistake and that's ok," "You don't deserve to be abused," "You are beautiful," "You are helpful," "People love and need you and would be devastated if you were gone." All negative thoughts should be recognized as what the abuser has brainwashed you and trained you to believe. They are lies, nothing more.

Coping Through Self-Harm

While some may give up in order to cope with the loss of control, others may decide to take back control and this can end up being very unhealthy in certain situations. In extremely controlling relationships, some may find that the only things they have control over concern their own body. Survivors may cope through self-harm, eating disorders, or using alcohol and drugs, all which exert control over one's own body.

Eating disorders include starving oneself (anorexia), binge eating and throwing up (bulimia), or severe over-eating leading to obesity. Eating disorders can be used as a way to gain control either by complying with the abuser or rebelling against the abuser. For example, a survivor who deals with fat jokes, fat nicknames, and putdowns about her weight may turn to anorexia or bulimia as a way to both give in to the abuser to lose weight and also to gain back some control in a situation where she feels as though she has none. Or she may decide to overeat in order to have control and to rebel against the abuser. When the abuser makes a snarky remark like, "You're eating *another* cookie?" the survivor may decide to eat three more just to spite him. In this way, she feels a sense of control over her life and her body. The survivor feels a sense of control when she gets to be the sole decider of what and how much she eats.

Self-harm, I believe, is a way of coping with extreme control and emotional abuse. Self-harm is the act of hurting oneself by cutting, biting, pinching, burning or scratching one's self, or by other means. This can also extend to ripping one's own hair out. Self-harm may have three purposes which feel relieving in the short term but which are very harmful long term.

First, self-harm may be similar to self-deprecating thoughts in the sense that if you can hurt yourself more than the abuser can hurt you, then in a way, you no longer feel hurt by the abuse. So, in this way, self-harm seems protective.

Second, self-harm may be a way to feel control in a situation that is chaotic and spiraling out of control. An individual who feels cornered, who feels as though they have no control and no way out may cut themselves or bite themselves to feel some control.

The third and last purpose that self-harm may have is to relieve the negative emotions induced by the abuse. The survivor feels frustrated, sad, angry, hopeless, and cornered. The survivor feels trapped emotionally, mentally, and physically. Not only is the survivor not allowed to leave the abusive situation but the survivor is also not allowed to express any of her negative emotions about the situation. Thus, it is through self-harm that the survivor feels a relief of the negative emotions and tension, while also gaining a sense of control. In fact, research has shown that individuals who self-harm come from homes in which they experienced maltreatment as a child (WHO, 2007).

Some survivors may cope with the loss of control and abuse by drinking or using drugs. Drinking and drug use puts the survivor into an altered mind state which may make the survivor forget about the abuse for a while, feel very good while intoxicated, and help the survivor deal with the loss of control due to the lack of care that drugs and alcohol induce. Although these are immediately pleasant short-term effects, they can also have negative outcomes like addiction, overdose, and death.

Other Coping Mechanisms

Survivors might also use coping mechanisms which make the violence seem less severe. These are: dissociation, denial, minimizing, and survivor violence.

Dissociation can be thought of as "checking out" or emotional numbness to the situation. Over time, to deal with the stress and trauma of emotional, verbal, and physical abuse, the survivor may learn that their emotions do not help the situation but instead make the situation worse. In abusive situations, responding to the abuser in a calm, cool, collected, and intellectual manner can be life-saving. Therefore, the survivor may learn to stop responding emotionally to situations. In other words, the survivor learns that detaching themselves from their emotions can help deescalate the situation. The survivor who is experiencing dissociation is present physically but seems to be preoccupied. The survivor who has successfully detached from her emotions may seem coldhearted to others as though she can't relate emotionally. She may not show empathy for others, she may have a hard time expressing her emotions and she may act intellectually when the situation would normally call for an emotional reaction. Emotional numbing can be protective in abusive relationships because remaining calm and unemotional helps to deescalate violent encounters. However, in the long term, emotional numbing may result in emotional detachment which can have negative outcomes for the survivor.

The survivor may also deny the abuse or minimize the abuse to make it seem less severe. Part of this is due to brain washing. The abuser has told the survivor over and over that the abuse was the survivor's fault and that if the survivor had not done X, Y, or Z, then the abuser would not have had to become physically violent. Because of this, the survivor starts to believe the abuser.

Furthermore, the survivor doesn't want to believe that the person she fell in love with and the person who she believes loves her would actually harm her. She wants to believe that the abuse was a one-time error that was caused by something that can be prevented. Therefore, minimization and denial of the abuse keep the survivor from analyzing and seeing the situation for what it is. In essence, minimization and denial protect the survivor's ego. It prevents the survivor from the realization that she has chosen to be in a relationship with a man who says he loves her but also hurts her. Moreover, because the survivor fails to see the relationship as abusive, she stays, and she is prevented from examining herself to understand the previous relationships and her own flaws which have contributed to her continuing to choose abusive men.

Lastly, the survivor may cope with impending violence by provoking the assault to make it less severe. This is called "survivor violence" (Samsel, 2013). For example, most survivors know when the abuser is "looking for a fight." This is the tension building phase, where the survivor feels that the physical abuse is imminent. During this time, the survivor may provoke the abuser by slapping him, calling him names, throwing things at him, etc. to provoke the violence that she knows is coming. Survivors learn quickly that this strategy, although it leads to abuse, often leads to a lesser violent outburst than what would have happened if the tension continued to build.

What is interesting about survivor violence though, is that it allows the survivor to gain some control over the situation. By provoking the abuse, the abuse will not be as severe. In some ways, the survivor is trying to control the extent of the abuse. But also, when the survivor feels cornered, provoking the abuser is a way to gain back a sense of power, control and autonomy.

For example, if the survivor has removed herself from the room to deescalate a situation, but the abuser follows her, stands in the doorway to block her exit and then berates her for the next 30 minutes, she will no doubt feel a loss of power and control over the situation. She is cornered and she has to listen to him berate her and she has to remain calm and comply with him in order to avoid the impending violence. However, when he turns to leave, she yells, "That's right, walk away! You coward-ass motherfucker!" Provoking the abuser can be a way of rebelling against the control the abuser has over the survivor. It is as though the survivor is determined not to give up control over everything. The survivor regains a sense of power with that statement.

CHAPTER 11
LEAVING

If you are ready to leave the abusive relationship, you should be aware that leaving is the most dangerous time in the relationship. "...Abused women are at the highest risk for further harm or actual death from the point ending the relationship to about 2 years postseparation." (McFarlane, et al., 1999). Interviews with men who have murdered their intimate partners reported that the woman's separation or threats of separation from their partner were the most influential events leading up to the murder (Tjaden & Thoennes, 2000). Thus, the most dangerous time for the survivor is when she leaves the abuser.

Remember that abuse, stalking, and murder are all linked together. It is estimated that between 29% and 54% of women murdered by their intimate partner were in physically abusive relationships (Felder & Victor, 1997). One study found that as high as 76.5% of women murdered by their intimate partners had been previously physically assaulted by the same partner (Moracco, Runyan, & Butts, 1998). Of women who were murdered by their abusive partner, 88% were stalked after the relationship had ended (McFarlane, et al., 1999). Therefore, if you have not already left, it is really important to come up with a safety plan while still living with the abuser and it is also important to plan to leave safely.

Safety Planning

The first step to leaving is designing a safety plan. This is a plan which will help you to stay safe while you continue to live with the abuser until you are able to leave him. Think about the things that can trigger an argument with your partner. If you know that your partner becomes more angry and violent when he drinks, then drinking is a trigger. If your partner becomes angry and violent when there is a mess, then you know that a messy house is a trigger for your partner. When you begin to recognize what triggers your partner, you can be proactive in order to keep yourself safer.

Go to safer spaces within your house or apartment during arguments. Avoid going into rooms where there are weapons (kitchen, garage, etc.) and where you will not be able to escape (bathrooms, bedrooms, closets, pantries, etc.). Avoid being cornered. Think about which rooms are the safest in your residence and go there when you feel like an argument is going to occur. Before an argument occurs, think about ways to leave safely. Can you leave through the front door? Is leaving through the garage an option? How about leaving by the fire escape, is that possible? Determine which windows you will be able to safely get out of if you need to. Make sure that you keep your important documents (driver's license, birth certificate, social security card, etc.) in either a safety deposit box that only you have access to or in your wallet or purse. Make sure to keep your keys and purse/wallet together and put them in an easily accessible place, in case you need to leave quickly.

Talk to your trusted friends or family about the abuse. Create a safe word with them that will alert them to call the police and send them to your residence for you. This word should be something that you do not use regularly. This word, if texted or said, will tell your friend or family member that you are in immediate danger and that help is needed. When your friend or family member receives this word as text or hears you say it, they should call the police and send them to your residence immediately. My safe word was "red." If I texted just the word "red" to certain friends, they knew what to do. You may want to come up with something more clever and incognito, like "saffron sauce" or "jade jewelry." However, remember to keep it very simple. If you are in fear for your life, you want something that can be texted quickly and easily and can be remembered. Furthermore, make sure that the word or phrase that you use will not alert the abuser.

Planning for Emergency Leaving

Often, survivors leave during or immediately after a violent incident in order to protect themselves from further violence or more extreme violence. In this emergency situation, the survivor may grab what she can and go. This may mean that the survivor leaves everything behind. Because of this, it is important for the survivor to plan for these types of emergencies.

The first important task in planning for emergency leaving is to create a couple of "go bags." These bags contain all of the necessities you might need for a one or two-night stay at someone's house. In each bag, you should pack: clothes for two days, (underwear, socks, pants, t-shirts) toiletries, (shampoo, soap, toothbrush, toothpaste, razor, contact solution, feminine hygiene products), clothes to sleep in and an extra phone charger. If you have your own vehicle and your partner does not borrow it or search it, you could leave one of the bags in the trunk and leave another bag with a friend. If you do not have a vehicle or if it is unsafe to leave your go bag there, you can leave it with another friend or at your office.

Second, if you do have a vehicle, it is important to prepare for it to be used in a time of emergency. If your partner keeps the gas tank of your vehicle on empty, try to buy a gas can, fill it with gas, and keep it hidden for emergencies. If you have nowhere to hide it, you could ask a trusted neighbor to keep it for you. If your partner takes the keys from you and makes you ask for them, get another copy of keys made when you are out with the car. Copies of keys can be made at your local hardware store, at your local locksmith's, and at your local dealership. Make sure you keep the key hidden in a safe place that the abuser will not find but that is also easily accessible to you in an emergency. If your partner does not search your belongings, it may be easiest to keep it in your purse.

Another important thing to keep in mind is that when you leave in an emergency, you will probably be leaving with no money. So, it is a good idea to hide some money from time to time to keep it in an emergency fund. Make sure it is hidden well and easily accessible in case you need to leave suddenly. A bank safety deposit box is a good idea if you want to build yourself an emergency nest egg, but the bank may be closed when you need it. Keep at least enough for gas and some food for one or two days on hand.

It may be important to buy and hide a burner phone. This is a cheap cell phone that you can buy at any store that sells electronics. This will allow you to call the police in times of danger if the phone lines are cut, or if the abuser denies you access to a phone. Furthermore, if you leave and take the phone with you, you will be able to call friends to pick you up.

Because you never know when you will need to leave, I really recommend keeping prescriptions that you take on a daily basis in your purse, or in your go bag. This is true for important papers as well.

Lastly, it is really important to memorize friends and family member's phone numbers in case you leave without your phone. Also, ask a trusted friend who knows about the abuse if they will commit to picking you up at any time if you are in need of a ride. Try to avoid enraging the abuser. If you need to lie and say that you are going to take a walk to think about what he said in order to get away, then lie. Arrange a secret pick up spot with your friend ahead of time. That way, when you call your friend, they already know where to meet you. This could be in the same neighborhood a couple of blocks over or it could be at a gas station, etc. Arrange to stay at a friend's house that the abuser does not know about. Make sure this is a friend that the abuser is not familiar with and does not know the location of their residence.

These steps will help you leave safely in the short term and in emergency situations. Although many survivors leave their partner for good in an emergency situation, emergency planning does not prepare you for the smoothest transition to leaving the abuser. This is because all of your property is left behind, you leave with essentially no money, no plan, nothing. That is why it is so important to plan to leave the abuser if at all possible.

Planning to Leave for Good

I left Abuser 3 in an emergency. He had just physically assaulted me, I was terrified and I wanted to get out for my safety. It was nighttime. I was in my pajamas. When I left, I grabbed my purse, threw on my house shoes and ran out the door. I literally left with nothing. I did not have any underwear, shoes, or clothing. I had no toothbrush, toothpaste, soap, shampoo, razor, or facewash. I had left my contacts and contact solution. All of my important papers were left in a safe in Abuser 3's house. Abuser 3 had spent all of my money and I had bills to pay. I left behind all of my books, computer, and schoolwork.

This put me in a very powerless position. I had no choice but to call Abuser 3 and negotiate with him in order to get some necessities. As most abusers do after violence, Abuser 3 was in the honeymoon stage and he wanted me to come home. Not wanting to go back to him put me in a difficult situation. I knew that I could not tell him outright that we were not getting back together. This would enrage him and it would make my life a living hell. So, I chose to lie. I told him that I was afraid and that I needed some time to think about things. He accepted this. Because he knew where I was staying (at my parents') and because he thought I would come back, he allowed me to have some toiletries and one pair of clothes. Honestly, I was too scared to get them. I didn't want to go back in that house. I was so worried that Abuser 3 would become more violent with me. So, my dad went to pick up the things Abuser 3 was willing to give to me. As punishment for leaving, he gave my dad clothes I never wore. These were ill-fitting clothes that I kept for cleaning and laundry day purposes. He did the same with shoes too.

Because I knew I did not want to go back to him, I immediately went to the pawn shop after I got dressed. I always wore a lot of jewelry that I never took off. This gave me the opportunity to get money for necessities. I sold all of my jewelry. I was able to get enough money to buy a couple of outfits from Goodwill and put gas in my car.

It was during this time that Abuser 3 really ramped up his ingratiating behavior. He was 100% in the honeymoon phase. At first, because I did not understand what he was doing or what the honeymoon phase was, I started to believe the lies that he told me. I started to believe that I was responsible for some of the abuse and that he loved me. I started to believe that he would never hurt me again and that he didn't really mean to hurt me. BUT, at the same time, in the back of my mind, the alarm bells were still sounding. I still felt terrified of him but I also still felt love for him. And it was because of these mixed feelings that I asked one of my friends who has a degree in counseling to help me. She immediately took me to a shelter where the helpful staff interviewed me and then educated me on domestic violence. After they taught me what I needed to know about domestic violence, I realized that I was in an abusive relationship. Understanding the patterns of abuse, the cycle of violence, and how much danger I was really in, I knew I never wanted to go back to him. Because I did not plan ahead when I originally thought about leaving him, before the last violent episode, I made things much worse on myself. I gave Abuser 3 the upper hand. Because I left with nothing, Abuser 3 could use my property as a negotiating tool, as something he could hold hostage.

This is exactly what he did. After I did not come back to him within the first couple of days, Abuser 3 quit everything he was doing. I mean he quit going to work and he quit going to school. He effectively stayed home all day. His purpose for doing so was that if I was going to come get my things, he would be there in order to persuade me to come back to him, start a fight, or prevent me from getting my things.

I attempted to get my things once by myself. I swung by the house in hopes that Abuser 3 would not be home. Of course, he was. I tried to talk to him in a calm manner where I explained that I was leaving and that I wasn't coming back and that I was there to get my things. This went horribly. He began to cry furiously and when that didn't work, he began to get angry with me. He used all of the tactics he had been using on me and talked me into circles. I realized that the situation was escalating, I wasn't going to be able to talk to him like a normal human being, and that he wasn't going to let me go. I told him the things that he needed to hear in order to calm down so that I could leave. I told him that I just needed space and time to think things through. I told him that I would think about coming back. I told him that maybe I would go to counseling with him. I knew in my heart that these were all lies. I never wanted to be with him again. All I wanted was a safe way to get my things. I left again with nothing.

After that episode, Abuser 3 started to realize that I might not actually come back. This is when he really stepped up his ingratiating behavior and he really began to stalk me.

I made one last attempt to get my things from him. After safety planning with my mom and dad, we all three went to Abuser 3's house. Our plan was for my mom to stay in the car and dial 911 if things got out of hand. My dad came in the house with me for moral support and to deter violence. I made them aware of all of the weapons in the house before we went over. We agreed that if Abuser 3 would not let my dad come in with me, that we would just go. I did not want to be in that house with him by myself. Thankfully, he allowed my dad to come in with me.

I told Abuser 3 that I was there to get my things. I think he realized at this point that I meant business and that I was really leaving him. I was terrified. Abuser 3 owned a lot of guns and I was terrified that because he now knew I was leaving him, he was going to shoot me. Abuser 3 continued to stand in front of me and get in my way, not allowing me to get my items. He barked at me, "Can we talk about this first?!" In order to calm the situation, I appeased him. I followed him into the room. He tried to shut the door but I wouldn't let him. "If you want to talk, talk, but I'm not talking with the door closed." He said anything that he thought would make me stay. He minimized, denied, and blamed me for the abuse. He refused to take responsibility for his actions. He also made a million empty promises.

As he talked, I continued to pack my things. I tried to not antagonize him, so I packed very slowly, and continued to look at him while he talked to me. I also answered all of his questions. I got what I could, which wasn't much. I felt the situation was turning into the same situation that had happened before when I tried to get my things. The conversation was circular. Abuser 3's aim was to get me to come back to him by any means necessary. He did not care about my thoughts, feelings, or perspective of the matter. He was not listening to me. Only his perspective mattered. Only what he wanted mattered. Because I could see that it was going nowhere quickly, I grabbed as much as I could as quickly as I could and I told my dad that it was time to go. I made it out of there with underwear, socks, important papers, and some school books. That was it.

As we loaded the three trash bags of items into the truck, Abuser 3 blocked us in. I was sitting in the backseat and Abuser 3 came up to my window. He continued to talk to me and wouldn't let us leave. His body was so close to the truck that my dad would have hit him with the mirror and ran over his toes if we tried to back out of the drive way. It was during this moment that I was the most scared. Thankfully, my dad was able to convince Abuser 3 to let us go. He suggested that we both write each other letters explaining our sides and try to work it out that way. I agreed so that we could leave. However, at this point, I knew in my heart that I never wanted to see or talk to Abuser 3 again.

I eventually got my things through an unexpected avenue. I was fortunate. The university that I attended really helped me in this situation. Because we both attended the same university, I was able to file a complaint against him for domestic violence through the school. The school has their own justice system which needs less convincing evidence to convict someone of domestic violence than the state. Thankfully, the university found Abuser 3 guilty of simple assault. At the same time, because he was stalking me, I was able to place a no contact order on him as well. This meant that if he continued to contact me, stalk me, or harass me in any way, the university could expel him. Because he was found guilty, the school ordered him to pack up all my belongings, place them on his driveway, leave the house, and allow my dad to pick up my belongings at a mutually agreeable day and time.

Although I considered this a win, it was also a loss in a sense. Although I got most of my things back, the number of things and what I was given back was controlled by Abuser 3. So, in essence, he was able to control me one last time. He used the opportunity to punish me. It was October when I finally got *my personal belongings. I had left him in May. For 6 months, I lived with only the essentials. When I unpacked my items, I realized how he had punished me: he had kept all of my winter clothes. He returned my summer clothes. Most of my favorite clothes were gone. He kept my computer and my winter coat. He kept my winter shoes. BUT, it could have been much worse. He could have set fire to all of my things. Or he could have sent them back completely destroyed. So, I am very thankful for what I did get back.*

However, my point here is that leaving the abuser for good during an emergency situation is not the ideal way to leave. You set yourself up for great heartache and headache. You also set yourself up for a situation in which you don't get your things back. That is why, if you have not already left, but know that you want to, I recommend creating a plan before you are ready to leave.

In order to plan to leave for good, you will need to outsmart the abuser. You will need to learn to lie and to withhold information from him. Remember that this is for your best interest and for your safety.

The first thing to do is to open a new bank account at an entirely different bank in your name only. This will set you up for financial independence from the abuser. If you have your own bank account that the abuser does not have access to, disregard this first step. Second, you will want to start taking money from your joint account and putting it into your new account. If the abuser has his own account which you do not have access to, or if the abuser watches the money in the joint account carefully or requires you to ask him for money, you will need to come up with clever ways of getting the money. You could possibly take small amounts of cash out when you go grocery shopping, if the abuser does not go with you. Another way to get money is by taking a little at a time from the change jar. Another possibility is to ask the abuser for money for something he has agreed to before. For example, you could ask the abuser for $20 for gas but then only put $10 in the tank. Or perhaps you tell the abuser that you would like to buy your lunch 2 days a week. But, instead of buying your lunch, put the money in your other account. Only you can come up with the best way to do this as you know the abuser and what he is likely to believe.

You will want to put money into your new account without getting caught. Perhaps make a deposit once a week, or once every other week. It is very important to not spend this money. It will be used for rent, utilities, phone, and other services once you leave the abuser.

If you do not have a job, try to convince the abuser to let you get one. If you can get him to agree, this will increase your financial independence and give you more money which you can save for moving. Furthermore, having a job will ease your transition into living on your own. You will be able to pay your own bills when you leave which will open up more housing opportunities.

You should also begin to look for affordable housing. This may include renting a room from someone who already has a house, asking a friend or family member if you can stay with them or rent a room from them, or even renting an apartment. The easiest transition would probably involve staying with a friend or family member until you are able to get back on your feet. This is because renting an apartment or a house requires a lot more effort: finding one, filling out paperwork, passing a background check, passing a credit check, completing a walk through, getting the keys, and paying the first month's rent and deposit.

Once you have secured a place to stay, start slowly moving things over to the new place while still living with the abuser. DO NOT tell the abuser that you are leaving yet. You want to make sure that you get the majority of your things over there before he finds out. Try to think of excuses for why things are missing before the abuser notices. That way when he asks you, you have a believable answer ready and you aren't taken by surprise.

For example, if your closet is starting to look a little bare because you have been moving your clothes to the new place, you could say that you gave some of your clothes to a charity or that your friend asked to borrow some things. If you know that the abuser will not go into the attic and check, you could tell him that you put some things in the attic because you were trying to declutter. However, that could be problematic if the abuser demands that you get them down from the attic and put them back.

Make sure that you only move things to the new place when you know the abuser will not be home. If he is at work or school, that is the best time to move items. Also, do not move a lot of items at once. It is more likely that the abuser will notice if he comes home and the majority of your clothes are gone. You could put one item of clothing into a purse each day. You could take an 'extra' pair of shoes to work under the pretense that your feet hurt later in the day. Take an extra sweater to work and leave it there. Wear more clothes than you need, such as a tee shirt and an over-shirt, then leave the tee shirt at your storage location. Put a small purse within a larger purse or tote bag. Wear two pairs of underwear and socks. Make some excuse to get vital papers such as your job needs another copy.

When you are ready to leave fully, the best plan of action is to call up your friends in advance and plan a moving day when you know that the abuser will not be home for some time. If you know that the abuser is going out of town for a couple of days, this would be the best time to move all of your things, or the rest of your things to the new place. If you know that the abuser will be at work from 8am to 5pm on Tuesday, then that is the best time to move. It might be a good idea to have someone remain at his workplace and keep an eye on his car. If he decides to leave work unexpectedly, you can either abort the plan or speed it up and get out quickly.

Ask for your friends' help in advance. Prepare in advance for the fast move. Have your friends bring boxes, duct tape, bubble wrap, trash bags, and trucks or any vehicles that will help you move your things. Take the most important things first, such as a computer or school books, vital papers, any cash you know to be lying around the house, items such as a heavy winter coat that you couldn't 'sneak out' earlier. Move things into the vehicles as they're ready to go. Don't leave it all piled up to take out at once. Try to get all of your things moved in one trip.

The larger the number of trusted friends that you have help you the better. First, they can help you pack your things faster. Second, there will be more vehicles which means less trips. Third, they can help you move large items like a bed. And fourth, most importantly, if the abuser happens to come home while you are in the middle of packing, the more people that are there will deter the abuser from becoming violent. Also, they can help protect you from the abuser in case he does become violent.

However, your friends do need to know the situation that they are walking into. They need to know about the abuse and it is really important to safety plan with them ahead of time. Let them know where the weapons are in the house. Let them know what the signs are that the abuser is about to become violent. Allow them to bring what they need to bring in order to feel safe. Discuss code words and escape routes. Let them know that no items are more important than everyone's safety. One friend could even serve as a lookout who texts if the abuser is on his way back home. Lastly, make sure that the friends know that they are not to tell the abuser where your new residence is.

It is important that the abuser does not find out that you are leaving. If he finds out, it is very likely that he will try to prevent you from leaving. He may quit his job, quit school, keep the kids home from school, and use other tactics to prevent you from moving your things. The abuser will make your life miserable in order to keep you from leaving him. He may cause fights, become violent, destroy your property, physically stand in your way, or continue to put your things back as you take them out. If the abuser catches you in the process of moving, he may cause a scene, become enraged, or become physically violent. He may even follow you to the new place. This could make it easier for the abuser to stalk you once you have left. If at all possible, try to leave when the abuser is gone and try to go someplace that the abuser does not know about.

Now, if you are unable to convince the abuser to allow you to work, if you are unable to open up a new bank account or take money from the abuser, if you do not have a car and don't know where to get transportation, and you still want to leave but it feels impossible, get help from your local shelter.

Shelters are available to anyone in an abusive relationship. What I mean is that, even if you aren't sure if you are in an abusive relationship, you can go to a shelter and they will educate you on abusive relationships which will allow you to decide whether or not you are in one. Beyond education, shelters can help you with safety planning, provide you with psychological counseling, and help you plan to leave if that is what you want to do.

The people at the shelter are there to support you as you make your own decisions. They do not force you to do anything. Shelters can help you escape and hide from the abuser, they can provide transportation to a safe place and they can provide you with housing and money. Some shelters have job training and will help you find a job. Shelters can provide you with legal help through lawyers who give their advice to you for free. Furthermore, shelters work with local police to provide you with police protection and support if that is what you choose. The goal of the shelter is to educate and support you while you make the best decisions for yourself. If you need help finding a shelter, please see the resources section of this book.

After You Have Left

You can absolutely expect to encounter the honeymoon phase and ingratiating behavior from the abuser after you leave him. During this time, the abuser can become very persuasive in his efforts to get you to come back. If you start to feel your will bending and you start to think that maybe you should go back even though you were firm in your belief of leaving earlier, please see a counselor that deals with abusive relationships before going back. Learn as much as you can to make the most informed and best decision possible. If you aren't sure how or where to see a counselor or cannot afford to go to a counselor, go to a shelter. They have counselors on staff that are trained in abusive relationships that will educate you on the matter free of charge.

Please understand that it is very possible that after leaving, the abuser will stalk you. If you are receiving unwanted calls, texts, emails, visits, etc. from the abuser, it is likely he is harassing and/or stalking you. If your local shelter offers legal support, I recommend exploring all your legal options regarding stalking there. You may be able to file a report, press charges, get a no contact order, or file a restraining order. The personnel at the shelter will be able to explain all of your options so that you can choose the best plan of action. Furthermore, they will be able to help you create a safety plan and educate you on what to do if the abuser/stalker becomes violent. Also, you can refer back to the stalking section to get an idea of how to make yourself safer.

It is very possible that the abuser may become violent. He may destroy your property or leave you threatening notes. He may break into your house or office. It is important to keep your go bags ready in case you need to leave suddenly. If the abuser does become menacing, have the shelter's number or your case worker's number programmed in your phone so that you can make plans with them to go into hiding. If the abuser becomes violent with you, tries to break into your home, or threatens you, call the police immediately. Remember that your life is more important than anything else. Going into hiding is a very smart option and can save your life!

If at all possible, I really recommend going "No Contact" with the abuser. Firmly tell the abuser that you are NOT interested in a relationship, you no longer want to have ANY contact with him, and that you no longer want to see him. You can tell this to him in an email. There is no need to put yourself in danger by telling this to him face to face. You do not owe him anything. After you go "no contact" make sure that you in fact abide by this rule! Do NOT call, text, or email him. Do not meet with him. Do not hang out with him. Completely ignore him! Make it harder for him to contact you and find you.

Do all the things previously mentioned: Change your phone number. Get a new email address. Change your address or get a P.O. box. Move to a new residence. Delete your social media accounts. Park your car in a garage so that the abuser doesn't know where you live. Tell your family that they have to go no contact with him also, this is for your safety!

If you have contact with him after telling him that you do not want contact with him – your "no" just turned into a "maybe" or even a "yes" in his mind. When you give an inch, the abuser will take a mile. If the abuser sees that you are caving, that you will respond to emails after you explained you do not want to have a relationship, the abuser will interpret that as though there is still a possibility that you do want a relationship. This gives them "permission" or justification to continue to pursue you. This means increased honeymoon and stalking behaviors.

I realize that there may be cases in which going completely no contact with an abuser is impossible. For instance, if you share children with the abuser, there may be times where you are required by law to have contact with him in order to discuss when and where and how the abuser will get to see the children. In this case, I recommend going no contact as much as possible. Only discuss the bare minimum with the abuser. I also really recommend seeking a lawyer knowledgeable in this area. They will be able to help you navigate these murky waters. They can explain your options and help you come up with a safety plan in order to protect yourself and your children.

Hopefully, after some time, the abuser will realize that you are a lost cause and he will move onto someone else. This is the best-case scenario. However, if the abuser does not get the message and does not leave you alone, then you need to know that you are in danger. If the abuser is stalking you, make yourself a much more difficult target by following the recommendations listed in the stalking section of this book. Furthermore, make sure that you leave a paper trail. Document all the abuser's stalking and harassing behaviors. Keep any proof of those behaviors that you might have.

If the abuser becomes violent, call the police right away. Although it is frightening, at the very least, make a police report of the violence. That way, there is more evidence if needed later on. It is also wise to talk to the police about what your options are. You may be in a position where you can press charges, request a protective order, or request a restraining order. However, in some cases, this may only provoke and enrage the abuser, putting yourself in more danger. You know the abuser and what will enrage him. So, you know what is best for you to protect yourself from him.

CHAPTER 12
AFTER-EFFECTS OF ABUSE

Besides immediate physical harm, domestic violence can also result in post-traumatic stress (PTS), anxiety, depression, and future illness. Because stress is experienced differently by different people, not all responses to domestic violence are the same. Some survivors may experience post-traumatic stress while others experience depression. Others may experience all of the adverse outcomes. Some survivors may not experience any of the adverse outcomes. Sometimes, the adverse outcomes are not experienced until some time has passed, while others may experience the effects immediately.

PTS
Post-traumatic stress, which can be a long-lasting disorder or a short-term response, occurs after a traumatic incident in which the victim feels terrified, helpless, powerless, or vulnerable. Some examples of situations which may cause post-traumatic stress are natural disasters (earthquakes, hurricanes, tornadoes), accidents (car accidents, accidental explosions, a plane crash), criminal acts (mugging, kidnapping, rape, domestic violence), and dangerous jobs (soldier, police officer, fire fighter). By no means is this list complete. Any traumatic situation in which a person feels fear and/or powerlessness has the potential to cause post-traumatic stress.

Symptoms of post-traumatic stress include: re-experiencing the event through images, memories, nightmares, hallucinations, thoughts, or flashbacks, avoiding discussing the event or remembering the event, avoiding places and things that are reminders of the event, trouble remembering parts of the trauma, avoiding participating in activities, less responsiveness, lack of expressing a normal range of emotions, feeling as though the future is uncertain, inability to sleep, becoming irritable easily, inability to concentrate, focusing on perceived threats (hypervigilance), and being startled easily (Kearney & Trull, 2012).

These symptoms normally show up 3 to 6 months after the traumatic event. Sometimes, however, the symptoms can show up later than 6 months after the trauma. This is considered "delayed onset" (Kearney & Trull, 2012). Furthermore, the symptoms of PTS can last months or even years. It should be noted that although 50% of adults in the U.S. will experience a traumatic event in their lifetime, only a small percentage (5% for men and 10% for women) will develop post-traumatic stress (Taylor, 2009).

Anxiety

Anxiety lies in the middle of the spectrum of fear, in between worry (low levels of fear) and fright (high levels of fear). Anxiety consists of thoughts, physical symptoms, and behaviors. Like worry, anxious thoughts can consist of beliefs of future harm or helplessness. Physical symptoms of anxiety may include: dizziness, shaking, sweating, dry mouth, racing heart, muscle tension, and shortness of breath. When people feel anxiety they often behave in a way that is avoidant. In one way, avoiding things that you feel anxiety about can protect you from harm. However, if the anxiety is caused by something not life threatening (like taking an exam) the avoidant behaviors can disrupt your daily life. When these emotions begin to interfere with daily life, it may be considered an anxiety disorder.

Generalized anxiety disorder is the tendency to worry excessively and have anxiety about daily events (paying bills, work problems, housework, health problems, etc.). However, the worry and anxiety are out of proportion to the threat. For example, a person might worry excessively about waking up late and set five alarms although they have never missed an alarm before. Besides excessive worry and anxiety, those suffering from generalized anxiety disorder may also experience: restlessness, fatigue, inability to concentrate, irritability, muscular tightness, nausea, upset stomach, and inability to sleep.

Panic Attacks

Panic attacks are feelings of intense fear when no actual threat is present. It seems as though the feelings of panic come out of nowhere. Panic attacks last for a short amount of time and consist of feelings of dread, like something terrible is about to happen. They include physical symptoms such as: feeling as though you can't breathe, racing heartbeat, sweating, dry mouth, feeling like you are choking, muscle contraction, chest pain, numbness and tingling in the face and arms, and dizziness. Some panic attacks can be predicted because they are triggered by a specific situation. Anxiety, panic attacks, and post-traumatic stress symptoms are all related to each other. Panic attacks are severe forms of anxiety. As such, anxiety and panic attacks lie on a spectrum from mild symptoms of anxiety to extreme symptoms of panic attacks. While panic attack symptoms are extreme anxiety symptoms, panic attacks themselves cannot kill you.

Sometimes it helps to view anxiety on a scale. *I chose a 1 to 10 scale to illustrate the spectrum of anxiety symptoms that I have experienced in my personal life. It should be noted that I do not typically experience the symptoms in this particular order. Sometimes I start at a 10. Other times I experience worried thoughts (1) and nothing else. Sometimes I start at a 4, then skip straight to a 1 and then feel no anxiety at all. It should also be noted that I may feel a mixture of these symptoms and label myself a different number. For example, I might experience tense muscles, clenching teeth, and have shortness of breath but only label myself a 1 for that day. Likewise, I may have a full-blown panic attack where I am gasping for air and having irrational thoughts and I label myself an 8. My point is, the scale below is a rough guide to help you understand the increase in severity of symptoms of anxiety. I typically label myself a 10 (regardless of the symptoms) if I feel completely out of control of the panic attack and have extreme irrational fear. I often label myself a 1 when I feel some anxiety but it is not really interfering with my daily life.*

Mild Anxiety					Severe Panic Attacks				
1	2	3	4	5	6	7	8	9	10
Worried thoughts	Muscle tension	Stomach ache	Nausea	Feeling fear and dread	Heart racing	Shortness of breath	Vomiting	Chest pain	Belief, feeling and thoughts that you are dying
Clenching teeth			Irrational thoughts			Dizziness	Diarrhea	Gasping for air	Numbness and tingling in face, arms, and hands
Muscle contraction and stiffness									

Anxiety often comes from experiencing something traumatic. Because living in an abusive relationship is traumatic, the survivor may experience anxiety after leaving. The anxiety may come about for many reasons (fear of retaliation from the abuser, fear of being located by the abuser, fear of getting into another relationship with another abuser, etc.) The anxiety may be so severe that the survivor experiences panic attacks. The anxiety and panic attacks may occur in situations that seemingly have nothing to do with the abusive relationship (i.e. a crowded bar), but I believe they can still be linked back to it.

Trauma may make an individual feel like they are no longer invincible. You realize you are no longer immune to bad things happening to you. Trauma can make the individual appreciate that their life is finite and there is no guarantee that they will live to see tomorrow (a PTS symptom). The fear that bad things may happen to you in the future can cause some individuals to become hypervigilant, searching their surroundings for possible threats in order to protect themselves from future harm (also a PTS symptom). In certain situations, I believe that hypervigilance can cause panic attacks. This is because searching for threats can become extremely overwhelming and overstimulating.

For example, an individual experiencing hypervigilance goes to a crowded bar to watch sports. This individual is tasked with attempting to absorb all of the information they can about every person in the bar in order to prevent harm coming to themselves from another person. This means observing and taking in all of the facial expressions, conversations, emotions and body languages of all of the patrons around them. It would be necessary to constantly scan the room for potential danger cues. The hypervigilant individual is conducting all of this covertly while still attempting to maintain their own normal bar patron behavior. All of this sensory information can become completely overwhelming to the hypervigilant individual triggering panic attacks in large crowds. This is because it is virtually impossible to process all of the information around you in order to feel safe. If you attempt to do so anyway, anxiety is increased, not decreased because there are too many opportunities for bad things to happen to you. Thus, going into areas where there are a lot of people may cause extreme anxiety.

For domestic violence survivors, anxiety may have evolved out of dysfunctional patterns of responding to the abuser. Living in a constant state of fear and worry about what will cause the next argument or bout of physical violence can be a protective mechanism for the survivor. The anxiety and worry get the survivor to behave in ways that may keep the abuser calm and could thwart potential violence. This continues as an unconscious pattern of behavior for the survivor even after the threat of physical violence is gone. After leaving the abuser, it is important for the survivor to listen to the anxiety. The anxiety points to triggers of abuse, or what the survivor had to do in order to prevent abuse. Triggers are situations which cause anxiety. When triggered, the survivor is re-experiencing the abuse unconsciously, through anxious feelings. In essence, the survivor's body is warning her that the thing that caused her anxiety, the trigger, is what used to lead to abuse in the past. In the abusive relationship, the survivor became anxious which alerted her to the potential forthcoming abuse. This is the tension building phase in the abusive relationship.

For domestic violence survivors, panic attacks may come from the chronic stress of living in an abusive relationship. After you leave abuse, panic attacks are likely to worsen (Moitra, et al., 2011). This may be related to control. When living in an abusive relationship, the survivor often gives up control over the majority of the decisions in order to avoid abuse. After leaving the abuser, the survivor is left with making all of the decisions which exponentially increased her options, often overnight. This can feel completely overwhelming. Furthermore, in the abusive relationship the survivor was often punished for making "incorrect" decisions. This may cause the survivor to feel anxiety about making decisions in general. Because of the overwhelming amount of decisions and the anxiety that has been trained into the survivor when making decisions, she may experience panic attacks. One way to sum this idea up is: we worry about what we *can* control when we aren't in control and we worry about what we *can't* control when we are in control. Unfortunately, the survivor may worry about what she can and can't control when she finally has control.

Depression

Depression, which can be a long-lasting disorder or a short-term episode, consists of feelings of overwhelming sadness or feelings of emptiness that occur almost every single day, all day. Symptoms of depression include: feelings of disinterest in the things that were once pleasurable, feelings of extreme tiredness and sluggishness, inability to sleep (insomnia) or excessive sleeping (hypersomnia), unexplained weight gain or weight loss, feelings of insignificance and unimportance, feelings of unwarranted guilt, inability to concentrate, inability to make decisions, thoughts of suicide, thoughts of death, and attempted suicide (Kearney & Trull, 2012).

For domestic violence survivors, depression may have stemmed from learned helplessness. Learned helplessness is the idea that a punishment is inescapable and uncontrollable and therefore, nothing can be done to prevent it or escape it. Unfortunately, the person enduring abuse learns that nothing works and so they give up trying new ways to prevent it or escape it (Gluck, Mercado, & Myers, 2008). Learned helplessness occurs over time when the survivor endures inescapable emotional, verbal, or physical abuse. The survivor effectually believes that nothing works to stop the abuse and so they give up trying.

Illness

One last unfortunate effect of abuse is illness. Researchers have found that stress has adverse effects on immune functioning. Our immune system is what functions to keep us well, to fight off disease and sickness. As we encounter stressful events, from everyday stressors, to natural disasters, to chronic stress from abuse, our immune system reacts, and these reactions can cause us to have an increased vulnerability to sickness and disease. Some researchers believe that the negative feelings associated with stressful events (anxiety, depression, and worry) may impact the immune system negatively.

Specifically, worry has been found to be associated with decreased T helper cells which help regulate immune responses (Kemeny, Cohen, Zegan, & Conant, 1989). Similarly, depression has been directly linked to compromised cellular immunity. Most interesting, is the fact that researchers have found that physically and psychologically (verbally and emotionally) abused women showed compromised immune functioning compared to non-abused women (Garcia-Linares, Sanchez-Lorente, Coe, & Martinez, 2004). In addition, Post-Traumatic Stress Disorder has been linked to short term and long-term changes in immune functioning (Taylor, 2009). Thus, it is likely that illness will occur sometime after experiencing trauma.

It is important to understand that illness may not present itself immediately after the trauma or stressful event. In what is known as the "let down effect," the immune system response is "turned down" which lessens its response and makes you feel less stressed. It is after this, that illnesses often surface (Colino, 2016; Schoen, 2001; Taylor, 2009). Because of the delayed time between stress and sickness, it may take even more time for an illness to present itself after a major trauma (such as domestic violence) especially if the individual experiences PTS. This is because PTS extends the stress response. Therefore, it is likely, that after PTS symptoms subside, the individual may fall ill.

Survivors may engage in coping behaviors which serve to protect them from the stress and anxiety of abuse and this in turn can protect survivors from illness. The first is optimism. Having an optimistic attitude, or "looking at the bright side," allows the survivor to cope with the stress of the abuse while reducing the survivor's risk of becoming sick. Although optimism is protective in this sense, it may be hurtful in other ways. Optimism may show up as minimization of the abuse, denial of the abuse, and belief that the abuser will no longer become violent with the survivor after he promises the abuse will never happen again, which all serve to keep the survivor in the abusive relationship.

One coping mechanism which helps buffer the effects that stress has on illness is social support. Having a good social support system means having friends and family who you can lean on in times of need. This may include people to talk to, stay with, borrow money from, or even hug. Having individuals to lean on during hard times really helps relieve stress. Therefore, the more social support a survivor has, the more likely she will be protected from the adverse effects of stress. Unfortunately, one of the key red flags of an abusive relationship is isolation. Isolation acts to remove the survivor's social support so that the survivor has to solely rely on the abuser, making it harder for the survivor to leave the abusive relationship. It may also mean that once the survivor has left the abusive relationship, because of her diminished social support, she is more likely to become ill.

Some other protective coping activities are: personal growth, finding the meaning in life, working on socially supportive relationships, meditation, and exercise, may all help to relieve stress which in turn reduce the immune response making illness less likely or less severe (Taylor, 2009).

One other way to deal with the trauma of an abusive relationship is to go to individual counseling. Counseling can offer many other coping tools, social support groups, and help with the after-effects of abuse. Many shelters offer free counseling to survivors of domestic violence and I really recommend exploring this option.

What did after-effects of abuse look like to me? *I experienced many of these ill effects after leaving Abuser 3. Specifically, when dealing with Abuser 3's abuse and stalking, I developed a post-traumatic stress response. The symptoms really started to present themselves about 3 months after leaving him. Specifically, I had an extreme startle response. I remember hearing dishes being put away and jumping out of my skin because the loud noise frightened me so badly. When I had heard the noise, I immediately thought that Abuser 3 was throwing a brick through the window. I always felt on high alert.*

I constantly wondered if Abuser 3 was going to be waiting for me when I got home. Was he going to follow me home? Was he going to be waiting by my car after I got out of class? Was he going to set the house on fire when I slept? Was he waiting for me on a rooftop, a mile away, ready to shoot me? He had bragged that he had great aim and a lot of practice. Did he plant a homemade bomb in my car? Were my tires going to be slashed when I got out of work? Was he going to start a defamation campaign against my character to our mutual friends?

These were legitimate questions I had and feared. He was 100% capable of doing any of these things. When I left him, I feared for my life and my safety and rightfully so. Because of this constant fear and alertness, I had an inability to concentrate. I was incapable of planning. If you know about these two things (concentration and planning) they are extremely important in escaping and dealing with the fear effectively. So, essentially, the fear short circuited my brain to where I was incapable of calming myself or making a plan to help myself deal with the fear. Unfortunately, because my mind was always racing, I couldn't think clearly long enough to figure out what to do to keep myself safe, which would have helped reduce the fear I had.

So, these symptoms were circular. The fear caused my mind to race, an inability to concentrate, and an inability to plan, and because I couldn't plan or concentrate I felt more fear. This becomes compounded when we add diet and sleep to the mix. Because of the heightened fear I felt, I wasn't able to eat like I normally would and I couldn't sleep at night. I often ate junk food, and because the fear made me feel sick, I ate very little. Low blood sugar (from improper nutrition) and exhaustion (from not sleeping) made me susceptible to panic attacks and basically blocked me from being able to control my anxiety. As you would guess, these are circular too. The more fear I had, the less I slept and ate, and the less I slept and ate, the more fear I had. These symptoms lasted MONTHS. It felt like forever. I honestly believed that it would never end. I started to become depressed because the symptoms from the post-traumatic stress response were so overwhelming.

But I held on. I got help. I went to individual counseling. I also went to group therapy for women who had been through trauma. Both of these gave me tons of coping tools to help with the stress. I learned to eat healthier, to eat more protein, and to make sure that I ate regardless of how I felt. I learned other tools for stress release: coloring in a coloring book, soaking in a bath, gardening, getting a massage, yoga, deep breathing, and exercising, are a few.

I was taught cognitive behavioral techniques such as letting emotions flow through you and not getting stuck in them. Acknowledge that you feel the emotion but don't get sucked into the emotion.

When I left Abuser 3, I left with nothing and I was being stalked; there were times when I felt overwhelmingly sad, frustrated, enraged and sorry for myself all at the same time. I would get stuck in these emotions. I would think about all the reasons I felt these feelings and I would become so worked up that I would sob uncontrollably and wouldn't be able to breathe. Allowing myself to go there brought on panic attacks. I learned not to go there.

Try not to think about all of those things that make you feel all of the negative emotions. It is better to try to take a different approach. Tell yourself, "Yes, I feel enraged, frustrated, sad, and sorry for myself and I have a right to" and then try to move on to something else. Getting bogged down in the emotions makes everything a million times worse and it doesn't fix the situation. It is not helpful.

Thankfully, for me the PTS symptoms faded away after several months. It was fully gone by a year.

With that being said, I still deal with anxiety and panic attacks. I noticed quite quickly after I left Abuser 3 that the anxiety was informative. My anxiety told me about the things that I had to do to avoid abuse. Exploring my anxiety and asking myself why I was feeling anxiety really helped me deal with it and overcome some of the grooming or "training" that Abuser 3 put me through.

For example, after I had left, I realized I had extreme anxiety when I got up at night to use the bathroom. After thinking about this, I realized it was because of all the rules around nighttime that I had lived with. Abuser 3 would become enraged if anyone turned the bathroom light on at night, no one was allowed to flush the toilet at night, or make noise. Essentially, anything that might possibly wake him up at night caused me anxiety.

My way of dealing with my anxiety has been to explore my feelings and stay in the struggle. What I mean is I would figure out why I was feeling anxiety; I would explore the reasons for the anxiety. What rules were there surrounding this thing? What behaviors were surrounding this thing? What would happen if I did this thing? What would happen if I didn't do this thing? This helped me figure out where I was being controlled.

I found I had high anxiety in many places and doing many things. I had panic attacks going to malls (there are too many controlling things to list about shopping with Abuser 3 that relates to this). I had anxiety about the shower curtain (it had to be pushed to the opposite side of the bath, away from the toilet). I had anxiety about cooking (the kitchen had to be clean at all times). Hell, the first year after leaving Abuser 3, I barely left the house because I felt so much anxiety, even at home. When I started dating again, I starting feeling so much anxiety again. If a place to eat was mentioned and I didn't want to eat there I had extreme anxiety about it. If I didn't want to watch something, I felt high anxiety about saying no. This is because above all else, abusers hate the word "No."

In order to deal with all of the anxiety I felt, after figuring out why I was having it and what it was from, I would "stay in the struggle." For example, one night, it was my normal, non-abusive boyfriend's turn to make dinner. A series of events unfolded which frustrated him greatly. First, he came home sweaty from a bike ride, full from a big lunch, and tired from a long day. He did not feel like cooking dinner.

However, he put his feelings aside and cooked anyway because it was his turn. During his cooking, he began to grow more frustrated with the heat of the kitchen, dropping food on accident, and then dropping a full cup of water that splattered everywhere. He was frustrated at the situation, at the series of events that were unfortunate. As his frustration grew, he began to do what most normal people do when they are frustrated: curse. He took his frustration out on the dishes, handling them roughly.

However, as his frustration grew, so too, did my anxiety. A knot began to form at the pit of my stomach. My whole body grew tense. As I sat on the couch reading a book, the anxiety I felt made me want to get up and help him to remove his frustration. I felt like it was my responsibility to ease his frustration, to fix his problems, and it wasn't. (This is an example of having bad boundaries. I am still working hard to create good boundaries).

In the past, this is exactly what Abuser 3 would have wanted. Abuser 3 had trained me through negative and positive reinforcement that when he showed anger or frustration, I needed to fix it for him, or remove the frustration in order to protect myself from Abuser 3's anger. Abuser 3's anger and frustration became a trigger for me.

My non-abusive boyfriend was frustrated with the situation, not with me. He wasn't trying to manipulate me into cooking the dinner for him. He was expressing his anger with the situation. However, my mind was still trained from the abusive relationships I lived in.

In the abusive relationships I was in, frustration and anger, wherever they originated from, ended up being cast upon me unless I fixed it. The negative emotions were used by Abuser 3 to manipulate me into doing things for him. If Abuser 3 started off as frustrated with the situation, it quickly turned into frustration and anger with me because he believed that he shouldn't even have to make dinner. He should not have to clean the kitchen; that should be my responsibility. Thus, he would feel justified in his anger towards me about having to make dinner because he believed that I should wait on him hand and foot. He believed that he shouldn't even have to ask me to make dinner for him, I should just already know that he didn't feel like doing it and I should take it upon myself to get these things done before he had a chance to do them.

So, because Abuser 3 did not receive the special treatment he believed he deserved, he felt that he was justified in his anger towards me. And then, after receiving those anger cues from Abuser 3, if I did not jump up and fix it for him, he would punish me. This could be in the form of an argument ("You knew I needed help, and yet, you sat there on your lazy ass doing nothing! You are the most selfish person I have ever met!"), giving me the silent treatment, flaking out on his other responsibilities, kicking me out of the house, or becoming violent.

So, when my normal, non-abusive boyfriend started to show frustration, I became triggered. I felt extreme anxiety which made me feel like I needed to get up and fix it for him so that I could avoid the anger and punishment that I had become accustomed to in my past abusive relationships. Normally, in the abusive relationships, I would allow this anxiety to motivate me to get up and take over the situation to remove or at least reduce the other person's frustration. I believed that by doing so, I was protecting myself from the escalation of the situation into violence. It was also immediately "rewarding" for me in that it reduced my anxiety as well. However, when I acted on my anxiety in abusive relationships, it was also immediately rewarding for the abuser. It taught the abuser that all he had to do was become frustrated or angry at me and I would give in to him. He was being rewarded for his manipulation of me. Once I realized this, it really motivated me to do the opposite of what I would normally do in these situations.

Thus, when my normal boyfriend became frustrated, instead of hopping up, immediately reacting to the anxiety I felt and the frustration he felt, I sat there and did nothing. I stayed in the struggle. I allowed myself to feel the anxiety without acting upon it and I allowed my boyfriend to endure his frustration without acting on it. Doing this helped me learn several valuable lessons.

First, his frustration is his responsibility and not mine. This lesson is about boundaries (which will be discussed in more detail later). It is not my job to remove or prevent his frustration. I can choose to support him emotionally if he wants to talk about his frustration or I can give him a hug to help him relieve some of his stress but I should not try to fix it for him. That is not my responsibility.

Second, he is allowed to feel frustrated and I should let him. Letting others feel negative emotions is an important and valuable experience. Negative emotions often teach us the most about life and boundaries. Specifically, experiencing negative emotions often teaches us strength, resiliency, and autonomy. We also learn when to ask for help from others and we learn when we can handle the situation by ourselves.

Third, this was a test for myself that I could feel a negative emotion (anxiety) and not act on it. It was very important for me to let myself feel this emotion, explore where it was coming from and then let the situation unfold and not do anything at all. Observing the situation as it unfolded helped me learn new responses and unlearn the abusive training that I have been taught. It showed me that, unlike Abuser 3, my normal boyfriend was not going to punish me for not fixing it for him. It taught me that my boyfriend can feel frustration and not take it out on me. I learned that he could be angry and frustrated with his situation and not punish me for it. It showed me that after he dealt with his anger and frustration (all by himself!) that he could come back to me and be loving and normal.

So, staying in the struggle (feeling the anxiety and not giving in to our automatic response) is very important to unlearn the "training" we received in the abusive relationship. It means fighting the anxiety and not giving in to it. It means doing the thing that causes you anxiety.

For me it meant pushing the shower curtain next to the toilet, leaving the kitchen dirty, not fixing other peoples' frustrations, saying no to things I didn't want to do, and forcing myself to go to malls.

Now, since the malls gave me panic attacks and not just anxiety, that one I had to take much slower. I would go to the mall and have the panic attack in the parking lot. I would wait until I was able to calm myself down. Then I would start to walk inside where I would start to have a panic attack again. I would go in, stay for a few minutes and then leave. I repeated this process until I no longer had panic attacks on the way there or in the parking lot. I would only have them on the walk to the mall. Then I eventually would only have panic attacks when in the mall. Now, I do not have panic attacks at the mall at all anymore. In fact, I go to the mall whenever I want and I really enjoy it! I push myself to overcome the anxiety and the panic attacks by making myself do the thing that I am scared to do. (This is actually a psychological technique called exposure therapy). This retrains me that these things no longer result in violence or fear of violence.

Now, I am not completely free of anxiety today. However, I am a completely changed person from when I first left Abuser 3. My quality of life is exponentially better and I know how to deal with anxiety when it happens. Lastly, I want to talk about illness. Sickness really hit me about a year after I had left the abuse. I became very ill with a bacterial infection which took several rounds of antibiotics and a couple of months to get over. I still experience upper respiratory infections and sinus infections more than I ever have in my entire life. I get them several times a year and I typically deal with multiple illnesses at once (ear infection, sinus infection, bronchitis, and laryngitis together). But, hopefully, as time marches on, my immune system will continue to grow stronger. I believe that eventually, I will get back to normal.

CHAPTER 13
BECOMING LESS
ATTRACTIVE TO ABUSERS

Another effect of abuse that survivors might deal with is the feeling that you have no idea who to trust. You might feel as though your natural built-in alarm system to detect violent and harmful individuals is broken. You may feel that you have a "victim stamp" placed on your forehead that is broadcasting to all the potential predators around you that you would make the perfect victim. These are all normal feelings. Thankfully, these can be overcome too.

Now that you have learned how to recognize abusers for what they are, it is possible for you to make yourself less attractive to them. Becoming less attractive to abusers means setting clear boundaries and being consistent with consequences when those boundaries are broken. All of the knowledge you have learned thus far will allow you to avoid future romantic relationships with abusers. In the case that the abuser is your family member which is harder to avoid, you will be able to protect yourself from the abuse because you are able to recognize the behavior for what it is and you will be able to set clear protective boundaries.

Boundaries

For a complete and thorough discussion on boundaries, I really recommend reading Cloud and Townsend's book, *Boundaries: When to Say Yes, How to Say No, to Take Control of Your Life.* It is an easy read which will keep your attention to the end. It is extremely informative and very helpful in learning what boundaries are and how to implement good ones.

When you begin to stand up for yourself, by telling people no to things you do not want, you will feel anxiety. This is because you are setting boundaries that you have never set before. You are telling people no, when you have never had your "no" respected. In abusive relationships, the abuser does not take "no" for an answer. They do not respect your "no." When you do tell the abuser no, you encounter more abuse, until you give in to the abuser. Thus, you have been trained that "no" is not an acceptable answer. You have been trained to give in to them.

Boundaries boil down to knowing when to say yes and when to say no and standing firm in that decision. Boundaries are really important to the healing process. Having great boundaries will not only protect you from abusers, but will also allow you to spot them early on before you become too involved with them. This is because abusers will test your boundaries within minutes of meeting you and if you have good boundaries in place, not only will you fail their test, but you will also recognize that they are testing you. Knowing what they are doing (even if they aren't consciously aware that they are testing your boundaries) will give you the ability to proceed with caution and make good decisions that put your safety at the forefront. Therefore, it is important to learn what boundaries are, build them up, and practice implementing them.

What Are Boundaries?

Boundaries, similar to a fence, separate us from other individuals. Boundaries not only keep others out but also keep ourselves in. Boundaries define what behavior we are willing to accept and what behavior we will not put up with. They define our own behaviors: what we are willing to do and not do. Boundaries declare what is our responsibility and what is another's responsibility. Having boundaries means knowing when and how to say no as well as yes.

In order to know what good boundaries are, I think it is easiest to first learn what bad boundaries are. We can have bad boundaries with ourselves and with others. Both are harmful to ourselves and our relationships.

With ourselves, bad boundaries come in many forms: overeating, not exercising, staying up all night when you have to go to work the next day, working nights and weekends (when you've already worked a 40-hour workweek), drinking in excess, gambling, drug use, excessive tardiness at work, not asking others for help when you need it, excessive shopping, and not paying your own bills due to things like gambling, drug use, giving others money, excessive shopping, etc. These are just a few examples of how we fail to place boundaries on ourselves.

When we have bad boundaries with ourselves we are telling ourselves yes when we should be telling ourselves no. This works with other people too. When we have bad boundaries with others, we are telling them yes when we should be telling them no.

Some examples of bad boundaries with others are: lending money to irresponsible people, enabling others in their poor decisions, doing something for another person when we don't want to, changing your no to a yes when a person gives you enough grief about it. Most of the examples of bad boundaries with others involves taking the responsibilities of others onto ourselves.

When we lend other people money, it doesn't always mean that we have bad boundaries with others. It depends on the situation. Lending money to a person you just met, a person who has a history of being irresponsible, or a person who has a history of not paying you back, is indicative of bad boundaries. It shows that you are saying yes to people when you should really say no.

When a person consistently gets behind on their bills, does not pay others back, or expects you to give them money when they have done nothing to earn it, this shows their irresponsible ways and their entitled attitude. These should be red flags to you. You should recognize that people like this are more users than givers. They will take from you and expect you to continue giving to them while giving you nothing in return.

Similarly, enabling others in their poor decisions is an example of bad boundaries. For example, if you give your drug-addicted friend or family member a place to stay, money, or you pay their bills, etc. you are enabling them in their drug addiction. As harsh as this sounds, you are not allowing them to struggle in their own bad decisions. You are not allowing them to face the consequences of their actions. Those consequences that you are helping them avoid could be a great motivator in changing their behavior for the better. But, while you pay their bills, give them food and money and a place to stay, those consequences will never become real to them. In a relationship like this, you are the one sacrificing, you are the one constantly giving, while the other is constantly taking.

When we say yes to people asking for help when we really want to say no, we are exhibiting both the bad boundaries we have with ourselves (because we aren't respecting our own no) and bad boundaries with others (because we should be telling them no). For example, imagine your friend is in the process of moving and calls you up the morning of the move to ask for your help. This is the first you have heard of them packing and you are given last minute notice. Your friend expects you to help and you want to help but you already have a full day planned. You don't want to cancel your plans but if you don't help you will feel guilty, so you agree.

In this example there are several issues. First, your friend has bad boundaries. She has not taken into consideration that you have your own schedule, needs, wants, desires, and plans. Instead, your friend expects you to drop whatever you have going on and come to their aid. (This is entitlement. Your friend believes that what she is doing is more important than what you have planned). Second, because she is your friend, you feel obligated to help her and to prove that you are good friends. This guilt is used to manipulate you into helping your friend move. Third, you are exhibiting bad boundaries because you agree to help instead of saying no. By helping your friend, you reaffirm her knowledge that if she can make you feel guilty, she can get you to do what she wants. Furthermore, you have also reaffirmed to your friend that she does not have to take your perspective or your plans into consideration. If she calls you, you will give up what you are doing to help her. Moreover, your friend is not learning any consequences from asking you to help at the last minute, so this becomes an acceptable format for asking for help.

Good boundaries would involve telling your friend that you want to help her but that you can't because you have already made plans that you are not willing to cancel. Good boundaries would also involve explaining that if she wants help from you in the future she should call you in advance so that you can make sure that you are available to help. It is important with good boundaries to stand firmly in your "no" even as others try to persuade you.

When you say no in a firm but loving manner, you are showing the other person what behavior you are unwilling to put up with. In this instance, you will not put up with being called last minute and guilt-tripped into helping. It also makes the other person endure the consequences of their actions. Because your friend did not plan ahead, she learns from her mistake by not having your help. She has to deal with her consequences by attempting to find others to help her or doing it herself. She learns that if she wants your help in the future, the best course of action is to call you ahead of time.

However, if your friend called you last minute to ask for your help moving because of some emergency instead of inconsideration, then you would most likely want to say yes and ditch your other plans, and doing so would not indicate bad boundaries.

When we change our answer from a no to a yes, we are showing that we are easily persuaded (manipulated) into changing our decision. In this situation, if we allow ourselves to change our answer, we are not respecting our own boundaries and we are also showing the other person that if they want to get us to do what they want, all they have to do is apply a little pressure. Similarly, by not taking no for an answer, the other person is disrespecting our "no" which is disrespecting our boundaries and ultimately our person.

Now, this does not mean that we need to be stubborn and stick to our answer all the time. It is ok to be persuaded in some things. However, you really need to know yourself and what you want in order to know whether to allow yourself to be persuaded or to stick with your no. You also need to take into consideration the other person's motives. Are they taking into consideration your needs, wants, and desires? Is saying "no" protective of you? By persuading you are they getting what they want? Are they being selfish?

To illustrate, let's assume a guy asks you out on a date. You say no for one reason or another, but instead of hearing you, he ignores you and continues to pressure you. Instead of walking away, he steps closer to you. He rests his hand on your arm while he explains all the reasons you should go on a date with him. He tells you how beautiful you are. Maybe he tells you that you will never get another opportunity to go out with him. Or perhaps he tells you that you will regret not going out with him. If these tactics don't work, maybe he becomes angry. He calls you a stuck-up bitch or a slut and walks away. By now, I hope you have noticed that all of the tactics to persuade you to go out with him are abusive controlling tactics discussed earlier in this book. In this example, the abusive controlling tactics used are: manipulation, ingratiating behavior, excessive talking, guilt trips, and name calling.

These are red flags that he has bad boundaries, he does not respect your "no" (your boundaries), and his behavior is a perfect example of what your relationship with him will be like in the future. Except in the future, it will be much worse. In this example, your boundaries are being tested by an abuser within minutes of meeting you to determine if you will be an easy victim.

When dealing with this type of situation, it is imperative that you stand firm in your no, recognize the tactics for what they are, and protect yourself from this person by every means necessary. If we ask ourselves the questions posed earlier in regards to this situation, we find that by him persuading you to go on a date, it only helps him and not you. We also find that it is absolutely not protective of you. In fact, if I were in this situation, I would feel extremely uncomfortable that this man is not taking no for an answer and that he is trying to force me to go on a date with him. This would lead me to ask myself some very appropriate questions about him. If he is willing to force me to go on a date with him, is he willing to force me to have sex with him? This is an extremely valid question and you already know the answer. If they are willing to force you to do this, they are willing to force you to do other things. Lastly, by persuading you, are they getting what they want? Absolutely. In fact, by getting what they want they are making you *NOT* get what you want. In other words, their motives are purely selfish. They do not care about your feelings or what you want. They only care that they get what they want, and at any cost; that they win.

I hope you are recognizing the abusive theme here in this example. They are being extremely selfish and entitled when they disrespect your boundaries. They believe that they should get special treatment (entitlement). Specifically, they believe that you should give up what you want to give them what they want.

Most often, when we exhibit poor boundaries we are taking on another person's responsibility as our own. Boundaries define what is and isn't our responsibility. For example, it is not our responsibility to pay an irresponsible person's bills who spent all of their money on non-necessities (like clothing, electronics, alcohol, restaurants, drugs, etc.). It is not our responsibility to help someone who, through poor planning, called us last minute. It is not our responsibility to fix other peoples' lives, to prevent them from feeling anger or frustration, or to remove the consequences of their actions. When we say yes to people when we really want to say no, we are often taking on their responsibilities as our own. We are allowing our guilty feelings, our anxiety, their anger, their punishment of us, or their criticism of us, to persuade us that whatever is happening is our responsibility.

Creating and Implementing Boundaries.

Having good boundaries is not about controlling others. It is self-protective. It is about defining behavior that you will and will not accept from others (and from yourself) and standing firm in the decision to not put up with those behaviors. It is also about initiating and following through with consequences when the other person disrespects your boundaries (not in a punishing way but in a self-protecting way), or not removing those consequences that would naturally happen to those individuals because of their actions (e.g. letting the person sit in jail instead of paying their bail).

For example, if you are dating a man and he calls you a bitch and you are practicing good boundaries, you should immediately notice that this is behavior that you will not put up with. Hopefully you also realize that this is verbal abuse and to protect yourself from future abuse, you should nip this in the bud immediately.

So, you tell your date that his behavior is unacceptable. If he is angry with you, he can tell you that he is angry with you and then he can explain what has happened that he feels angry about. But, he can do so without name calling. Then you place a boundary down. You might tell him that when he can speak to you with respect and without name calling, that is when you will have a conversation with him, or maybe you tell him that if you ever hear him speak that way to you again that you will no longer be dating.

Whatever boundary you lay down, it is imperative that you follow through with it. If you decide to remove yourself from the hostility but you are willing to talk to him when he talks to you with respect, then make sure that you do just that. If you decide that you will opt out of the relationship if he calls you a name again, then you need to make sure that you are serious about that decision when you say it and that you really do end the relationship if he calls you a name again (whether it be bitch, selfish, slut, or whatever).

Having good boundaries is about recognizing what is and what is not your responsibility. It is about recognizing what is someone else's problem that they have to deal with on their own. When we take on someone else's responsibility, we are preventing them from learning the lessons in life that they need to learn. For example, if you have a friend who drinks too much and they call you to pay their bail, when you have good boundaries you will recognize that this is not your problem. It is not your responsibility. They made bad choices and now they need to suffer their consequences. You bailing them out of jail will prevent them from learning a hard life lesson that they need to learn.

Boundaries, as you can see from the examples above, are ways to define who we are. It lets the other person know what behavior we will and will not accept from them, what behavior we will and will not accept from ourselves, and they define what responsibilities are ours versus others. When we have good boundaries, we are standing up for ourselves. We are saying, "This treatment of me is unacceptable and I will not stand for it." When we have good boundaries we are also saying, "If you continue to treat me poorly, I will remove myself from the situation to protect myself." It is also saying, "I will not remove your consequences or take on your responsibilities when you have made bad decisions and need to learn from them." Having good boundaries is not about trying to force the other person to act how we want them to act. We allow the other person to act poorly, but we do not put up with it. In essence, the other person can do what they want but we don't have to put up with it.

So how do we create good boundaries?

We first need to figure out what behavior we will and will not accept from others. You probably have a good idea of what these behaviors are now after reading the abusive tactics. We don't want to put up with disrespectful behavior. We don't want to put up with abusive tactics. Our goal in practicing good boundaries is to start small and build up so that way, when we start to date we can see when someone is testing us (breaking small boundaries or using very subtle abusive and controlling tactics). And trust me, you will be tested, by strangers, friends, family, and potential significant others.

The most important part of practicing good boundaries, I think, is to remain self-protective, to remain fair but firm in the consequences, and to follow through with the consequences.

Start small. Practicing boundaries is extremely hard. You have lived a life where you have had minimal to no boundaries and the boundaries that you did have were bulldozed over by abusive others. So, you will want to start with things like choosing a restaurant to eat at for dinner or telling a friend that you really don't want to eat at the place they picked. Speak up when a time to meet doesn't fit your schedule. Tell the waiter that your steak is undercooked. Change out of uncomfortable shoes.

It seems silly, but when you begin to practice good boundaries, you start to realize how much shit you have been putting up with for the sake of not making waves and not starting arguments. You begin to realize how much shit you put yourself through as well, like wearing uncomfortable clothing because the abuser liked it or eating food you hate because you wanted to avoid criticism. Give yourself permission to throw out a gift someone gave you that you just don't like. You don't have to hold on to it out of obligation. Give the ugly hand knitted sweater to Goodwill. It's allowed.

Once you have a good handle on the small things, go a little bigger. Start saying no to people. Not for fun, but for real reasons. When that impulsive friend calls you at 7am and asks you to help them move – today, right now and this is the first you have heard of it, say no. Say no to the telemarketers. Say no to the door to door salesman. Say no to the coworker who wants you to cover their shift. In other words, stop putting up with all the shit you used to put up with.

When you start to tell people no, you will feel anxiety and guilt. That is ok. Let those feelings remind you that you are doing what is best for *you* – for once – and that it is ok to have those feelings. You don't have to act on them. They are reminders that you are doing what you should be doing.

You will find that some people will ask you to do things for them when you are in front of a group of people (to force you to say yes out of obligation because you don't want to look bad in front of others) or when you are in a hurry (because you will not have time to think and it is automatic for us with boundary problems to say yes when we don't have time to think about it). In these situations, note what this person is doing. It is manipulative and it is controlling. Also, the first few times, you will probably answer yes automatically and then kick yourself later after you realize what just happened.

This occurred several times to me and it was very irritating because I didn't want to say yes, I wanted to say no! And, since I was trying to practice good boundaries I felt I let myself down because of this sneaky tactic. When this happens, it is a great time to practice saying, "I don't know, I will have to look at my schedule and get back to you." In this case, you may encounter someone who is going to rush you to give them an answer. They will pressure you for an answer now. The best response to someone pressuring you for an answer right then is, "If you need an answer now, it has to be no."

Also, when you begin implementing boundaries, start practicing on people who already have good boundaries. They will be understanding and supportive of you which will strengthen your resolve to follow through. You will be surprised at how many people are totally cool with you telling them no and will try to compromise with you. You will also be surprised at how many really great people you have around you that will be unfazed by your boundaries (in a good way).

What I mean is that some of the people you are friends with, who you will practice boundaries on, will not even notice that you are placing boundaries down. There will be no arguments, no fights, no resistance, just respect and caring for your needs and desires. This is because these people are not abusive and are not controlling and they want what is best for you. To them, boundaries are a normal part of their everyday life. It does not upset them when you do what you want or have a different opinion than they do or want to go to a different restaurant. They will compromise and they will respect your wishes as you respect theirs.

You will also deal with people who are opposed to you having boundaries. They will fight back against you. When you begin to practice boundaries, you will start to see who is controlling and manipulative and abusive because they will use the tactics on you to try to force you to remove your boundaries.

The best response to resistance is to try and remove yourself from the situation so that you can gain some clarity. Abusers will often try to create some urgent situation so that you don't have time to think about what is happening, you just react to the emotions you feel. The abuser will either tell you that you have to make a decision right then or the abuser will start an argument about the answer you have already given him. This is a way for the abuser to get you to feel feelings of urgency, anxiety, fear, or guilt which typically motivates you into action. Removing yourself from this will slow the process down and remove the emotions so that you can recognize what they are trying to force you to do and understand what tactics they are attempting to use against you to get you to do what they want. In these situations, the best answer is, "I need to think about it. I'll get back to you."

After you remove yourself from the urgent-feeling situation (rarely is there an actual need for a response right then), you can then begin to process the situation. You can begin to see the tactics the abuser used to try to get you to do what they wanted. You can also really think about the decision you need to make. Ask yourself important self-protective questions to come up with a solid answer.

- If I do this, who does it benefit?

- Who does it hurt?

- Would I be taking on more responsibility than I should?

- Does it allow this person to escape responsibility or to have less responsibilities?

- Do I want to do this?

- Do I have time to do this? Has this person helped me in the past?

- How has this person treated me in the past?

- If I was in this position and I asked that person to help me with the same thing, would they help me?

Hopefully, by answering these types of questions, you will be able to tell whether this person is manipulative and is using you or if this person really needs help. Hopefully it will also allow you to determine whether you have the ability and desire to help them.

If the person is being manipulative and would never help you when you needed help, you should definitely say no. If the person has been abusive to you in the past, you should say no. If the person has been respectful to you in the past and would help you in the future and you have the ability and time to help them, then say yes. If the person is sincere and has been good to you in the past and would help you in the future, but you do not have the ability or time to help them, then say no. As you will want to help in this last example, you can help them in other ways. For example, if they need money but you don't have it, you can point them to other ways that they might be able to get money or reduce their expenses so they have money. Maybe you know of a food pantry where they won't have to worry about buying groceries that week. That would help them save some money. Maybe you know of someone who needs some work done on their house that could give them some extra cash. When we want to say yes but we have to say no to protect ourselves from burn out, we can still help in other ways. We can be emotionally supportive. We can give advice and point them in the direction of others who may be able to help them.

When you make a decision and place a boundary, you need to stand firm in that decision and boundary. This is very important. When we stand firm, we tell the other person that none of the tactics they use on us will work. And those who are abusive will attempt to use many tactics to control you, to force you to change your position, to force you to remove your boundaries. Once you bend on one boundary, the abuser knows that he can make you bend on all of your boundaries with enough force or abusive tactics. In this instance, your boundaries are being tested.

So, when you are tested and the book of tactics is thrown at you, the abuser is hoping that they can stir up enough emotion in you to get you to act, and when you act, it will be out of automaticity, out of emotion, and will be in the abuser's favor. Therefore, do not let your anxiety move you into action. Allow yourself to feel the anxiety and do nothing. Take note of how the situation unfolds and remember how the other person is acting. This will inform you as to whether they are abusive. Do not let your guilt move you into action. Again, allow yourself to feel guilty. But remind yourself that it is not your responsibility. It is not your job to save the world or to save others from themselves. Do nothing. Do not let their anger or frustration move you into action. They are allowed to be angry and frustrated. It is their anger and frustration, not yours. It is not your job to fix it for them or to fix them. Allow them to feel those feelings but do not fix it. You can be emotionally supportive, give them a hug and allow them to vent. Notice if they are using their anger to get you to take on responsibilities that are not yours. If so, realize that those are not your responsibilities and that they are not your problem. Do not let their urgency move you into action. If they need an answer that badly, they can figure it out without you.

Do not allow their criticism of you to move you into action. Notice that they are criticizing you for that purpose, to make you feel guilty or responsible for something that is not your responsibility. Do not let their punishment move you into action. Remind yourself that punishment is one of the key features of an abuser. Note that the person is using criticism and punishment. Use your good boundaries to remove yourself from that relationship to protect yourself from abuse.

When you stand firm in your boundaries, it shows the other person that they cannot force you to do what they want. They will not be able to bulldoze your boundaries which means they will have a very hard time manipulating you in the future. Although the resistance can be very difficult at first, take the resistance as a learning experience. Every time you implement good protective boundaries of yourself, and someone fights against them, you now see who that person is. You can now see their tactics, you can see their abuse, and you are no longer blind to it. You might feel disappointed because you now realize that one of your good friends is controlling, manipulative, and abusive, but you have learned something very valuable. Now, you can protect yourself against their caustic behavior.

When I started practicing good boundaries, it was very strange. I was so surprised to find that many of my friends were very supportive and had zero reactions to my implementation of boundaries. Lots of them didn't even realize that I was doing anything. I would tell them no and it wouldn't even faze them.

It was no big deal.

I also started to recognize abusive, controlling, manipulative behavior more easily. I no longer felt blind to it.

Much of the time, you don't catch the abuse as it is happening, you only have a visceral, bodily reaction to it. It's almost as if your body knows that it is abuse before your mind figures it out. You will feel anxiety. You will walk around more stiffly. You will feel anger or frustration but not really understand where it is coming from. And then, when you get home and have time to think about it, you will realize all of the tactics that were used on you.

I was disappointed to find that some of my friends were manipulative and abusive. I realized it when I began to set boundaries. I was shocked to find that a friend that I felt safe with, that I trusted, was actually very emotionally and verbally abusive. I would go out with this friend and feel frustrated and on edge during our time together. When I would come home and reflect on the things that were said, I was surprised to find how many of them were verbally abusive. I would find myself realizing that in one outing, this friend called me lazy, putdown my creativity, undermined my decisions, and just generally made me feel like shit.

Recognizing this allowed me to protect myself from it. I have the ability to choose to hang out with this person or not. I can decide to confront this person or not. I can be on alert for this sort of behavior in the future.

Another friend, I realized was extremely manipulative. She would ask me to do things for her in a way in which it was hard to say no. She would ask me in front of other people. Or she wouldn't ask me at all, it was more like, "You can do this for me, can't you?" When I stood up to it, placing down some boundaries, she immediately began to fight against them. She used tactics such as name calling and mind fucking. When I confronted her with her manipulation, she tried to make me believe that I was the one who was manipulating her! Eventually, I realized she was not really a friend. As I stood up for myself and others that she was attempting to use, it became clear that I had to cut ties with this person in order to protect myself. Although it was disappointing, I also felt proud of myself for seeing the abusive behavior and for standing up for myself and having good boundaries. In the end, I was able to have control over myself and my actions which protected me from further harm.

Creating boundaries is all about defining who you are and what behaviors you will not put up with. Having good boundaries is explaining to the world what is and is not your responsibility, and how you will protect yourself from people who do not respect you or your boundaries. When you begin to implement boundaries, start small, with manageable things and build your way up to larger boundaries. Start practicing boundaries on people who already have them. They will be more supportive of you which will strengthen your resolve. Lastly, learn from other's reactions to your boundaries.

You are now in self-protective mode and the ball is in your court. You have the power and control to decide what behavior you will and will not accept. If someone is being abusive to you, you have the power and ability to decide to be around them. You no longer have to take shit from others. You can leave that relationship. You don't have to answer that person's phone call. You do not have to answer the door when that same person shows up at your house with no invitation. You do not have to go on another date with a guy who makes you feel bad about yourself. You don't have to talk to that family member who constantly criticizes you. You don't have to be friends with verbally abusive or manipulative people.

Revel in your ability to recognize those subtle abusive tactics. You have come so far! You are no longer blind to it! Celebrate every small boundary placed. It is a great step forward! Remember those who support and respect your boundaries. Keep them close as they are great friends and good to practice boundaries with. You will learn so much from them! Lastly, read the boundary book: *Boundaries: When to say yes, how to say no, to take control of your life.* It will give you so much more information than what I have been able to summarize here. It was seriously a game changer for me.

Becoming a Survivor

Unfortunately, when living with an abuser for a substantial time, we become trained in responses which are submissive but also protect us from the abuser's violence. However, these characteristics alert other abusers that we would make a "good victim" and also show people that our boundaries are not very strong.

One of the first things we can change which will tell the world not to fuck with us, is our body language. As you have lived with an abuser, you have learned that certain things really set him off. Looking at other men may cause fights with the abuser. Anything said in public to others will be scrutinized by the abuser and can cause arguments. Being too polite or not polite enough to others in public can cause fights with the abuser. All of these things can trigger our body language when we go out.

We might learn to look down at the ground to avoid eye contact with others so that they don't speak to us. Maybe we look down to avoid being accused of "eye-fucking" some guy. We might learn to say very little when talking with others because we have been accused of flirting with the waiter in the past. Perhaps we learned to speak very quietly because the abuser criticized us for being too loud. Maybe we learned to fake smile while in public because the abuser continually asked us, "Would it kill you to smile or are you always just a bitch?"

Looking at the ground, seeming timid, being quiet, slouching, not looking at others directly, and even being too friendly can send signals to others that we are easy prey. At the very least, it suggests that we will not put up much of a fight.

We can project a strong fighter stance to the world by standing up straight and looking around. This shows others that we are alert and aware of our situation. We can look others in the eyes which shows them that we are not timid or meek. Changing ourselves from being overly nice to being direct and even having "resting bitch face" shows others that we will not put up with shenanigans.

As Gavin de Becker explains, "A woman is expected, first and foremost, to respond to every communication from a man. And the response is expected to be one of willingness and attentiveness." .... "Women are expected to be warm and open, and in the context of approaches from male strangers, warmth lengthens the encounter, raises his expectations, increases his investment, and at best, wastes his time. At worst, it serves the man who has sinister intent by providing much of the information he will need to evaluate and then control his prospective victim" pg. 68.

Gavin recommends being clear, firm, and non-negotiating when saying no and when rejecting a man. He specifically states, "I encourage women to explicitly rebuff unwanted approaches..." Yes, you might be considered "cold" or you might be called a "bitch" but at the same time, when you do not want to go on a date with some guy, you are setting a clear boundary down and following through with it. His reaction will show you his intentions.

I have to admit, that changing my demeanor from always pleasant to resting bitch face has had its advantages. Before, when I went around always smiling and being super polite to everyone, looking down at the ground, and acting timid, guys and men approached me constantly. Often for stupid things, and many times, I was approached about really inappropriate things. Sometimes I would be stopped by men in the grocery store asking me about foods or where they could find different items, other times they would compliment me.

But the worst was the unwanted approaches that turned into inappropriate confrontations. For example, one time I was waiting in line at the local Chicken Express. This was during the busiest time of the day – dinner, where many families were in line with their children and were sitting at tables eating together. A man got in line behind me. He noticed that I had piercings. He then began an inappropriate, unsolicited, unwanted conversation with me about his piercings (which were on his penis). I was mortified. I felt stuck and embarrassed.

Another time, I was in line to buy groceries at the local grocery store. A man got in line behind me and noticed that I had many TV dinners in my basket. He then commented, "What happened, your mom never taught you how to cook?"

I have had many encounters with men who have no boundaries, who believe it is ok to say inappropriate things to women. I believe that since I started using "resting bitch face" no one really approaches me anymore. I am perceived as less approachable by men because I seem cold and bitchy and I am totally ok with that.

Other ways that we can make ourselves look less like victims to others is to attempt to undo some of the other abusive "training" that we have experienced. Some of the things we have learned to do to protect ourselves include: apologizing for every little thing (even things we can't control), over helping, not asking for help when we need it, shutting down emotionally, and using some of the tactics ourselves (guilt trips, passive aggressiveness, and manipulation).

When living in an abusive relationship, we learn that to avoid arguments and even physical violence, sometimes it is just best to apologize for whatever is happening that is pissing the abuser off. We apologize that the food wasn't done by the time the abuser wanted it, we apologize for the waiter getting the abuser's order wrong, and we apologize when the abuser has had a bad day at work. We basically apologize anytime the abuser is angry or frustrated in attempts to calm him down so he will not turn his anger onto us.

Similarly, when apologies don't work, or when we feel we need to add more to the apology to get the abuser to become less angry, we try to fix it for him by over helping. We might volunteer to do the dishes too since the food wasn't finished until late, we might talk to the waiter to smooth things over or to get him to fix the order, or we might go out of our way to relieve the abuser of his responsibilities to "make up" for his bad day.

However, apologizing for everything, fixing things for the abuser, and over helping are all bad boundaries. When we do this, we take on someone else's responsibility. When we apologize for things that are not our fault, we are saying that we are responsible for something we really aren't responsible for. Often, we apologize for things we can't control. This is also taking on responsibility that is not ours. Fixing things for the abuser tells the abuser that we are responsible for his feelings and for him having a good day when this is not our responsibility. It is not our responsibility to make him happy or to fix it for him.

When we apologize, fix it, or over help, we are also adding to the cycle of violence. We are sending a signal to the abuser that all he has to do is get angry or frustrated enough and we will take over his responsibilities. He will not have to do any of the things that he does not want to do if he just acts angry enough. This is very rewarding to the abuser. By fixing it, apologizing, or over helping, we reinforce his abuse of us.

Along the same lines, when living with an abuser, we learn that he will not be there for us the way we are there for him. We learn that he is not supportive, he is not a caretaker, and he will not help us when we really need it. After experiencing many arguments when asking for help, we learn to not ask for help at all. We suck it up and we do it ourselves. But this too shows that we have bad boundaries. When we don't ask for help, we take on more responsibility than we can handle. So, we have to unlearn this, or overcome it. In relationships with non-abusive individuals, we have to continue to ask for help when we need it. We also need to avoid taking on more responsibility than we can handle.

Lastly, when living in an abusive relationship, we learn that regular ways of communicating do not work with the abuser. Being direct bites us in the ass. Asking for what we want puts us in a situation where that can be used as a bargaining chip to get us to do something we don't want to do. Asking the abuser to stop doing something is used to start fights. Saying no to the abuser is met with hostility and resistance. And so, we try to find other ways of saying no, getting the abuser to stop doing what he's doing, and asking for what we want. Unfortunately, the other ways we get the abuser to do what we want is by using the abusers' tactics: guilt trips, passive aggressiveness, and manipulation.

We use guilt trips and manipulation to get what we want without having to ask for it, and we use passive-aggressiveness to get the abuser to stop doing what he is doing without having to ask him to stop, and we also use passive-aggressiveness to say no to things we don't want to do without having to actually say no.

I have found myself being passive-aggressive in my new relationship (with my non-abusive boyfriend) when he was doing something that I didn't like and I was too afraid to confront him about it. In past abusive relationships, confronting the abuser to tell him to stop doing things that I didn't like ended in arguments and violence.

We have to be conscious that we have had to use some of these tactics ourselves to avoid verbal, emotional, and physical violence. Once we recognize that, we can really make an effort to be direct, and ask for what we need and want. This goes back to practicing boundaries as well. When you become stronger in practicing boundaries, you will have the strength to ask a friend or a boyfriend to stop doing things that you don't like. You will also feel strong enough to say no to things you don't want to do. And knowing how it feels to have the tactics used against you, when you do give someone a guilt trip and they point it out to you, you can be sincere in your apology and attempt to no longer use guilt trips but to ask directly for what you need and want.

None of us is perfect. But you can work toward becoming a better person and this is going to include times when you don't like the things that you find yourself doing. You will realize that you have manipulated someone into doing something and if you feel bad about this and you work hard to not do this anymore, you will succeed. Don't be disparaged, don't give up. Recognizing that you had to use some of these tactics to survive is half the battle. Because you recognize it, you can change it.

CHAPTER 14
FORMING NEW NON-ABUSIVE
RELATIONSHIPS

The Abuser's Test

When you begin to get out there and date again, several fears will creep into your mind: Will he be abusive? Will I be able to recognize the abusiveness if it happens? How long until I know if he is abusive or not? You have every right to be fearful and these are all valid questions.

After leaving, we also feel as though we have a "victim stamp" placed on our forehead alerting all other abusers to the fact that we have been victimized. It feels like there is some sort of radar or tracking device that shows the abusers where we are at, because after all, by the time we figure out we have been in an abusive relationship, it is likely that there have been several before it that we didn't recognize either.

Abusers can recognize who will make a "good victim" but it has nothing to do with stamps, radars, or tracking devices. It has to do with the abuser's test. Abusers will test your boundaries very quickly after meeting you.

They will test you in ways to see if you will stand up for yourself, to see if they can get you to change your no into a yes, and in ways to see how strong your boundaries are. In Gavin de Becker's book, *The Gift of Fear*, he says, "No is a word that must never be negotiated, because the person who chooses not to hear it is trying to control you."

Have you ever been approached by a man who asked you out on a date and when you said no, he kept trying to find ways to convince you to change your mind? Maybe he just wouldn't leave your table (even after inviting himself over and then being rejected), maybe he uses his charm to convince you, maybe he says something like you're too bougie to go out with him anyways, maybe he continues to buy you drinks even after you have refused them, maybe he promises to take you somewhere expensive if you say yes.

All of these are tactics to get you to change your no to a yes. These are absolutely red flags that this person is disrespectful of your boundaries and is controlling. In fact, these are good indications that if you do go on a date with this person, there is a very good chance it will be much harder to get rid of him later, and the control will become much worse. If he can get you to change your no into a yes so quickly on this one thing, he can get you to change your no to a yes when he wants to have sex with you, move into your house, share bank accounts, borrow your money... you get the picture.

What is interesting is that these tactics just mentioned which are explained in depth in Gavin de Becker's book are also tactics of rapists, kidnappers, and robbers. Each uses these tactics to force others to do what they want: Forced Teaming, Charm, Too Many Details, Type Casting, Loan Sharking, The Unsolicited Promise, and Discounting the Word "No."

I will briefly describe these, but I highly recommend reading his book. The knowledge that he provides in his book allowed me to "reset" my intuition so that I could recognize these early warning signals when I was dealing with potentially dangerous men. What is interesting, is that you will see so much similarity between men who are abusive to their girlfriends/wives and men who commit other crimes like rape, kidnapping, and burglary.

The first tactic is *Forced Teaming*. I discussed this tactic more thoroughly in the tactics section of this book. You can notice this tactic being used when the person you are saying no to creates a situation that has to be solved immediately and forces you to team up with him. The abuser may simply take something you said and make it his problem. For example, if a guy approaches you in a bar and asks you to go with him somewhere else and you reply that no, you can't go because you have to feed the dog when you get home, he may create a forced team by saying something like, "We can get that taken care of, no problem!" You should notice that he is ignoring your no, he is inviting himself over to your house, and he is creating an even more awkward situation because now you have to figure out how to uninvite him to your house even though you never invited him. In this instance, he is attempting to make it very hard for you to say no, which means that it is even more imperative that you do say no.

Charm and Niceness is the second tactic and one of the hardest to recognize. This one was also spoken about in the tactics section of this book. Essentially, abusers use charm to make you feel like you can trust them, to convince you to let your guard down to change your no into a yes.

The third tactic is *Too Many Details* which also goes along nicely with charm. Men who do not want to hear no may combine their charm with excessive talking (which was also discussed in the tactics section of this book) to distract you from your uncomfortableness in the situation. With this tactic, the abuser will use excessive details while talking to distract you from the fact that they are trying to force you to change your no to a yes. It also works to get you to lower your guard because excessive talking and too many details, combined with charm, make a person seem "relatable," "funny," and even "trust worthy." Just remember that it is not sincere. It is used for a purpose: to control you.

The next tactic that abusers use to test you is *Typecasting*. This is similar to reverse psychology but with the use of putdowns. The abuser uses a putdown in order to get you to do the opposite. For example, if the abuser anticipates that you will say no to him when he asks you on a date, he may preface that with, "I was going to ask you out but you're probably too bougie to go out with me." With Typecasting, recognize that the abuser is putting you down with the intent to make you do what he wants. He believes that he can get you to go out with him by putting you into a position where you feel you have to prove to him that you are not bougie. It is extremely manipulative.

Loan Sharking, another way that the abuser might test you, occurs when he makes you feel indebted to him so that you will do what he wants. He may buy your table an expensive bottle of champagne. Perhaps he pays for your tab or dinner before he walks over and asks you out. When he does something nice for you, it makes you feel obligated to return the favor. It makes you feel indebted to him. That way, you are more likely to say yes when he asks you for a date.

I think the context is really important for this one. For example, I don't believe that a guy is testing your boundaries if he buys you a drink before asking you on a date. I think buying someone a drink is like the universal symbol for "I am into you" and is not necessarily dubious. However, if his niceness is extravagant, unsolicited, or makes you feel uncomfortable, it is because loan sharking is at play. He is being overly nice and helpful to make you feel indebted to him. He either wants to make you feel like you owe him a date or if you are on a date with him, he wants to make you feel like you owe him sex. Either way, loan sharking is a way to force you to change your no into a yes.

The *Unsolicited Promise* is another tactic mentioned in the book. Upon meeting and asking you out (and after you say no) the abuser will promise you something (unsolicited) in order to convince you that his motives are pure (they aren't) and to get you to change your no to a yes. For example, a guy asks you to go to dinner with him and you say no, he then says, "I will make it worth your while, you will have a great time and I will have you home early if you want, I promise!" With the unsolicited promise, the abuser is trying to convince you to go out with him by promising whatever he thinks you want to hear in order to change your no to a yes. Understand that these promises are hollow. They are used as bargaining chips to get you to do what you do not want to do (and once you change your no to a yes, the promise goes out the window).

The last tactic mentioned in Gavin de Becker's book is *Discounting the Word No*. With this tactic, the abuser literally ignores your no. They will not take no for an answer. This should send alarms all through your body. If this guy does not take no for an answer now, what else will he not take no as an answer to? The answer is, whenever he wants you to say yes, he will ignore your no!

The tactics that Gavin de Becker explains in his book are used by rapists, serial killers, and robbers – immediately upon meeting you in order to convince you to do what they want you to do. Though these tactics are used in extreme cases, they can also be used by potential future partners who are abusers.

Abusers also may use other more-subtle tactics to test your boundaries on dates. While the abuser tests you, they are also exposing their controlling, jealous, and abusive ways. What is important is that you practice good boundaries and keep your eyes peeled. While they test your boundaries, you will be able to see them for who they really are.

Some of the subtle tactics abusers use to test your boundaries are: ordering your food for you, asking you who is texting or calling you, ignoring you when you say that you don't want dessert, ordering another glass of wine for you after you have said that you don't want anymore, refusing to let you take an Uber home, becoming extremely angry easily, being rude to the waitress/waiter, and using any of the tactics discussed earlier in the book (such as calling you names, putting you down, criticizing you, etc.).

Some abusers will order your food for you at a restaurant. Ordering your food for you if you haven't decided what you want, limits your options and removes your choices. The abuser has literally chosen what you will eat. If you have already chosen what you want to eat and told the abuser about it, him ordering it for you removes your autonomy. It places you in a position of subservience. Now, I realize that for this latter example, some may argue that he is being a gentleman or it is endearing. But I would argue that if you are on your first couple of dates with this man, then it is very likely a test.

If he orders for you and you haven't made up your mind, take this opportunity to place a boundary down. Tell everyone at the table that you will order for yourself. If you need more time, tell the waiter you need more time. If your date speaks over you and tells the waiter again that you will have (whatever it is he ordered for you) please realize that this is a huge red flag. It is extremely controlling. He is disrespecting you and your autonomy. He is telling you that he knows what is better for you than what you know is best for you. Understand that this is abuse. Get up and leave. Simply end the date. Ghost him. Do whatever is necessary to never speak with or come in contact with that person again. Recognize that this person is abusive and that if you continue a relationship with him, it will get much worse.

Now, if you have told your date what you want to eat and he orders for you, it is still a good opportunity to place a boundary down. Implementing good boundaries will alert you to abusive and controlling individuals when they begin to fight you on said boundaries. In essence, you are testing the abuser as he is testing you.

Tell your date that while you appreciate the gesture, you would like to order for yourself from now on (or something to the effect). You will learn from his reaction what to expect from future interactions. What you have asked is a normal thing to ask. It is not extreme. So, if he reacts in an aggressive or passive-aggressive way, you know you have a possible controller/abuser on your hands. He may say something under his breath like, "You can't even do anything nice anymore without someone taking offense to it." Or he might be outright aggressive saying something like, "God. Why are you being such a bitch? I was just trying to do something nice."

If the guy you are on a date with ignores your no for any reason, (i.e. you don't want dessert but he orders it anyway, you don't want more wine but he orders another glass for you, you want to take an Uber home but he insists on driving you) this is also a huge red flag. This shows that while he may be ignoring your no for small things now, if you continue to date him, he will ignore your no for much larger things in the future. By ignoring your no, he is also showing that he believes he knows what is best for you more than you know what is best for yourself. Remember that this is how abusers think.

If the guy you are on a date with asks who is texting or who is calling you, this is also a red flag. It is none of his business who is texting or calling you. It shows that he is already being jealous and suspicious of you. This will only get worse later on. Conversations like this, where you give in to this type of behavior by telling him who is texting or calling, lead to other more severe controlling behaviors like going through your phone or placing spyware on your phone to track what you are doing. There is absolutely no reason why he should be distrustful of you. Likewise, there is no reason for him to be jealous. You should recognize that this behavior is extremely unacceptable and if you continue to see him, the behavior will become much worse.

While you can learn a lot from these situations, it is sometimes hard to tell if someone is abusive just by one date (unless of course he becomes physically assaultive, stalks you, threatens you, or uses intimidation). When those tactics are used, know that this person is absolutely abusive.

However, we can learn what behavior to expect from the person we are dating and what his disposition is. We can learn whether he is disrespectful towards us and whether he fits the abusive theme (selfishness, entitlement, and feeling justified in their behavior). Learning this will allow us to determine whether he's abusive. We can also ask him the hard questions on a date which will tell us more about his values: Where does he believe a woman's "place" is? Does he believe women can have fulfilling careers and a family life? If he had kids, how would the workload be split? How are the responsibilities divided?

Of course, some of these questions can make a woman look desperate to become married and have kids, which is unsavory when you are beginning to date someone. However, you can reword these questions to still talk about the overall theme of women and duties and housework to see what types of traditional beliefs a man still holds onto. Or you could simply ask him about his life growing up and whether he agrees with the methods that he experienced then, which can give you great insight as to what he believes.

What he tells you – those beliefs will inform you of what he would expect in a relationship and whether those expectations meet with yours. Remember that abusive men tend to hold onto extremely traditional beliefs that women should stay home, cook, clean, take care of the children, and take care of the man while the man goes out and makes money. Abusive men also typically believe that if a woman is going to have a career, it needs to come second to her household duties.

You can also "test" your dates to determine whether they are abusers. One great test that you should definitely do is conduct a background check on anyone you are going to go on a date with (before the date). Background checks are cheap and fast, you can get them done over the internet and they usually only cost a couple of dollars. You will need your date's birth date, full name, and possibly a current address. Many of these things you can find online. You can ask them their full name before you go on a date with them. Then, if you feel uncomfortable asking them their birthday, you can try finding it through Facebook or other social media sites.

When you run a background check you want to look out for

any criminal record. If they have assault on their record, sexual assault, domestic violence, armed robbery, or child molestation, that is a huge red flag. If you find any of these, I would definitely cancel the date and go no contact. Past behavior is the best predictor of future behavior. This means that if they have criminal charges related to being violent on their record, there is a good chance they will be violent with you in the future.

Test your date by not answering his calls, texts, or emails while you are at work. Observe his reaction. Does he text you incessantly? Are you getting a barrage of calls and texts from him? Does he become enraged or passive-aggressive? When you talk to him later that night, does he ask you a million questions? Does he ask you what you were doing, where you were at, or who you were with? Does he accuse you of cheating or lying about what you were doing? These are all red flags that he is abusive and controlling. First of all, it is none of his business where you have been or what you have been doing. I would not entertain those questions and I would not answer them. Second, there is absolutely no reason for him to not trust you. You haven't done anything to cause distrust and this is the beginning of the relationship where you are getting to know each other. If he is already acting as though he doesn't trust you, this is a sign that he is very controlling.

Another way to test your date is by a having a girls' weekend instead of going out with him. I don't necessarily mean canceling a date with him. Instead, plan a weekend with the girls in advance, one that you haven't already made plans for. Again, you will want to observe his reaction. Does he act jealous? Is he angry? Does he start a fight with you about it? Does he try to make you feel so miserable that you consider calling off the girls' weekend? When you go, does he call you and text you repeatedly? Does he show up where you and your friends are at, uninvited? Is he waiting for you, uninvited, at your residence when you get home? These are all red flags of abusive behavior. He is showing you that if you continue dating him, he will isolate you from your friends and family, he will not allow you to have your autonomy, and he will not allow you to do things that don't involve him. In a normal relationship, you should be able to hang out with your friends without your partner, and he should be able to do things with his friends without you there.

The idea of testing your date, is to determine how he will act in normal, everyday dating type situations to determine if he is abusive and controlling. A normal, non-abusive man may not like that you want to have a girls' weekend instead of hanging out with him, but he can respect it and accept it. Testing your date will reveal whether they are disrespectful, jealous, controlling, entitled, and whether they will discount your no. These are all indicators of abusive behavior.

While Dating

You may be wondering how much time? How long until I should move in, how long until I know that he is not abusive? How long until it's ok to get married? Most people on average date for about a year to two years before they move in together. On average, most people will date for two or more years before they marry.

Learning if someone is abusive may also take time. Abusers typically do not become severely abusive right away. Remember that they typically need to hide their abusive ways in order to keep the survivor confused so that she stays in the relationship. Abusers are often very loving and attentive, especially in the beginning and especially after they have been abusive.

So, take the relationship slowly. Allow yourself time and get to know them slowly. Abusers will try to rush the relationship by love bombing, getting you to move in with them very quickly, and proposing to you very quickly. This is so that they can have more control over you while limiting more of your options for escape. Countering these things by taking it slow will allow you to recognize more of his behavior that is controlling and abusive before you become too serious with him.

Continue placing good, strong boundaries down and observe your date's actions. Abusers hate boundaries. They will resist them, fight you on them, and will use many tactics to get you to remove them. Sometimes they will just flat ignore your boundaries. If your boundaries are being ignored, trampled on, or you are being coerced or forced into removing those boundaries, you are dealing with an abuser.

While dating, if you're dealing with more subtle controlling behaviors like the silent treatment, guilt trips, ingratiating behavior, self-degradation, interrupting, and excessive talking, I would suggest approaching the situation as cautiously optimistic. Continue to observe and note the behavior. Continue to place boundaries. Continue to watch how he reacts to your boundaries. I believe you will learn over time if he is a good guy or if he will become abusive.

As I tell my friends, I personally believe it takes about a year for the other person's "crazy" to come out. What I mean is, it takes a fairly long time to really get to know someone. They will be on their best behavior in the beginning of the relationship – everyone is. So, it is going to take a while before they let down their guard and tell you like it really is. It will take about a year before you know how they argue. And that is important.

Witnessing how someone argues will tell you a lot about the type of person they are. Do they punish you? Do they ignore you? Do they fight dirty and say the most hurtful thing they can to cut you deeply? We all get angry with each other but in healthy relationships, we can express our anger and still hear the other person's point of view. We can take it into consideration even if we don't agree with it. We can still love while we are angry. We want resolution not dissolution. Therefore, if your partner fights dirty, ignores you, calls you names, says the most hurtful things, punishes you - that really indicates that he is abusive. He is using abusive tactics to get you to do what he wants. His goal is not resolution. He wants to conquer you.

Back to the original questions. To know if someone is going to be abusive, you will have to take your time, watch and wait. Abusers typically start with subtle abuse before they move on to physical abuse. If you recognize subtle abusive tactics are being used on you, and you recognize that he is selfish and entitled, then you need to recognize it is abuse that you are dealing with and do everything in your power to self-protect.

As for moving in together and marriage, I would suggest taking it slow. Do not be rushed. Allow yourself a year to get to know him before moving in. You need to know what you are getting into. Once you move in, it will be harder to end the relationship than if you are not living together. Same with marriage. It is much harder to leave a marriage than a boyfriend. Along the same lines, protect yourself sexually. It is much harder to leave a man you have children with than someone you otherwise have no ties to.

When you do decide to move in or get married, take care to protect yourself. Have your own money in your own bank account that he does not have access to. Do not share bank accounts. Split the bills down the middle. Put your name on the lease or the mortgage. These will put you on equal footing in the beginning of the relationship. There will be no power dynamic in which one person has more power over the other. He will not be able to tell you how to spend your money, he will not be able to spend your money for you, and he will not be able to say things like "Get out of my house!"

Talk about how you will divide and share responsibilities before moving in together. Do not take on more responsibility than what is yours. Split the household chores in half. Don't do his laundry. Have your own transportation. Split household expenses down the middle. All of these things will protect you from being taken advantage of. This gives you more options and allows him much less control over you. In addition, you will be coming into this relationship on equal ground. There will be no power differential. He will not start off having more power than you. This sets you up for a fair and equal relationship, not one based on power and control.

CHAPTER 15
CONCLUSION

Originally, when I encountered physical assault in the relationship with Abuser 3, I was stunned, but I wasn't sure that I was in an abusive relationship. Thankfully, a great friend took me to a domestic violence shelter where I was given free counseling when I arrived. As they educated me as to what an abusive relationship was, my heart sunk and I felt sick. Every fact matched what I had been dealing with in my relationship.

Learning that I had been in an abusive relationship was a total shock to my system. I had so many questions: How did I miss the signs? How did I not recognize it as abuse even when he became physically violent with me? Why didn't I see it coming? What other behaviors were abusive that I didn't recognize? How many other relationships had I been in that were also abusive? Why do I continue to choose abusive partners? How do I recognize abuse in the future so that I will not fall prey to it any longer? Why do I continue to be targeted by abusive individuals? What is it about me that encourages this type of person to seek me out? Why are abusers abusive? Do they enjoy hurting others? Do they love it? Is there some kind of personality issue with them?

All of these questions led me on an intense book-reading journey. I consumed so much information about abuse to be able to learn the answers to my questions and to be able to help myself overcome the situation that I had been in. It was an eye-opening experience. As I read, I realized that I wanted to be able to put all of the information that I had learned into one book so that others could answer these questions too. And that is where this book was born. My goal was to give you as much information as possible to help you in any way that you might need. I wanted to give you all of the information that I wish I had before I made the decisions that I did. Maybe you will be able to do better than I did. I hope you will be able to do better than I did. I hope that I have provided the answers to your most important questions.

HELPFUL RESOURCES

Link to finding a shelter near you:
www.domesticshelters.org

National Domestic Violence Hotline:
1-800-799-7233
1-800-787-3224 (TTY)

Link to a great website about abusive relationships:
www.abuseandrelationships.org

Link to stalking information:
http://victimsofcrime.org/docs/src/stalking-a-handbook-for-victims.pdf?sfvrsn=2

https://www.womensaid.ie/download/pdf/digital_stalking_guide_v2_nov_2012.pdf

RECOMMENDED READS:

"The Verbally Abusive Relationship: How to Recognize It and How to Respond" by Patricia Evans

"Why Does He Do That?: Inside The Minds of Angry and Controlling Men" by Lundy Bancroft

"Boundaries: When to Say Yes, How to Say No to Take Control of Your Life" by Henry Cloud and John Townsend

"The Gift of Fear: Survival Signals That Protect Us from Violence" by Gavin De Becker

"The Battered Woman" by Lenore E. A. Walker

"If You Had Controlling Parents: How to Make Peace with Your Past and Take Your Place in the World" by Dan Neuharth, Ph.D.

REFERENCES

American Psychiatric Association (2013). *Diagnostic and Statistical Manual of Mental Disorders* (5th ed.). Arlington: American Psychiatric Publishing.

Anderson, K. L. (2008). Is partner violence worse in the context of control? *Journal of Marriage and Family, 70*(5), 1157 – 1168. http://dx.doi.org/10.1111/j.1741-3737.2008.00557.x

Arbuckle, J., Olson, L., Howard, M., Brillman, J., Anctil, C., & Sklar, D. (1996). Safe at home: Domestic violence and other homicides among women in New Mexico. *Annals of Emergency Medicine, 27*, 210-215.

Archer, D. (2017). *The manipulative partner's most devious tactic: Spot the warning signs of love bombing early and recover faster with these tips.* Retrieved from http://www.psychologytoday.come/blog/reading-between-the-headlines/201703/the-manipulative-partners-most-devious-tactic

Bancroft, L. (2002). *Why does he do that?: Inside the minds of angry and controlling men.* New York: G.P. Putnam's Sons.

Baum K., (2009). Stalking Victimization in the United States, *Bureau of Justice Statistics Special report*, 1 – 16.

Block, C. R. (2003). How can practitioners help an abused woman lower her risk of death? In J. Ashcroft, D. J. Daniels, & S. V. Hart (Eds.) Intimate Partner Homicide. *National Institute of Justice Journal, 250*, 4 – 8.

Breiding, M. J., Smith, S. G., Basile, K. C., Walters, M. L., Chen, J., & Merrick, M. T. (2014). Prevalence and Characteristics of Sexual Violence, Stalking, and Intimate Partner Violence Victimization – National Intimate Partner and Sexual Violence Survey, United States, 2011, *Centers for Disease Control and Prevention Morbidity and Mortality Weekly Report, 63*(8), 1 – 18.

Brewer, G. & Abell, L. (2015). Machiavellianism in long-term relationships: Competition, mate retention and sexual coercion. *Scandinavian Journal of Psychology, 56*, 357 – 362.

Browne, A., & Williams, K. (1993). Gender, intimacy and lethal violence: Trends from 1967 through 1987. *Gender and Society, 7*, 78 - 98.

Buckels, E. E., Jones, D. N., & Paulhus, D. L. (2013). Behavioral confirmation of everyday sadism. *Psychological Science, 24*(11), 2201 – 2209.

Buss, D. M. (1992). Manipulation in close relationship: Five personality factors in interactional context. *Journal of Personality, 60*(2), 477 – 499.

Buss, D. M., Gomes, M., Higgins, D. S., & Lauterbach, K. (1987). Tactics of manipulation. *Journal of Personality and Social Psychology, 32*(6), 1219 – 1229.

Campbell, J. C. (1992). "If I can't have you, no one can": Power and control in homicide of female partners. In J. Radford & D.E.H. Russell (Eds.), *Femicide: The politics of woman killing* (pp. 99-113). New York: Twayne.

Carton, H. & Egan, V. (2017). The Dark Triad and intimate partner violence. *Personality and Individual Differences, 105*, 84 – 88.

Casserly, M. (2010). Why so few self-made billionaire women? *Forbes Entrepreneurs.* Retrieved from: https://www.forbes.com/2010/06/18/richest-women-billionaires-entrepreneurs-forbes-woman-power-women-oprah-winfrey.html

Cloud, H. & Townsend, J. (2002). *Boundaries: When to say yes, how to say no, to take control of your life.* Grand Rapids, MI: Zondervan

Colino, S. (2016). The real reason you get sick after a stressful period has ended: It's called "the let-down effect." *Healthy Living.* Retrieved from: http://www.huffingtonpost.com/entry/let-down-effect-sickness_us_568d60e0e4b0a2b6fb6e510b

Deane, C., Morin, R., Parker, K., Horowitz, J. M., Wang, W., & Brown, A. (2015). Women and leadership: Public says women are equally qualified, but barriers persist. *Pew Research Center: Social & Demographic Trends.* Retrieved from: http://www.pewsocialtrends.org/2015/01/14/women-and-leadership/

de Becker, G. (1997). *The gift of fear: Survival signals that protect us from violence.* Boston: Little, Brown.

Ellis, D., & DeKeseredy, W. S. (1997). Rethinking estrangement, interventions, and intimate femicide. *Violence Against Women,* 3, 590-609.

Emory, L. R. (2016). *This is when most couples first say "I love you."* Retrieved from: https://www.bustle.com/articles/136238-t

Evans, P. (1996). *The verbally abusive relationship: How to recognize it and how to respond.* Holbrook: Adams Media

Corporation.

Felder, R., & Victor, B. (1997). *Getting away with murder: Weapons for the war against domestic violence.* New York: Touchstone.

Freud, S. (1989). *Introductory lectures on psychoanalysis.* New York: Horace Liverlight.

Furnham, A. Richards, S. C., & Paulhus, D. L. (2013). The dark triad of personality: A 10 year review. *Social Personality Psychology Compass, 7*(3), 199 – 216.

Garcia-Linares, M. I., Sanchez-Lorente, S., Coe, C. L., & Martinez, M. (2004). Intimate male partner violence impairs immune control over herpes simplex virus type 1 in physically and psychologically abused women. *Psychosomatic Medicine, 66,* 965 – 972.

Gluck, M. A., Mercado, E., & Myers, C. E. (2008). *Learning and memory: From brain to behavior.* New York: Worth Publishers.

Johnson, M. P. (1995). Patriarchal terrorism and common couple violence: Two forms of violence against women. *Journal of Marriage and Family, 57*(2), 283 – 299. Retrieved December 20, 2015, from http://www.personal.psu.edu/mpj/1995%20JMF.pdf.

Jonason, P. K. & Ferrell, J. D. (2016). Looking under the hood: The psychogenic motivational foundations of the Dark Triad. *Personality and Individual Differences, 94,* 324 – 331.

Jonason, P. K. & Webster, G. D. (2012). A protean approach to social influence: Dark Triad personalities and social influence tactics. *Personality and Individual Differences, 52,* 521 – 526.

Jones, D. N. & Figueredo, A. J. (2013). The core of darkness: Uncovering the heart of the Dark Triad. *European Journal of Personality, 27,* 521 – 531.

Kearny, C. A. & Trull, T. J. (2012). *Abnormal psychology and life: A dimensional approach*. Belmont: Wadsworth, Cengage Learning.

Kellerman, A. L., & Mercy, J. A. (1992). Men, women, and murder: Gender-specific difference in rates of fatal violence and victimization. *Journal of Trauma, 33*, 1-2.

Kemeny, M. E., Cohen, R., Zegans, L. S., & Conant, M. A. (1989). Psychological and immunological predictors of genital herpes recurrence. *Psychosomatic Medicine, 51*, 195 – 208.

Kiire, S. (2017). Psychopathy rather than Machiavellianism or narcissism facilitates intimate partner violence via fast life strategy. *Personality and Individual Differences, 104*, 401 – 406.

Lev-Weisel, R. (2007). Intergenerational transmission of trauma across three generations: A preliminary study. *Qualitative Social Work, 6(*1), 75 – 94.

McCarrick, A. K., Manderscheid, R. W., & Silbergeld, S. (1981). Gender differences in competition and dominance during married-couples group therapy. *Social Psychology Quarterly, 44*(3), 164 – 177.

McFarlane, J. M., Campbell, J. C., Wilt, S. Sachs, C. J., Ulrich, Y. & Xu, X. (1999). Stalking and intimate partner femicide. *Homicide Studies, 3*(4), 300 – 316.

Mededovic, J. & Petrovic, B. (2015). The Dark Tetrad: Structural properties and location in the personality space. *Journal of Individual Differences, 36*(4), 228 – 236.

Moitra, E., Dyck, I., Beard, C., Bjornsson, A. S., Sibrava, N. J., Weisberg, R. B., & Keller, M. B. (2011). Impact of stressful life events on the course of panic disorder in adults. *Journal of Affective Disorders, 134*(1-3), 373 – 376. doi:10.1016/j.jad.2011.05.029.

Moracco, K., Runyan, C. W., & Butts, J. D. (1998). Femicide in North Carolina, 1991-1993: A statewide study of patterns and precursors. *Homicide Studies, 2*, 422-446. National Women's

History Project (n.d.). Timeline of legal history of women in the United States. Retrieved from: http://www.nwhp.org/resources/womens-rights-movement/detailed-timeline/

Paulhus, D. L. (2014). Toward a taxonomy of dark personalities. *Current Directions in Psychological Science, 23*(6), 421 – 426.

Paulhus, D. L. & Williams, K. M. (2002). The Dark Triad of personality: Narcissism, Machiavellianism, and psychopathy. *Journal of Research in Personality, 36*, 556 – 563.

Perry, J. (2012). Digital stalking: A guide to technology risks for victims. *Network for Surviving Stalking and Women's Federation of England*, 1 – 73.

Petrosky, E., Blair, J. M., Betz, C. J., Fowler, K. A., Jack, S. P., & Lyons, B. H. (2017). Racial and ethnic differences in homicides of adult women and the role of intimate partner violence — United States, 2003–2014. *Morbidity and Mortality Weekly Report, 66*, 741–746. doi: http://dx.doi.org/10.15585/mmwr.mm6628a1.

Rasmussen, K. R. & Boon, S. D. (2014). Romantic revenge and the Dark Triad: A model of impellance and inhibition. *Personality and Individual Differences, 56*, 51 – 56.

Rod, M., Puhlik-Doris, P., Larsen, G., Gray, J., & Weir, K. (2003). Individual differences in uses of humor and their relation to psychological well-being: Development of the Humor Styles Questionnaire. *Journal of Research in Personality, 37*(1), 48 – 75.

Rutgers, (2017). Center for American Women and Politics. *Fact Sheet: Women in the U.S. Congress 2017*. Retrieved from: http://www.catalyst.org/knowledge/women-government

Ryan, K. M., Weikel, K., & Sprechini, G. (2008). Gender differences in narcissism and courtship violence in dating couples. *Sex Roles, 58*, 802 – 813.

Samsel, M. (2013). *Abuse and relationships.*
https://www.abuseandrelationships.org

Schoen, M. (2001). *When relaxation is hazardous to your health:
Why we get sick after the stress is over and what you can do now
to protect your health.* Calabasas, CA: Mind Body Health Books.

Semenyna, S. W. & Honey, P. L. (2015). Dominance styles mediate
sex differences in Dark Triad traits. *Personality and Individual
Differences, 83,* 37 – 43.

Sharps, P. W., Campbell, J. C., Campbell D. W., Gary F.,
& Webster, D. (2001). The role of alcohol use in intimate
partner femicide. *Journal on Addictions, 10,* 1–14.

Smith, M. (1990). Patriarchal ideology and wife beating: A test of a
feminist hypothesis. *Violence and Victims, 5*(4), 257 – 273.
Retrieved December 20, 2015, from
https://login.ezproxy.uta.edu/login?url=http://search.proquest
.com.ezproxy.uta.edu/docview/208554970?accountid=7117

Smoker, M. & March, E. (2017). Predicting perpetration of intimate
partner cyberstalking: Gender and the Dark Tetrad. *Computers
in Human Behavior, 72,* 390 – 396.

Soenens, B., Vansteenkiste, M., Luyten, P., Duriez, B., &
Goossens, L. (2005). Maladaptive perfectionistic
self-representations: The mediational link between
psychological control and adjustment. *Personality and
Individual Differences, 38*(2), 487 – 498.
http://dx.doi.org/10.1016/j.paid.2004.05.008

Sonkin, D. J., Martin, D., and Walker, L. E. A., (1985). *The male
batterer: A treatment approach.* New York: Springer Publishing
Company, Inc.

Spence-Diehl, E. (1999). *Stalking: A handbook for victims.* Holmes
Beach, FL: Learning Publications, Inc. Storey, J. E., Hart, S. D.,
Meloy, J. R., & Reavis, J. A. (2009). Psychopathy and stalking.
Law and Human Behavior, 33, 237 – 246.

Swogger, M. T., Walsh, Z., & Kosson, D. S. (2007). Domestic violence and psychopathic traits: Distinguishing the antisocial batterer from other antisocial offenders. *Aggressive Behavior, 33,* 1 – 8.

Taylor, S. E. (2009). *Health psychology.* New York, NY: Mcgraw-Hill.

Tjaden, P., & Thoennes, N. (1998). *Stalking in America: Findings from the National Violence Against Women survey* (NCJ 169592). Washington, DC: Department of Justice, National Institute of Justice.

Tjaden, P. & Thoennes, N. (2000). *Extent, nature, and consequences of intimate partner violence: Findings from the National Violence Against Women survey* (NCJ 181867). Washington, DC: Department of Justice, National Institute of Justice.

Walker, L. E. (1979). *The battered woman.* New York: Harper and Row.

WHO (2007). *The cycles of violence: The relationship between childhood maltreatment and the risk of later becoming a victim or perpetrator of violence.* Retrieved from: www.euro.who.int/_data/assets/pdf_file/0008/98783/E90619.pdf

APPENDIX A

Example Stalking Behaviors Record						
Date	Time	Stalking Behaviors	Location of Incident	Witness Info	Police Report #	Officer Info
20-May	9:15am - 8pm	Jim called 20 times	Work phone & Cell	Andrea 888-888-8888	1234567	Darvis; Badge #2112
21-May	7:30am	Jim showed up at my work	222 W Northstrop Lane	Vanessa 222-222-2222	1234567	Darvis; Badge #2112
22-May	3:21pm	Received 3 letters from Jim	255 Corner Street	N/A	N/A	N/A
23-May	All day	Was emailed by Jim 5 times,	He emailed my personal email; called my cell	N/A	1234568	Darvis; Badge #2112

Fillable Stalking Behaviors Record						
Date	Time	Stalking Behaviors	Location of Incident	Witness Info	Police Report #	Officer Info

ABOUT THE AUTHOR

Dr. Audrey Snowden is the author of *The Hidden Abuser: Learn to Recognize Subtle Abusive Behavior* which integrates her own experiences in abusive relationships with her insights as an Experimental Psychologist.

While in graduate school, Audrey survived an emotionally, verbally, and physically abusive relationship. Surprised, she realized this wasn't the first abusive relationship she had been in. After going on an intense journey to understand abusers and why she continued to select them for partners, she decided to write a book detailing the answers to her questions.

Audrey earned her Ph.D. in Experimental Psychology from The University of Texas at Arlington in 2017. While in graduate school, she studied emotional decision making and group processes. She currently lives in Burleson, Texas, with her partner Mike and their cat Friday.

If you would like to contact Audrey Snowden, Ph.D.:
Dr.AudreySnowden@gmail.com
https://www.facebook.com/hiddenabuser/

Made in the USA
Middletown, DE
30 December 2020